# Families
# & Time

# Understanding Families

*Series Editors:*   *Bert N. Adams, University of Wisconsin*
*David M. Klein, University of Notre Dame*

This book series examines a wide range of subjects relevant to studying families. Topics include parenthood, mate selection, marriage, divorce and remarriage, custody issues, culturally and ethnically based family norms, theory and conceptual design, family power dynamics, families and the law, research methods on the family, and family violence.

The series is aimed primarily at scholars working in family studies, sociology, psychology, social work, ethnic studies, gender studies, cultural studies, and related fields as they focus on the family. Volumes will also be useful for graduate and undergraduate courses in sociology of the family, family relations, family and consumer sciences, social work and the family, family psychology, family history, cultural perspectives on the family, and others.

Books appearing in **Understanding Families** are either single- or multiple- authored volumes or concisely edited books of original chapters on focused topics within the broad interdisciplinary field of marriage and family.

The books are reports of significant research, innovations in methodology, treatises on family theory, syntheses of current knowledge in a family subfield, or advanced textbooks. Each volume meets the highest academic standards and makes a substantial contribution to our understanding of marriages and families.

The National Council on Family Relations cosponsors with Sage a book award for students and new professionals. Award-winning manuscripts are published as part of the **Understanding Families** series.

*Multiracial Couples: Black and White Voices*
Paul C. Rosenblatt, Terri A. Karis, and Richard D. Powell

*Understanding Latino Families: Scholarship, Policy, and Practice*
Edited by Ruth E. Zambrana

*Current Widowhood: Myths & Realities*
Helena Znaniecka Lopata

*Family Theories: An Introduction*
David M. Klein and James M. White

*Understanding Differences Between Divorced and Intact Families*
Ronald L. Simons and Associates

*Adolescents, Work, and Family: An Intergenerational Developmental Analysis*
Jeylan T. Mortimer and Michael D. Finch

*Families and Time*
Kerry J. Daly

Kerry J. Daly

# Families
# & Time

## Keeping Pace in a
## Hurried Culture

UNDERSTANDING
FAMILIES

**SAGE Publications**
*International Educational and Professional Publisher*
Thousand Oaks   London   New Delhi

*For information address*:

SAGE Publications, Inc.
2455 Teller Road
Thousand Oaks, California 91320
E-mail: order@sagepub.com

SAGE Publications Ltd.
6 Bonhill Street
London EC2A 4PU
United Kingdom

SAGE Publications India Pvt. Ltd.
M-32 Market
Greater Kailash I
New Delhi 110 048 India

Printed in the United States of America

**Library of Congress Cataloging-in-Publication Data**

Daly, Kerry J.
    Families and Time / author, Kerry J. Daly.
        p.  cm.  —  (Understanding families; vol. 7)
    Includes bibliographical references and index.
    ISBN 0-8039-7340-3 (cloth: acid-free paper). — ISBN 0-8039-7341-1
(pbk.: acid-free paper).
    1. Family.  2. Time—Sociological aspects.  I. Title.  II. Series.
HQ728.D25  1996
306.85—dc20                                                          96-25178

This book is printed on acid-free paper.

96  97  98  99  10  9  8  7  6  5  4  3  2  1

Sage Production Editor: Sherrise Purdum
Sage Typesetter: Marion Warren

*This book is dedicated to my own family—*
*Helen Theresa, Johanna, and Ben—*
*whose love, patience, and care*
*sustain me through time.*

# Contents

# Preface

Consciousness is often irrevocable. I used to take great delight as a child when someone told me to imagine a black-and-white cow in a green field and then insisted that I stop thinking about it. My relative powerlessness at chasing the image from my mind led me to try out this phenomenological trick on others who similarly had difficulties in dismissing the images of such cows from their consciousness.

As I wrote this book, time took a central place in the way that I viewed the world. Increasingly, I interpreted my experience through the lens of time. My consciousness of time had become irrevocable, and like the cow that couldn't be chased away, time came to dominate my ways of thinking about and experiencing everyday life.

The idea for this book came out of my research with fathers of young children. Using qualitative interviews as my data collection technique, I asked questions about how they saw themselves as fathers, who their important influences were, and how they perceived their relationship with their children. As I reflected on their responses, I was struck by the dominance of time metaphors in their descriptions of their relationship with their children. They lamented about *not having enough time* with their children, they strategized about *how to make time* to be with their children, and most important, they repeatedly emphasized the value of *spending time with their kids*. Time appeared as a dominant currency in their experience of family: It was the measure of value in their relationship with their children. It was with this sensitization about the importance of time to men that I began to look more broadly at the meaning and importance of time in families as a whole. When I began to look at the literature, I was initially struck by the relative absence of time in the family research. It appeared that most of what people were doing was to count the number of hours that family members committed to various activities as a way of understanding the stresses and strains associated with managing the family-work balance. What was missing in the literature was a comprehensive analysis of the *conceptual meanings of time for families.* Although various aspects of family time experience have been explored in the literature, there has been little effort to bring these elements of temporal experience together into a comprehensive whole. It was this apparent gap in our understanding that became the catalyst for this book.

In the course of writing this book, I had many different personal experiences that sensitized me to the multidimensional nature of time. One of the overarching changes in my experience of time occurred as a result of having a sabbatical. With sabbatical, the tyranny of institutional time structures is removed. When you don't have to teach classes or attend regular meetings, then the daily schedule is something that must be constructed rather than simply responded to. At the same time, however, I was very aware that I wasn't as free as I had expected. First, I realized that family schedules are bigger than just me. Children go to school and must be fed lunch and be picked up. My spouse was working, and as a result, there were several schedules that needed to be synchronized—just as if we were at home. Furthermore, the spatial move of living in another part of the country did not make my time unavailable to people at my home institution. Specifically, e-mail and fax machines meant that the response to graduate students, editors, and colleagues was expected just as quickly as if I were at home. Although sabbatical removed me from some of the temporal constraints of my work institution, it did not free me completely. Overall, I was left with a respect for the power of our daily timetables that came from two directions. First, I was more appreciative of my dependence on routine that arose in the course of trying to establish a new schedule for myself outside of the institutional structure of the university. Second, I was aware of how difficult it was to shake the persistent and steady pace of my life that continued during sabbatical by virtue of my embeddedness in the schedules of the people around me. The forces that maintained this pace ranged from the hours of my children's school day to the research progress of one of my graduate students in South America.

During my sabbatical year, I also experienced the death of my father. He died after struggling with Alzheimer's disease for several years. For me, his death was a profound and sobering realization that human time does not stretch out endlessly before us.

I also spent time during this year volunteering through our church to take a man in his 99th year for regular walks. When I breathlessly arrived at his house (because I always try to arrive just on time rather than early), I was always aware of the change in pace and tempo from my own plugged-in world. I would come from having impatiently checked my e-mail for a message at my office, to walking slowly and methodically up the lane lined with arbutus trees with a man whose stroke meant that each step was calculated and methodical. I was intensively aware of *slow*. I was also very aware of the dramatic change in historical context, for many of his reference points, reminiscences, and memories were rooted in the 19th century! I was always somewhat awed and humbled by his range of experience in time.

Over the past couple of years, I have also found myself as a father and husband shifting gears from having a wife who was initially an at-home mother to a wife as a graduate student to a wife who now works full-time in the workforce. The pace and intensity of our shared lives have changed dramatically through those transitions and have had a powerful influence on our lives together.

Overall, these experiences have alerted me to the importance of some of the central themes in the theoretical analysis of time: the power of schedules and timetables in the way that we organize our day-to-day lives, the embeddedness of our own schedules in the temporal structures of others, the finitude of time, the intertwining of individual lives and history, and the challenges that are associated with synchronizing the changing schedules of individual family members. These themes and others constitute the substance of this book.

Several comments are warranted to alert the reader about the style in which this book is written. First, the book is intentionally interdisciplinary in nature. Although I am a sociologist by training, time defies the neat boundaries of any one discipline. It has been a central focus in both ancient and modern philosophy. The social sciences have taken a modest interest in time through their relatively brief history, with the perspectives of sociology, psychology, and geography being represented most often in this book. Time has also been a focus in the interdisciplinary fields of family science and family systems theory, and these too are well represented throughout the book. Nevertheless, despite my efforts to present these various perspectives, I am quite sure that my sociological orientation has resulted in a more heavy weighting for that perspective in the book.

Second, this book is distinctively North American in its scope. Although many of the ideas are relevant to Western, postindustrial societies, culture plays an important role in the way that time is valued, perceived, and experienced. There is much that needs to be learned in an analysis of cultural variation with respect to time, but this is beyond the scope of this analysis. Of course, cultural variation is as much present within North America as it is present comparatively throughout the world.

Third, this book is intended for a wide range of audiences. It is primarily directed toward scholars from a variety of disciplines who share an interest in the family. Professionals and students who regularly teach about, or do research on, some aspect of family experience inevitably must deal with issues of time. Whether it is division of labor, caregiving, or developmental changes throughout the life span, time is a foundational theme. Those who focus in their scholarship on some aspect of the family-work interface may find this work particularly relevant. Time lies at the heart of families' efforts to work out the stresses and conflicts associated with the work-family balance. This book is also intended for therapists and educators who wish to help families cope with the escalating demands of a fast-paced technological culture.

Finally, this book is intended to be a theoretical book about time. In light of the move away from positivist assumptions about how to do science, *theory* has become a contentious term that can mean many things depending on the values, goals, and premises of the theorist. As a result of this, some comment is warranted at the outset about how I perceive theory. In contrast to the axiomatic, lawlike character of positivist theory, I view theory as a meaning structure. A meaning structure is a composite of ideas and explanations that provide insight into the dynamics, dimensions, and relationships of a particular phenomenon. These ideas and explanations are rooted in many sources, including our own conjecture as scientists; empirical evidence that portrays patterns of feeling, action, or behavior under specified circumstances; and our observations of the world around us that are shaped by the media, culture, and experience. Given the dynamic nature of these influences, theory can never stand still. It must always have an elasticity that allows for the incorporation of new information and ideas.

In keeping with these ideas, I propose this as a theory about family time. Although books tend to reify ideas in a way that most postpositivists find distasteful, they serve as an important medium for the exercise of ideas that are relevant to the topic at hand. Metaphorically, theories should be treated like bread dough that rises with a synergetic mix of ingredients only to be pounded down with the addition of new ingredients and human energy. It is my hope that these ideas will give rise to new ideas about the patterns and politics of family time. Equally, it is my hope that they will be kneaded and reworked as time goes on.

# Acknowledgments

Thanks to Dave Klein and Bert Adams, the series editors, and Jim Nageotte at Sage for believing in this book and being willing to support it.

# 1

# Conceptualizations of Time

We spend a regular portion of our lives asking the question "What time is it?" We expect and usually receive a relatively precise answer. By contrast, we do not usually scramble the words in the question and ask "What is time?" for we are unlikely to get the kind of straightforward answer that would allow us to move forward, in an uninterrupted fashion, with our daily routine. In fact, asking the latter question lays open the possibility of a kind of phenomenological crisis where the very core of experience and activity is called into question. To question time itself is to question a human construct that undergirds the way that we define reality.

The usually unproblematic nature of the question "What time is it?" attests to the taken-for-granted presence of time in all activity. Time is a foundational component of the sociocultural order that we take for granted and that serves as the basis for our decisions and actions. In fact, the normalcy of our social environment presupposes our taking for granted time as a background feature of the familiar world of everyday life against which we perceive social situations (Zerubavel, 1979). Time, by its pervasiveness, is present in all human

1

activity and can be seen as the "central organizing feature of family activities" (Presser, 1989, p. 536). It is a central part of our taken-for-granted reality that shapes daily schedules, commitments, and priorities. It gives concrete shape to a family's collective history as marked by anniversaries, birthdays, and shared key events. It lies at the core of our personal biography and serves as the basis for anticipating the way that events will unfold in the future. As such, time has an important place in the discourse about family experience. However, it is the embeddedness of time in the normalcy of everyday life that keeps it hidden from our critical gaze.

In the study of families, time has suffered from conceptual deprivation. Although time is implicitly present in matters of caregiving, work-family balance, or socialization, it resides in the recesses of the discussion. When time does enter the analysis, it has been treated as a value-neutral, reified quantum when measuring the division of labor or as a series of static "benchmarks" (Roth, 1963) that have come to symbolize key transitions for individual and family development. For example, with the dramatic increases in the number of women in the paid labor force in recent years, time diary studies have come to dominate the way that family scientists treat the analysis of time. In these studies, time is approached from an accounting ledger perspective. It is treated as a variable to measure the amount of time that family members commit to a variety of work, household, parenting, or leisure activities. It is also used conceptually as a way to divide the life cycle (Bengston & Allen, 1993) or the course of family development (Rodgers & White, 1993). In other analyses, time is used historically as a way to understand how present-day families are different from families of the past (Hareven, 1982; Schvaneveldt, Pickett, & Young, 1993). Although there have been varying degrees of theoretical development in each of these areas, the meaning of time for families has been insufficiently problematized. Rather than being the focus in family research, time is more often treated as an ephemeral concept that is taken for granted because it is ever present. It is implicit in family research because so much of the emphasis has been placed on "target issues" such as outcomes of family interactions and family pathology (Kantor & Lehr, 1976, p. 115). Little effort has been directed at understanding the social and political underpinnings of time as manifested in the day-to-day experiences and negotiations of family members. To this end, I endeavor in this book to develop a theory that focuses on the meanings, structures, and politics of family time. My goal is to allow time to percolate to the surface of the discussion in order for us to understand the degree to which it is pervasive in the experiential world of families. It is an effort to move time from its complacent and taken-for-granted position and make it manifest in the core of family activity.

To say that time has been insufficiently "problematized" (Davies, 1994) is to argue that we need to look beneath the surface of our everyday assumptions about time and begin to explore the conceptual richness that lies below. To "problematize time" at an experiential level is to place temporal concerns at the center of the day-to-day experience of work and family. At a conceptual level, problematizing time is to shake it off its common and universal understandings and to raise questions about its many meanings, dimensions, analytical levels, and implications. In this regard, the task of reconceptualizing and problematizing time is akin to the process of setting out to purchase a computer for the first time. At the start, time is like a computer: You know what it is and essentially how it works. Consequently, advertisements and first impressions suggest that it is as simple as purchasing any other household appliance. However, once one enters into serious inquiry, one is quickly confronted with a new language, endless configurations, and an overwhelming array of options associated with brand, power, components, and speed. Like the complicated world of computer hardware, when the seductively simple veneer of time is removed, there is a web of questions, contradictions, and puzzles that readily problematize the experience of time in families.

When we go beyond singular and objective definitions of time, "There lie hidden terrains of ambiguity, contradiction and struggle" that arise "not merely out of admittedly diverse subjective appreciations, but because different objective material qualities of time and space are deemed relevant to social life in different situations" (Harvey, 1989, p. 205). Time is not confined to one aspect of life, but it permeates all activity across many domains of experience. Although individuals may agree on an objective, external measure of time, it is experienced in diverse and changing ways. For example, as we age, we have differential experiences of time that arise in the course of individual development (Hendricks & Hendricks, 1976). Situations that vary by social class, neighborhood or ethnicity also incur different meanings of time. Street life in larger urban centers, for example, does not run by the rigid punctuality of the middle-class clock but, rather, according to the rhythms of "what's happening" (Horton, 1967). Gender, employment status, and family structure also play key roles in shaping different experiences of family time.

## Theoretical Premises of Time

A theory of family time must be viewed against the backdrop of theories of *social* time, which are different from theories of natural time. Whereas natural time is uniform, homogeneous, and quantitative, social time is imbued with meanings based on different frames of reference and experiences (Sorokin & Merton, 1937). From a Newtonian perspective of positivistic science, natural time is real and absolute in the measure of motion across space. Our clocks and calendars, for example, are based on the movement of the earth relative to the sun. Other forms of time measurement, such as sidereal time, are based on the apparent motion of the stars. Social time, in distinction from physical time, is "artifactual time," and although it may have quantitative and continuous aspects, these are usually arbitrary products of convention (LaRossa, 1983, p. 580). From a social time perspective, time derives from human activity as an imposed or nominal dimension of the world. Social time has no ontological status but is an artifact of our mode of social organization (Seltzer & Hendricks, 1986, p. 653). The implication of this is that the quantitative dimensions of clock time can serve as an adequate measuring tool in the natural sciences, but many time aspects of social life cannot be quantified, including experience, awareness, consciousness, or knowledge of time (Adam, 1988).

Social time has been conceptualized in many ways in the sociological literature. Symbolic interactionists speak of time in terms of its situated and socially constructed elements; phenomenologists refer to time as duration, motive, and intersubjective experience; functionalists are concerned with the social organization of time, temporal norms, and the synchronization of temporal orders; and

Marxists are most likely to deal with time in its commodified form. Sociologists, however, are relatively late arrivals in the long history of scholarship on time. Major thinkers such as Aristotle, Plato, St. Augustine, Kant, Whitehead, Hegel, Einstein, and Piaget are but a few of the serious contributors to the question of time. As Adam (1988) has pointed out, "the study of time destroys the sanctity of disciplinary boundaries" (p. 198) where sociologists, philosophers, physicists, psychologists, and geographers come together to grapple with the quandaries of time.

Although social time has been studied throughout history and across disciplines, it resists monolithic definition. In acknowledgment of this, Fraser (1978) argues that it is important to think of "temporalities" instead of time. If the emphasis of postmodernist ideas is the pluralism that directs us to talk about "families" instead of the family, then it also directs us to speak of many temporalities, instead of a structured monolithic system of time. In an effort to review these many temporalities, the next section gives an overview of some of the main metaphors that have been used in the social analysis of time. Because metaphors play a central role in defining how we conceptualize our everyday realities, metaphors of time give insights into the systemic underpinnings of thought, action, and language (Lakoff & Johnson, 1980).

## Traditional Models of Time: Circular and Linear Time

### CIRCULAR TIME

Circular models of time are driven by nature. Time is viewed as a cycle of seasons, as the cyclical rhythm of day and night, and through the human cycle of birth and death. Prior to industrialized technology and the wide-scale use of clocks, time was experienced as the repetitive periodicity of the weather, tides, seasons, and the movement of the planets and the stars. For families, cyclical patterns of work and rest, planting and harvesting, celebration and mourning, or growth and decay were tied to the cycles of the natural world. The past, present, and future were not as important as the naturally recurring ecological cycles. Circular models of time continue to dominate the patterns of experience for hunting-and-gathering and agricultural societies. Some religions too are based on circular models of time. For example, time is circular and repetitive for the Mayas, Hindus, and Buddhists with history repeating itself and lives being relived through endless cycles of reincarnation (Toffler, 1980).

Clocks, of course, did not remove the effect of nature on the experience of time but, rather, introduced a schism between time as a constructed, mechanical artifact and as a naturally recurring process of cyclical regeneration. Ironically, although the hands of a clock *go around in a circle* to measure time, the introduction of the clock has played a major role in separating the daily experience of time from the cycles of the natural world. Daily and seasonal rhythms continue to play an important role in our technological world, but they are in competition with the urgency of a clock culture that champions speed and efficiency. As Elias (1992) reminds us, a clock itself is not time but is a physical mechanism that bears a message that we have created and incorporate into our symbolic world. What clocks introduced into our daily experience was the precision of time. Whereas early agricultural societies divided time into relatively imprecise periods to perform tasks such as planting, milking a cow, or harvesting, the clock culture of an industrial society ran on the basis of precise standardized units that were interchangeable from one season to the next (Toffler, 1980). Hence, although families continue to have daily routines for determining who gets the bathroom first, mealtimes, and departures and arrivals for work or school, these have less to do now with cycles of nature and more to do with the complex organizational demands associated with living in a postindustrial culture. Furthermore, although these daily routines are still cyclical and repetitive at one level, they are dramatically more exact in the way that they are carried out and organized. Whereas the rhythm of everyday life was once shaped by the movement of the sun, it is now governed by commercial and organizational demands and constraints.

LINEAR TIME

Our experience of time has also been dominated by linear metaphors. Our orientation in everyday life is one of traveling through time with a wake of experience that we call the past and with a bow that cuts into the smooth surface of the future. The past comes before the present and the present comes before the future. These are cause-and-effect notions of time where we attribute our current state of being to decisions and events in the past. Our language of time is also linear insofar as we speak and write in past, present, or future tense.

Linear forms of time firmly took hold with the onset of industrial capitalism. Clocks not only divided time into standardized interchangeable units, but these neat and precise chunks of time were placed in a straight line that extended back into the past and forward into the future (Toffler, 1980). Although notions of the past and future certainly existed prior to the clock culture, the mechanization of time succeeded in making the passage of time more measurable and vectoral.

Indeed, the notion of progress, which is central to modernity, is rooted in a linear view of time. Wage labor under the factory system not only separated the public sphere of paid labor from the private domain of personal meanings (Zaretsky, 1976), but it also dictated the temporal organization of everyday life. Through their daily and generational reproduction of labor power, families fueled the engines of progress. In so doing, they marched in step on the track of progress. Our current economic climate in North America, which is still based on principles of more, cheaper, and better-quality products, continues to embrace the idea of progress by holding out an ever-higher standard of living for consuming families.

In noneconomic terms, notions of both aging and individual and family development are unidirectional in nature and assume a linear model of time. Time is seen as being "analogous to points on a line, in both direction and order; it is a unique standard by which everyone can be compared" (Hendricks & Hendricks, 1976, p. 31). From this perspective, not only is time linear, but it is also externalized and largely beyond the control of the individual. Individuals are seen moving along "time tracks" where "social and cultural conventions carve out time segments from the raw, existential world, providing direction-giving tracks of meaning upon which man travels through life" (Lyman & Scott, 1970, p. 189). Indeed, as some have argued, time has virtually no importance unless it is linear and brings irreversible change (Needham, 1943). Like "the refreshing river," time is an endless, irreversible flow of change and newness of forms (Needham, 1943). This is the "linear-vectoral" view of time where we have a "common conception of time as a continuous dimension" (Zerubavel, 1979, p. 2).

The linear conceptualization of time is what Mannheim (1952) referred to as the positivist approach to time in which there is "a measurable span of life" where "generation follows generation at regular intervals" and "where the framework of human destiny is comprehensible, even measurable form" (p. 276). Families have linear histories marked by a series of events, including birthdays, deaths, and anniversaries. Although some of the rituals that are used to mark these events are repeatable and cyclical, they typically represent the idea of progression through time—a directionality of success (as in marriage anniversaries), maturity (as in birthdays), or accomplishment (as in graduations). In each of these, movement along a time line is the implicit focus of the celebration.

## Time as an Economic Metaphor

Industrial capitalism gave birth to the association between time and money. Marx wrote about the transformation of time under the factory system, where labor power and time itself became a commodity. The clock was a precise measure of work activity that focused on the quantity of goods that could be produced within the smallest amount of time. In this regard, time is the measure of value attached to work, for like all commodities, the value of the labor power is determined by the labor time necessary for production (Pronovost, 1989, p. 4). As a commodity, working time is time that employers buy from their employees and that thereby entitles them to access. As a result, overtime is working beyond your regular public time, beyond what the employer is usually entitled to (Zerubavel, 1981, p. 156). The association of time with money and productivity spawned the idolization of efficiency as a key value in industrialized society. Max Weber (1958) cited at length Benjamin Franklin, who said not only that "time is money" but also that idleness therefore involved throwing away money. In *The Protestant Ethic and the Spirit of Capitalism*, Weber built on this theme to establish the association between the

Protestant work ethic and the appreciation of time as a precious resource to be allocated with diligence and frugality (Adam, 1993). The link between time and money is evident in our language when we speak of spending, wasting, and saving time.

For families, time as money governs the day-to-day routines that are set up around productive activity. With the onset of capitalism, the family's routines were determined in large part by the productive activity of the man of the house, who entered into the public sphere of paid work to meet the needs of the family. Family mealtimes, leisure time, and consumption activities were organized around the hours of his work. Now in families, there is either a single-parent head or a dual-earner couple who participate in paid work, resulting in a different complex of daily routines. In contemporary families, paid work schedules are juggled, housework and child care are negotiated, and free time is haggled over. Time has become the dominant currency in families. In keeping with the commodification of time, Schwartz (1982) argues that "opportunity costs" of time are most likely to be encountered in social systems that are highly coordinated through schedules, deadlines, appointments, and timetables. As society grows more affluent, money becomes less effective as a rationing device and time costs take its place. In families, the time costs of multiple schedules and competing organizational demands result in a variety of temporal conflicts and opportunity costs.

When time is a dominant currency, family members are seduced by the need for temporal efficiency. On the basis of the belief that time can be saved through the use of express lines, microwave ovens, drive-through tellers, e-mail, or instant food products, we seek to pack more activity into the time that is available. The irony is, of course, that when we pack more tasks into the extra time that we have saved, we then require another time-saving device to cope (Russell, 1992). In our industrialized culture, we have a speed fetish that values expediency over processes that take a long time.

## Dialectic Metaphors

Dialectic metaphors of time are concerned with contradictions in time or the tension of opposing forces in the experience of time. Fraser

(1978) postulates that the ontology of time is conflict: Specifically, conflicts are part of the universal condition of nature that involve an existential or constitutive tension. These opposing trends are part of "single integrative states" and, to be understood, must not be thought of as existing independently—only their conflict or tension can be regarded as real (Fraser, 1978, p. 28). Furthermore, these conflicts are unresolvable—they coexist as two opposing trends, regularities, or groups of laws. Perhaps the "tick-tock" of the clock comes closest to symbolizing the dialectics of time where either the tick or the tock are meaningless on their own. Only in the constant oscillation between the two is there a meaning of time. In this regard Needham (1943) emphasizes that our experience of time is a dialectic process because contradictions are at the root of our biological and social evolution.

Examples of these dialectics abound. There is dialectic between time that is instantaneous and time that is glacial (Urry, 1994). Glacial time refers to time that is evolutionary and involves an immensely long, imperceptibly changing process that happens over hundreds of millions of years. At the other extreme of incomprehensibility is the nanosecond, which deals in currencies of a billionth of a second. Time in this form is, for all intents and purposes, instantaneous, for it cannot be experienced or observed. It is just as far beyond conscious human experience as the notion of 600 million years. Clock time lies in the middle of these extremes, and because of its comprehensibility, it serves as the primary organizing principle for our industrialized world.

Oscillations between night and day also lie at the root of routine tensions between energy and fatigue. Although most people are diurnal in their patterns of wakefulness and activity, some are more nocturnal. Furthermore, as Melbin (1978) has pointed out, as services expand into the night, more and more people have changed the pattern of their wakeful life to "occupy" the night. Increasingly, we live in cities characterized as "sleepless Gorgons," where a growing proportion of individuals work outside their normal diurnal rhythms (Toffler, 1980). The dialectic of time is expressed on a daily basis in the interaction between the biological rhythms of the body and the rhythms of the solar system.

Existentially, there is an unresolvable conflict of time that is rooted in growth and decay and between death and eternity. At the same time, "our ordinary experience of time is one of unity: time embraces everything that was, is, or will be" (Fraser, 1978, p. 191). Although there is unity in the dialectic of time in experience, this unity is more difficult to preserve intellectually, with our limited conceptualizations of permanence and change.

Perhaps the most important dialectic of time is one that is located in the tension between time as consciousness and time as an organizational structure. Classic writings in philosophy and sociology have emphasized time as either a subjective experience or as a framework within which we operate. For example, Heidegger (1962) argued that time expresses the nature of being. Bergson (1965) focused on the experience of duration when he used the term *durée*. For Bergson, the ultimate reality is not "being" or being changed but the continual process of change itself. By contrast, Durkheim identified time as the key organizing principle of all social life insofar as it served as a uniformly imposed framework for all social activities. In this same vein, time is viewed as being among "the major parameters of the social order, and social life is structured and regulated in accordance with it" (Zerubavel, 1979, p. xxi). Although these classic perspectives emphasize time as either consciousness or social structure, they do not capture the dynamic interplay or the dialectical tensions that bring these perspectives together in lived experience.

More recent writers have proposed views of time that bring together these extremes into a dialectic view of time. Gurvitch (1964) presents a model of time based on the idea that individuals create the social order, which in turn acts back on them to affect their experience of that world. Likewise, time is part of inner experience that varies according to the context within which it is experienced. Perhaps the most important dialectical approach to time is found in Giddens's (1984) theory of structuration. This perspective places emphasis on neither the experience of the individual actor nor the existence of any form of social totality but on the way that "social practices are ordered across space and time" (p. 2). The theory of structuration rests on the idea that there is a "duality of structure" whereby the structural properties of social systems are seen as "both a medium and outcome of the practices they recursively organize" (Giddens, 1984, p. 25). Put in another way, the moment of the production of action is also one of reproduction of the structures within which that action occurs. Time is characterized by the double existence of the lived aspect and of abstract pure value. In its "lived" aspect, time is experienced as *durée;* as an abstract value, time is objective, and like money, is expressed in a universal and public mode (Adam, 1990). The power of this concept for the theoretical analysis of time is that actors and structures are both in temporal motion. Gone is the idea of structures as "social products" (Giddens, 1984, p. 26) and in its place is structure that is tied to human agents whose actions occur through a reflexively monitored "process" and "flow" (p. 9). From an ethnomethodological perspective but with the same focus, Garfinkel (as cited in Telles, 1980) emphasizes the reflexive nature of time: It is a constituent as well as a product of social behavior.

Kellerman (1989) also talks about the duality of time. Time can be seen as both a context and a composition. As a context, events and actions occur within time or are located in time. Time is compositional insofar as it can be seen as a "resource and factors for human action" (p. 1). Corresponding with this, time can be seen as both absolute and relative. Absolute refers to time as a framework or container for human action (passive context), whereas relative time refers to the active use of dimensions and resources by individuals and societies (active use) (Kellerman, 1989). Actions, which pertain to the way time is used, are influenced by values. These in turn influence societal conceptions of time. As a result, actions and conceptions undergo simultaneous change. This is the duality of structure whereby people's use of time creates new conceptions of time and uses of time are influenced by existing conceptions (p. 38).

Jaques (1982) also speaks of dual perspectives in temporal experience. Time that is viewed to be objective or real, such as the readings on a clock, is atomistic and is identified as the time of *chronos.* On the other hand, time is subjective, continuous, and flowing. It is the unbounded field of *durée* or *kairos.* In lived experience, these aspects of time live in relationship with one another. They are linked by the experiencing self with a continuous oscillation between these opposites.

Weigert's (1981) construction of time as a "fundamental dialectic of daily life" makes reference to the intricate relation between biographical time and social timetables. Through their participation in social roles, individuals play out the tension between their biographical experience of their social world and the collective social structure (Lewis & Weigert, 1981). The linkage between action and structure is conceived of as *time embeddedness* insofar as all social acts are fitted inside larger social acts (Lewis & Weigert, 1981). This has also been referred to as a process of "time reckoning" that is dependent on the interaction of inner time consciousness and social time schemes (Hendricks & Peters, 1986, p. 662). In a similar vein, Adam (1989) contends that time is "simultaneously abstracted and reified, experienced and constituted" (p. 468). She cautions that a focus on time necessitates an approach that transcends dualisms and dichotomous thinking and that instead highlights the multiple realities that bear on social life simultaneously. Understanding the relationship between actions and structure in relation to time involves a focus on the "interlacing of meaning, normative elements and power" (Giddens, 1984, pp. 28-29).

It is precisely this "interlacing" of meanings and structural realities that can serve as an important window on the dialectics of family time. Family members live in a tension between the experience of their own unique biography with all of its idiosyncratic desires and needs, and the structures and routines of both the family as a group and the organizations and institutions of the broader society of which they are a part.

## Acceleration Metaphors

In *The Time Machine*, H. G. Wells (1931) describes the peculiar sensation of time traveling: "As I put on pace, night followed day like the flapping of a black wing. The dim suggestion of the laboratory seemed presently to fall away from me, and I saw the sun hopping swiftly across the sky, leaping it every minute, and every minute marking a day" (p. 18). Like all good science fiction, Wells prods a nerve of contemporary sensitivity. Although the quantum dimensions of what constitutes a day have not changed, it appears that our experience of time in that day has accelerated dramatically. Like the time traveler, we seem to be putting on pace. Where once families toiled from sunup to sundown, they now vie for flextime, patch together a daily schedule of caregiving arrangements for children and aging parents, and on the way home, grab some fast food that will enable them to spend some precious time together before attending to the household duties. Of course, in the process of organizing and implementing these complex daily schedules, sunrise and sunset often go unnoticed.

Our day-to-day discourse offers a good deal of evidence to support the idea that we are experiencing the "acceleration syndrome." Parents crave to "spend more time with their children" and spouses "juggle their schedules." Children are relentlessly urged to "Hurry and get your shoes on" so that another day of drop-offs and pick-ups can be implemented without interrupting the daily routine. Family calendars that are filled with work, lessons, and appointments create an angst about "fitting it all in." The dominant discourse of current social time patterns is a discourse of "crisis" that rests on the notion of an ever-increasing acceleration of time (Pasero, 1994). The result of this acceleration is that we have become a "time-obsessed society" (Shaw, 1994, p. 81). Unlike Longfellow's poetic description in the 1800s, relationships are no longer silent ships passing slowly in the night but rather are screaming trains that go careening by each other in broad daylight.

Families live in a world of accelerated time demands. In response to forces such as industrialization, information technology, and the globalization of the world economy, families are caught in an "ever-tightening spiral of development" (Russell, 1992, p. 145). This spiral of development has condensed evolutionary changes taking millions of years to a time scale that has a series of technological revolutions occurring within a lifetime. Ours is a "time-compact" society (Lenntorp, 1978, as cited in Nowotony, 1992). The implications of the escalating pace of life for families is that there is "time scarcity" (Pronovost, 1989, p. 28) and "time famine." Family worlds are increasingly dominated by an angst about the availability of time. Family and work activities are "time-consuming," stress and role overload arise when there is insufficient time to complete the required tasks, and families frequently lament the shortage of time for being together.

With the recent historical shift from single-provider to dual-earner family models, time famine has become a more common aspect of everyday family experience. For many families, this is due to the necessity for both partners to work in the paid labor force in order to maintain an adequate standard of living. For other families, there are costs associated with the pursuit of an ever-higher standard of living. Time scarcity emerges in the course of material acquisition, for the more we want, the more we must work for it and the more extra time is required to purchase and maintain all of these things (Young & Schuller, 1988). The result is that the dual-earner household is likely to be "time poor" (Crouter & Crowley, 1990, p. 297). In keeping with this, Nock and Kingston (1984) concluded in their research that "while not an absolute zero-sum proposition, more time given to outside-the-home paid employment generally would seem to mean less time for family interaction, child care, home maintenance and leisure activities" (p. 333). As Hochschild (1989) concluded in her analysis of dual earner couples, overall there has been a "speed up of work and family life" (p. 9). In the end, we have all "become more and more subservient to the *tyranny of time* [italics added]" (Whitrow, 1988, p. 164).

## Summary

To theorize about family time, it must first be dislodged from its taken-for-granted hold on our lives. Because time is pervasive in all activity and embedded in the normalcy of everyday lives, it is infrequently scrutinized as a problematic force. Due in part to the perception that time is "out there" and beyond our control to change, it carries us along in a never-ending march of routines and schedules. However, time is becoming more problematic as family members work more, have less free time, and overall feel the speedup of work and family life. In the family literature, there has been considerable emphasis placed on documenting the changes in the number of hours that family members spend on various activities but considerably less effort committed to the exploration of the meanings of time for families. The goal of developing a theory of family time in this book is therefore contingent on two key conceptual shifts. The first of these is to problematize the everyday experience of family time by opening the taken-for-granted to scrutiny. This involves a shift from seeing time as a background feature of everyday life to seeing time as an explicit, foreground feature of everyday life. The second conceptual reorientation involves shifting attention away from cataloging the number of hours that family members commit to various activities and to focus instead on the meanings that time has for them.

The development of a theory of family time is, therefore, a theory of social time. Although theories of natural time emphasize time in its quantitative and absolute form, theories of social time focus on the socially constructed essence of time. In this regard, time is both a structural or cultural artifact and an ongoing project of individual construction. As a structural artifact, time is a set of globally agreed-on conventions that are based on adherence to the clock and universal rules about things such as time zones, schedules, or operating hours. Like any organizational artifact, time is based on compliance for its continued existence. As an individual construction, time is a form of consciousness that is experienced through awareness of time and the synchronization of activity through interaction. In this regard, time is experienced through many forms of awareness: being late, feeling rushed, or being overburdened by too many demands.

The metaphors that we have for time in our culture can serve as a set of sensitizing conceptualizations for the way that we approach the development of a theory of family time. Beyond the elementary questions of how much time we spend in family activities, we can begin to examine social time in a variety of manifestations. As the metaphors suggest, we have cyclical, linear, economic, dialectical, and acceleration constructions of time. Circular models of time are rooted in the cycles of nature. Although families continue to experience the cycles of life and death or night and day, the organization of their everyday life is shaped less by nature and more by the complex demands of a fast-paced, technological culture.

Linear models of time continue to play an important role in the way that we think about individual development and social progress. On the basis of notions of cause and effect and the sequential flow of the past, present, and future, linear metaphors emphasize movement along a line. For individuals, the directionality of linear time is marked by key transitions and celebrations that constitute individual biography. Collectively, key dates and social transformations are marked as history, with progress being the primary axis along which we have constructed these noteworthy events.

Because progress is the primary thrust of a modernist view of history, time is also manifested as an economic metaphor. Here, time takes on a commodified form and is directly associated with money. When economic progress is of primary importance in the culture, then time becomes the precise measure for assessing production and efficiency. For families, time has become a dominant currency in the difficult task of negotiating and organizing a complex set of schedules and timetables. The result is that there is competition for time in families in the same way that there is competition for money in the capitalist culture.

Time can also be understood as a dialectic metaphor that involves a state of tension and a recursive relationship between the lived experience and the structure of time. For families, this metaphor introduces the idea that their private experience of time is always embedded in the context of the larger social order. Managing the inherent tension between the personal and the public dimensions of time involves an ongoing process of "time-reckoning" where personal desires and wants must be correlated with structural schedules and constraints.

Acceleration metaphors of time have arisen in response to forces such as industrialization, information technology, and the globalization of the world economy. As the world puts on pace with respect to the exchange of information and commercial goods, so too has the family put on pace as a way of adapting to these changes. Significant within families has been the increasing propensity to work, which has left families with less time for themselves. Families have become time impoverished in the face of escalating demands.

Although each of these forms of time can be conceptualized separately, they come to bear on our lives simultaneously. What we call time is a complex network of relationships, and timing is essentially a synthesis or an "integrating activity" (Elias, 1992, p. 56). Experientially, all of these metaphors of time are less distinct and are inconspicuously incorporated into our everyday realities. An integrated theory of family time experience must in some way attend to the unity of these elements.

For heuristic purposes, however, there will be an examination of how various perspectives can illuminate separate aspects of temporal experience in families. In the chapters that follow, there will be an exploration of how families experience time in its myriad forms. In the first part of the book (Chapters 2, 3, and 4), there is an exploration of the patterns of family time. In Chapter 2, there will be a discussion of the relationship between family time and historical time and an analysis of how history has changed the meaning of family time. Included in this will be a discussion of postmodernist views of family time. In Chapter 3, there is a discussion of how time is socially constructed in families. There is an analysis of the meanings that time has for families and how those meanings are acquired. Time is explored as an orienting dimension where the past, present, and future serve as reference points for navigating through the patterns of past behavior and arousing the expectations associated with future possibilities. In addition, time is examined as an instrument for mapping individual and family identity. In Chapter 4, there is a discussion of "family time" as representing not only an experience of togetherness but an ideology with prescriptive elements.

In the second part of the book (Chapters 5-8), the emphasis shifts to an examination of the *politics* of family time. In this part, there is a focus on the underlying dynamics of control over time and how these are manifested in the relationship between families and the culture of which they are a part and within families on the basis of gender and generation. In Chapter 5, there is a discussion of the properties of time that subject it to control. Specifically, there is an examination of time as value and the manner in which time is objectified. The tendency to objectify time is critical for understanding the political dimensions of time. When time is treated as a standardized currency, it is susceptible to the dynamics of power and control. This chapter explores the implications of time as an unequally distributed resource.

In Chapter 6, the discussion focuses on the dynamics of control that arise between families and the many organizations of which they are a part. There is an exploration of institutional spheres that affect family time: work, education, and day care. Temporal norms play a vital role in the construction and maintenance of family schedules and routines. Dual-earner families in particular are preoccupied with the need to find a balance between the family and work. Control over time is a problem in everyday lives with role overload, stress, lack of flexibility, or competing demands, all resulting in the ongoing need to manage, preserve, and redistribute the allocations of time.

Gender is a key axis within families where there are conflicts over the control of time. In Chapter 7, there is a focus on the negotiations and conflicts between men and women as they vie for time in work, domestic, and leisure domains. Time is subject to power dynamics, with gender differences creating discrepancies within families regarding their control over time.

Control over time is also expressed in the relationships between generations, and this is examined in Chapter 8. Parents raise their children by controlling their time. As adults, they are faced with challenges of having their time controlled by the time that they must give to both their children and their aging parents.

In the final chapter, an integrated theory of family time is presented. Although each of the perspectives discussed earlier sheds light on various dimensions of our temporal experience, to understand the simultaneity of these many temporal influences, there is a need to put all the pieces back together. Here new questions are identified with the intention that these new questions will keep the theory of family time in play. Furthermore, there is a discussion in this chapter of the implications of our fast-paced world for family well-being. Taking control of time, reexamining values, and taking time seriously in education and therapy are discussed as means for contending with the tyrannizing effects of time.

# 2

# The Experience of Family Time in Historical Perspective

History is itself a temporal concept. Although there are many scholarly debates about what history is, three models will be discussed here in relation to family time. These include traditional or grand narrative approaches to history; dynamic models that are concerned with the active intertwining of individuals and families with their historical milieu; and postmodern ideas that are critical of metanarratives and instead focus on globalization, diversity, and the pace of change.

## Grand Narrative Views of History

Our traditional beliefs about the nature of history are perhaps best represented by the "march of time" metaphor. The history of the world can be conceptualized as a series of dated, critical events that have been documented by careful observers and that are widely believed to have really happened. History locates our present activity in the context of all past events. It is made up of a calendar of traditions, celebrations, crises, and transitions. The key characteristic of historical time, which distinguishes it from other kinds of time, is that it is time that has elapsed or is completed (Gurvitch, 1964). The historical method emphasizes the unique and unrepeatable character of the flow of events, which in turn reinforces the ties of cause and effect (Gurvitch, 1964). The word *story* is at the root of history and reflects the centrality of narrative for the cataloging of past events. Like any story, history is at some level an "artifice" and a product of individual imagination (Carr, 1986, p. 10).

From this perspective, the relationship between families and history is concerned primarily with the documentation of how families have changed in relation to major world events. Laslett (1972) speaks of the rejection of evolutionary theories that focused on the Darwinian succession of family forms in order to explain how "civilised monogamous man evolved from his Simian predecessors" (p. 4). This was popular in the 19th century and usually involved a strong moralizing tone whereby "the family was regarded as fundamental to society not only as its final structural unit, but as the receptacle of its values" (Laslett, 1972, p. 4). Carr (1986) offers a critical view of this approach, arguing that grand historical narratives "dress up reality" reflecting our need for "satisfying coherence" and, in a more cynical vein, seek to "put across a moral view of the world in the interests of power and manipulation" (p. 16).

One of the classic treatises to examine the changes in family form over the course of human history was Friedrich Engels's study of the emergence of the monogamous family. Based on the anthropological work of Lewis Henry Morgan, Engels (1967) examined how family forms were transformed on the basis of economic shifts from hunting and gathering to agrarian to capitalist-based societies. Although the linkages drawn by Engels between family structure and world historical events has titillated family theorists, it is of a scale that reduces the history of the world into several broad categories. In the same genre, other historical commentators have looked at the impact of wars on marriage patterns, reproduction, and family well-being. The classic work of Parsons and Bales (1955) is very much a part of this genre where the postwar economic prosperity of the 1950s gave rise to the standard, middle-class, suburban family.

As Giddens (1990) has described accounts of this sort, this is a grand narrative view of history that is evolutionary and that suggests there is a continuous flow of "real" events related in a cause-and-effect manner. Of course, as the philosophers of history remind us, the meanings and importance of these events is projected onto them by our concerns, prejudices and interests (Carr, 1986). Anthropological work by Malinowski and others in the early part of the 20th century seemed to put an end to these evolutionary ways of thinking by emphasizing cultural variations in the experience of history (Laslett, 1972). This anthropological work demonstrated there are other models of history that are quite different from a Western, linear and developmental conception of events. Commenting on the work of Lévi-Strauss, Carr (1986) contends that in some non-Western societies, time and change are devalued and in some cases denied. Similarly, in other cultures, an action or event does not derive value from its place in a narrative sequence but from its capacity to reflect other events and actions in a timeless symbolic scheme of affinities and oppositions.

The purpose of this chapter is not to dissect the grand narrative of family history. This requires the experience and methods of historians to adequately document and discuss how families have changed through time. There are many excellent scholars who have carefully examined the changes in family form and function through history. The purpose is, rather, to look at models that show how families are "intertwined" with their history. History from this view is not simply a progression of events but is a kind of narrative that involves families at the center as storytellers, protagonists, and audience (Kellerman, 1989).

## Dynamic Models of Families and History

Mills (1959), in his classic portrayal of the personal troubles and public issues dialectic, focuses on the interaction of biography and history. The experience of individual time is informed by history and in turn shapes the course of that history. Similarly, for Dilthey, "we are historical beings first, before we are observers of history, and only because we are the former do we become the latter" (cited in Carr, 1986, p. 4). Time and history stand in a reciprocal relationship where "our idea of history is based on that of time, so time as we conceive it is a consequence of our history" (Whitrow, 1988, p. 186).

Contemporary historians have emphasized the importance of looking at the connection between structures and everyday experience to understand the ways in which the regularities, patterns and structures are continuously and subtly remade (Elliot, 1994). The individual not only observes the historical world from the outside but is "intertwined" with it (Carr, 1986, p. 4). Furthermore, the family, as Elliot (1994, p. 60) argues, is a key "pivot" between individuals and structures. When families are both protagonists and audience of history, they are at the same time the product and producer of their family career (Hareven, 1994).

The temporal relationship between discrete lives and the larger processes of social change has been best articulated by Hareven (1982), who examined the "interrelationships between individual and collective family behavior as they constantly change over people's lives and in the context of historical conditions" (p. 6). When individual family members move from one role status to the next, they synchronize their activities with those of other family members and in response to historical conditions. Metaphorically, this is like a school of fish in the ocean where the activity of individual members is continuously being aligned with the actions and movements of other members in response to a variety of contextual cues (Hareven, 1982). The way that people respond to the historical conditions they encounter are shaped both by "the point in their lives at which they encounter these conditions and by the 'equipment' they bring with them from earlier life experiences" (Hareven, 1982, p. 355).

Individual time and family time are closely synchronized, for most individual transitions are related to family transitions. Specifically, because individuals carry on obligations to their family of origin and their families of procreation, these obligations cast individuals into various overlapping and, at times, conflicting, functions over the course of their lives.

Historical time affects individual and family time because the overall social, economic, institutional and cultural changes affect patterns of individual and family timing. However, as Elder (1974) points out, caution must be used in thinking about families as the passive victims of unidirectional environmental conditions. Rather, as he illustrates in his book about the children of the Depression, it is more prudent to view families as active problem-solving units who work out defensive and coping adaptations. For example, the age, the career stage, and the family stage at which individuals encountered the Great Depression affected their ability to cope with adversity (Hareven, 1982). What comes into play is the culture and experience from earlier life that individuals bring with them to these conditions and the networks within which they are enmeshed at that particular moment (Hareven, 1982). The focus on timing of transitions, as outlined by Hareven, provides insight into the way that priorities were established by families as they encountered various social and economic developments, how they revised their experiences in the face of new challenges, what kinds of choices they made when faced with constraint, and what kinds of options they exercised when dealing with a variety of choices. Indeed, as Elder (1974) observed in his study of Depression families, the persistent economic incapacity of the father meant that children were accelerated into adultlike roles and experiences. In the face of the father's diminished economic position, families became more labor intensive, which enlarged the household roles of the children. Hence, as part of their adaptive strategy, children's transitions to adulthood were accelerated to accommodate the prevailing economic challenges. Specifically, for boys, there was an early emancipation from family constraints and an expected maturity in the management of money; for girls, they were expected to be more dependable and to carry a greater portion of the domestic responsibilities (Elder, 1974).

    In a study of historical differences in the pattern of individual and family timing, Modell, Furstenberg, and Hershberg (1978) compared the transition to adulthood between youth in the late 19th century and in the early 1970s. The researchers concluded that the social timetable of becoming an adult has become more rigidly prescribed with more uniformity in the pattern of attending school, entering the workforce, getting married, and establishing a household. Consistent with the greater routinization of the transition, was the fact that the transition from family of orientation to family of procreation became more rapid. In this regard, growing up was more concentrated for youth in the 1970s, for it took less time to leave home, marry, and set up their own household. Of critical importance in explaining these life cycle and family transitions was the alteration in the nature and functioning of the household economy. In the 19th century, most families were dependent for a relatively long period of time (approximately 7 years) on the contribution of their laboring children to maintain the household economy. By contrast, the household economy of families in the 1970s depended on the contributions of the husband and the wife. As these data indicate, there is an interaction between the timing of family transitions and the structural constraints that were in operation at the time. Of course, in the time since Modell et al. carried out their research in the 1970s, we have witnessed additional changes in social and economic structures that have had a further impact on the transition to adulthood. Inflation, unemployment, and shifts in the labor market to service-sector kinds of jobs has meant for many young people prolonged periods of dependency on their parents.

Although much of the current literature pertaining to individual and family life cycles is based on fixed stages and the normative timing of various transitions, there are many indeterminant aspects of the life course or family experience that defy neatly sequenced normative timetables. Gergen (1980), for example, maintains that the life course is infinitely varied because it is open-ended and individuals constantly re-create their past, construct their present, and shape their future. Others, such as Seltzer and Troll (1986), take a moderate position, pointing out that the life course is partly self-determined and unique and partly influenced by common cultural expectations as well as by the observations of the life trajectories of previous generations. This is referred to as the "expected life history" and it involves the "structuring of a personalized future" (Seltzer & Troll, 1986, p. 755). Although age-graded systems and expectable normative transitions play a role in determining how this life course is shaped, it is also important to look at how various "family themes" are transmitted over the generations and how individual goals and expectations play a role in determining the actual course of life events.

There is evidence to suggest that the family life cycle occupies a smaller proportion of the life cycle than it once did (Hantrais, 1993).

This is due to a number of demographic forces: The average family size has declined; women are delaying the age at which they have their first child; divorce rates have risen over the past couple of decades; and individuals are living longer after the death of a spouse or other family member. The implication for women, in theory, is that there is more time for nonfamily-oriented activities and, in practice, more women are entering employment outside the home (Hantrais, 1993). However, despite these changes, paid work and family raising still coincide for women and "compete for their time to a greater extent than in the past at a critical stage of women's lives" (p. 142).

Two other demographic changes have had an impact on the experience of family time. For Hagestad (1986), changes in mortality patterns have not only expanded the duration of individual lives and family relationships, they have also made death more predictable. The consequence of this is that the death of a child or the death of a parent is more easily predicted. The implication is that deaths that are untimely become more of a crisis than perhaps they once were (Hagestad, 1986, p. 681). Fertility patterns have also changed, such that women have fewer and more closely spaced children. The implication of this trend is that generational lines are more clearly demarcated. Where once it was not unusual to find children and grandchildren who were the same age as a result of large families with generous spacing, this is no longer the norm. The implication for families is that some of the hesitance associated with creating and maintaining family attachments under conditions of high mortality have diminished somewhat, such that most people in our society have come to take long-term family bonds for granted and to invest in them.

The life careers of family members are not "nomadic" in the sense of being isolated and independent but, rather, are interconnected. Individuals hold contingent expectations about the lives of other family members, experience countertransitions as a result of other family members undergoing such transitions, build expectations about family change and stability, and are shaped by norms and symbols that are created in the family (Hagestad, 1986). One of these contingencies is expressed in the relationship between a parent and child's progression through a series of normal developmental tasks. When a child moves through the expected sequence of life events on time, the parent experiences the "reflected glory" of their child's success (Hagestad,

1986). By contrast, when children do not leave home on schedule to take on their tasks of adulthood, parents are often left with a sense of strain and personal failure (Hagestad, 1986). A dynamic model of families and history includes the intertwining of the individual and the intergenerational dynamics of time as they stand in relation to history.


## Time in Postmodern Culture

A historical account of family time must also be examined as part of the shift from modernist to postmodern ways of thinking. Whereas modernism is identified with the belief in linear progress, absolute truths, positivism, rational planning of ideal social orders, and the standardization of knowledge, postmodernism emphasizes hetero-geneity, fragmentation, indeterminacy, and a distrust of universal explanations (i.e., metanarratives) (Harvey, 1989). Consistent with this, Giddens (1990) outlines the essential elements of postmoder-nity:[1] Nothing can be known with any certainty; there is an abandon-ment of progress because history is devoid of teleology (based on functional purpose rather than cause); and there is a new social and political agenda (which includes ecology). Several themes are explored in this section. First, there is an exploration of modernity as way of establishing a baseline for the discussion of postmodernity. In the discussion of postmodernity itself, three themes are discussed: the disembeddedness of time, diversity and pluralism in relation to time, and the accelerated pace of change.


### THE MODERNIST BASELINE

Mannheim (1952), in his critique of positivism, gives some in-sight into the modernist ideas about progress that were based on "a mechanistic, externalized concept of time, and attempted to use it as an objective measure of unilinear progress by virtue of its expressibility in quantitative terms" (p. 281). Modernization focuses on the emer-gence of modern institutions driven primarily by technological and economic forces. Industrial capitalism is identified throughout the literature as giving birth to the modernist trajectory. When time was commodified under the factory system, machinery dictated a tempo that mirrored the clock (Rifkin, 1987). Speed, efficiency, and success were the necessary conditions for productive activity and the progress that it brought. Modernism was based on a time orientation that idolized the clock in the name of material progress. The emphasis on recurrence of natural cycles diminished in favor of the future promise of something that was bigger and better. Progress is steeped in materialism and it is unstoppable and relentless (Rifkin, 1987).

When a modern time structure is substituted for a traditional one, it runs of necessity on the time that can be measured on a wristwatch inasmuch as modern technology and modern bureaucracy presuppose temporal structures that are precise, highly quantifiable, and universally applicable (Berger, Berger, & Kellner, 1973). Modernism affected temporal structures on many levels, including the reorganization of everyday social life (e.g., making precise appointments for social activities, rather than coming by sometime tomorrow); bureaucratic activities need schedules for efficiency; and there are more planning activities (e.g., there are economic plans and forecasts, social policy plans, environmental plans, etc.) (Berger et al., 1973). For families, one of the ramifications of the technological advances associated with modernity was the economic shift from production to consumption. Whereas families were the primary productive unit in agrarian societies, under capitalism, they worked for wages and became consumptive units in the marketplace. The daily participation of family members in organizational structures gave rise to a "time budget" mentality in order to be "on time." This, in turn, put strain on the private sphere, where the search for satisfactory meanings for individual and collective existence became more "frantic" (Berger et al., 1973, p. 191).

Generations were a central part of the modernist explanation of progress insofar as generations "articulated, rather than broke, the unilinear continuity of time" (Mannheim, 1952, p. 281). Generations were in fact a key driving force of progress. The overlap of old and new generations expressed the rhythm of history and the curve of progress in a unilinear and chronological way. By contrast, the postmodern rejects unilinear notions of progress and expresses "an incredulity toward metanarratives" (Lyotard, 1984, p. xxiv). Whereas modernist "metanarratives" of history are evolutionary and emphasize grand unilinear depictions of the world, postmodern views are more likely to approach history as involving a series of discontinuities (Giddens, 1990).

## DISEMBEDDEDNESS OF TIME

One of the discontinuities associated with the postmodern is the way that time is separated from the flow of local experience. Disembedding is the lifting out of social relations from local contexts of interaction and their restructuring across indefinite spans of time and space (Giddens, 1990). In the face of globalization, the disembeddedness of time is a delocalization of time. When time is disembedded, it is disassociated from space and it loses the uniqueness of the immediate environment.

In the premodern world before clocks, time was closely tied to space (Giddens, 1990). You could understand "when" by reference to "where" insofar as the place was the site for temporal structures. Natural rhythms and cycles of the land were the place for repetitive social routines. In traditional cultures, then, experiences and actions were marked by a "temporality of repetition" (Giddens, 1990, p. 104) that could be readily placed within a context of time and space with little separation between the two. With tradition, there is respect or reverence for the past. Time and space are not empty or contentless dimensions but, rather, they are "contextually implicated in the nature of lived activities" (p. 105). In Giddens's words, there was little time-space "distanciation" (Giddens, 1990). In the modern world, the clock separated time and space. In the last half of the 19th century, "the machinery of modernization was grinding traditional society into piecemeal" (Shorter, 1977, p. 13). Specifically, the hum of machinery was driven by the clock, which expressed uniform, quantitative, or "empty" time. Indeed, at the heart of Marx's explanation of alienation is the idea that clocked labor time is transformed into abstract, exactly measurable physical space that strips time of its qualitative flowing character (Lukacs, 1922/1971). The universalizing of time across the globe (calendars, clocks) has separated time and space and further "emptied" and abstracted time (Giddens, 1990).

Harvey (1989, p. 293) makes reference to the use of satellite communications as playing a key role in the "collapse of spatial barriers" insofar as the time of communication is invariant with respect to distance. When the world's spaces can be collapsed into a series of images on the television screen, we are firsthand witnesses to the "annihilation of space through time" (p. 293). Changes in the marketplace have also made the goods of the world easily available: Chilean grapes sit next to avocados from California in the supermarket and Japanese sushi bars are neighbors of the Italian pizza parlor in the food malls (Harvey, 1989). This is the postmodern landscape where the spaces of the world collapse on each other (Harvey, 1989, p. 301). Furthermore, computer networks create "virtual communities" (Rheingold, 1993) where space is nothing more than a technological artifact. Whereas traditional communities are based on a physical place where interactions occur with bodies that are located in a tangible space, virtual communities require acts of imagination that are mediated by computer screens (Rheingold, 1993).

For families, the question becomes one of determining the effects of space annihilation on the sense of community. In his discussion of the transition from traditional to modern societies, Shorter (1977) refers to the family as a ship cut loose from its moorings. Where once great cables secured the family firmly to its place in the community and the larger network of kin and generations, modernization meant that the family drifted into the variable winds and currents of the high seas. To extend Shorter's metaphor to postmodernity, the ship has found its place in outer space, where the earth is viewed out the window and time zones have lost their meridian. Harvey (1989) suggests that spatial annihilation can have two divergent effects on families. On the one hand, families can take advantage of the tremendous diversity that accompanies the globalization of the world. There is a new opportunity created to take advantage of the broadened consumerism and the network of television and computer possibilities that allow for rapid access to information, escape, fantasy, and distraction. On the other hand, there is a move that rejects the ever-imploding collage of space and, rather, focuses on the search for personal or collective identity or the "search for secure moorings in shifting world" (Harvey, 1989, p. 302). The continued presence of a discourse that celebrates family values and yearns for a nostalgic view of families from the past are indicative of the continued need that individuals have for the family as the site of this "secure mooring." A third possibility, not identified by Harvey, is that families just keep working harder and going faster where time, space, and the sense of belonging are lost in a blurry effort to keep it all together.

Shaw (1994) elaborates on the effects of globalization. Picking up on Giddens's idea of "disembeddedness," she contends that the dispersion of organizations over time zones throughout the world has created new time pressures, new anxieties about time that go well beyond the traditional anxiety associated with getting to work on time. Faxes, conference calls, electronic mail, and the interdependence of global stock markets require a temporal coordination that goes well beyond one's immediate geographical context. This has resulted in constant sensitivity to time, pressure caused by the shortage of time, and a general and unquestioned discipline of time (Pasero, 1994). For families, the constant vigilance to the multiple demands of "world time" results in a hurried pace of life, an expectation of growing possibilities in the efficient use of time, and the potential for more competing exigencies in the individual use of time within families.

## PLURALISM

A discussion of time in postmodern culture must be attentive to the pluralism of time. One of the main tenets of postmodern thought is that there is an accelerated rate of change accompanied by "the constant newness of forms" (Cheal, 1993, p. 11). One of the manifestations of this flow of new forms is the emergence of new temporal forms. Whereas industrialization tied life to the tempo of the machine, in the postindustrial era of computers and information technology, there are many new forms of time that emerge. Instead of time being tied to the machinelike throb of mass production, it is being "demassified" (Toffler, 1980, p. 263). In other words, there is a shift toward more individualized schedules. In the day-to-day experience of families, new temporal forms, such as "flextime," "the double day," or "the full-time parent" are understandable within a culture that has the majority of both parents working in a paid labor force where part-time work and shifts not tied to 9 to 5 are becoming increasingly typical. Similarly, the "permanence" of marriage took on new meanings in light of the escalating rate of divorce and changes in life expectancy. Where once marriage was forever, it now has an embedded time ambiguity.

The pluralism of time is manifested in many ways. At one level, time is simultaneously present in many domains: historically (our location in the "march of time"), biologically (the age of the organism), psychologically (subjective experience of time), socially (shared definitions of time in interaction), and symbolically (as a socially and culturally produced abstraction). It also exists with respect to our orientation to the past, present, or the future and the effortless mental shifting that can return us to past experience or project us into an experience of our fantasies. Furthermore, there is diversity with respect to the meaning of time with age, gender, social class, ethnicity, and location all having a bearing on how time is experienced and defined. Consistent with the postmodern view, there are multiple manifestations of time that arise through various depth levels of social reality (social activity, collective mentality) to expression in various social elements (groups, classes, etc.) (Gurvitch, 1964). The multiplicity of time is concerned with, on the one hand, the many ways of being aware of time in various social frameworks and, on the other hand, the multiple manifestations of real time. This diversity pushes us to abandon the notion of an external, singular time structure in favor of a vision of time that is lived, diverse, and changing. It is precisely the variety and multiplicity of time that is at the heart of the postmodern view.

Furthermore, postmodern experience seems to heighten the number of choices that are available at any given time. Rorty (1990) refers to this as the experience of "contingency" whereby one's experiences are always qualified by the knowledge that other experiences were available at the same time. Decisions about how to use time are embedded in a wide range of possibilities, a radical diversity of individual objectives and the plural coexistence of different lifestyles (Pasero, 1994, p. 185). Consistent with these ideas, everyday time is the "product of negotiation between the imposing structures of the calendar, the workday, the schedules of broadcast television and the temporal patterns of household or family life" (Silverstone, 1993, p. 289). One of the consequences of these imposing structures is that our lives are in a continual state of interruption (Ventura, 1995). Cellular phones, beepers, and call-waiting features on telephones have normalized the expectation of constant availability and interruption. The result is that time is fragmented, contradictory, plural, and variable—all key elements of the postmodern condition. Consequently, the trend toward the individualization of needs and goals associated with time use has resulted in the presence of time on the social policy agenda. Examples include Sunday shopping, flexible work hours, compressed work weeks, and day care hours.

In contrast to the role of generations in articulating the continuity of time, Lasch (1979) warns that we are fast losing our collective sense of historical continuity. There is "a waning of the sense of historical time," where there is no longer a sense of "belonging to a succession of generations originating in the past and stretching into the future" (Lasch, 1979, p. 5). Shorter (1977) concurs, arguing that where once people learned their place in the eternal order of things by looking at the progression of generations that stretched behind them, they have now "lost interest in family lineage as a means of cheating death . . . and have let fall the ties which bind one generation to the next" (p. 8). This is the culture of narcissism where to "live for the moment is the prevailing passion—to live for yourself, not for your predecessors or posterity" (Lasch, 1979, p. 5). This is consistent with the burgeoning forms of time and the accompanying diversity of temporal experience. The result is a culture that is obsessed with the present and in which personal therapy supersedes religious continuity. The present is filled with a concern for the feeling of personal well-being, health, and psychic security (Lasch, 1979, p. 7). For families, this creates a dependence on certified experts. Traditional generational supports have atrophied, with the result that family members are more reliant on bureaucracies as a source of validation for their collective well-being.

Another manifestation of the greater diversity of experienced time is reflected in a drift away from the "linear life plan" of education, followed by employment followed by retirement (Best, 1978). Family time structures are also based on a set of expectations regarding the rhythm and timing of family change, where there is a gravitation toward wanting the normal sequence of family life consisting of marriage and childbearing and ending with the empty nest and retirement (Hagestad, 1986). However, there have been a variety of demographic changes that have made alternative life schedules more attractive. For example, better health care and increased longevity have expanded the time frame for the experience of education, work, and retirement (Desaulniers & Theberge, 1992). This has made second careers or adult learning in midlife more common. In addition, there are changes in family structure—such as decreasing family size, more dual-earner families, and more single-parent families—that give rise to many more alternatives in the way that life plans are experienced (Desaulniers & Theberge, 1992). As a result, the experience of family time is less likely to follow the traditional, unilinear paths that are typically presented in the family development literature. With the move away from the monolithic family, there is more diversity in the way that families experience time. For example, in shared custody arrangements, children move in and out of two different temporal domains—each with its own rhythm and schedule. In commuter marriages, spouses live in different temporal worlds with relatively low levels of intersection. The greater pluralism in family form gives rise to temporal pluralism.

### THE ACCELERATED PACE OF CHANGE

Acceleration, temporariness, and ephemerality are hallmarks of the postmodern condition (Harvey, 1989). As we put on pace in our lives, the constant newness of information, consumer goods, and values give rise to a temporariness where the new is exalted and pursued. At the same time, there is a sense that the pace of life has quickened so radically in recent decades that there is a certain numbness that accompanies rapid change and progress. Our culture has become jaded to the wonderment of technology and has simply come to expect that there will be regular announcements about better and faster telecommunications. The fast pace of time has itself become taken for granted.

Indeed, technology creates a new kind of impatience. Microwave ovens made conventional ovens seem slow. A computer with a 486 chip appeared slow when the Pentium chip arrived. Watching a movie with commercials is slow compared to taping the movie on the VCR and fast-forwarding through the commercials. Technology gives rise to an intolerance for waiting and a desire for immediate results and gratification. With regard to commodities, this is expressed in terms of the values and virtues of instantaneity (instant fast foods) and disposability (cups, plates, napkins, clothing) (Harvey, 1989). The cultural mentality of postmodernity has resulted in a heightened "temporariness" of values, things, and relationships (Lyotard, 1984). More specifically, in a "throwaway society" people are willing to throw away not only produced goods but also values, lifestyles, stable relationships, attachments to people, and received ways of doing and being (Harvey, 1989). In families there is a reduced sense of trust and commitment over the generations, with family relationships being much more disposable and temporary (Urry, 1994). The acceleration of time in all its forms has resulted in the rapid "write-off of traditional and historically acquired values" where the temporary contract is everything (Harvey, 1989).

The development of sophisticated technological communications has contributed to the acceleration of time. The introduction of telegraphy and the laying of the transatlantic cable in 1858 revolutionized communications in the 19th century (Whitrow, 1988). Wireless telegraphy was introduced in the early part of the 20th century, further accelerating the rate of dissemination for information (Whitrow, 1988). Now, we have fax and computer e-mail networks that can be transmitted instantaneously across the globe. The speed of these communications now places new demands on the receivers to respond not only promptly but instantaneously. Although the expansion of technology allows for a global network that operates on a principle of simultaneity, this may be more illusory than real (Nowotony, 1994). The overall effect of approaching simultaneity is not that time is of less importance but, rather, that the little temporal differences matter more (Nowotony, 1994). Specifically, the competitive edge grows sharper in such a climate because innovations that have the temporal advantage generate greater profits. Hence, simultaneity does not eliminate discrepancies in time but has the effect of accelerating the speed and competition of information exchange and the marketplace. Furthermore, underlying the apparent simultaneity of the plugged-in globe are growing inequalities between the rich and the poor or developing and technologically advanced societies where there is unequal access to technology (Nowotony, 1994).

Questions arise about the importance of punctuality in a culture that is bent on acceleration. One argument is that punctuality rises in importance with the perception that the pace of life is increasing (Shaw, 1994). High-speed networks, beepers, and cellular phones give rise to the expectation of an immediate response, thereby putting a fine edge on the meaning of punctuality. From another perspective, Toffler (1980) predicted that in light of an increase in personalized, rather than massified schedules (associated with mass production), punctuality would become more selective and situational. Although punctuality is still vital in situations where ritual and courtesy demand it, it may become less important "as the computer spreads and people are permitted to plug into and out of round-the-clock cycles at will" (Toffler, 1980, p. 271). It appears that although computers and telecommunication networks offer more flexibility in when information is accessed or transmitted, they do demand greater diligence when individuals are called on to respond.

Efficiency in the production of goods and services also entails an acceleration in exchange and consumption. In fact, as Harvey (1989) argues, if we are to understand what time is from a postmodern perspective, we must understand its relationship to the material practices and processes that serve to reproduce social life. By increasing speed and doing more in a shorter period, time is directly related to money, efficiency, competition, and profit (Adam, 1993). For example, improved communications and techniques of distribution have made it possible to circulate commodities through the market system with greater speed. At the same time, electronic banking, automatic debits, and plastic money have speeded up the flow of money from consumers (Harvey, 1989). Families, as consumptive units, are thereby not only faced with a wide array of goods and services for purchase but are in a position to buy these with a sense of immediacy. Our culture has an "appetite for the new" where tradition and traditional practices are not as important as incoming information and goods (Giddens, 1990, p. 39). The mass market has accelerated dramatically with splits into "ever-multiplying, ever-changing sets of mini-markets that demand a continually expanding range of options, models, types, sizes, colors and customizations" (Toffler, 1980, p. 248). Most goods either are available locally or can be shipped express in a couple of days. Moreover, with the many credit options available, there is little need to wait. So too with services. Entertainment, education, and health services have escalated dramatically and provide a dizzying array of choices from videos delivered to the door to distance education courses on CD ROM. With this acceleration in the marketplace, there is a "collapse" of the future time horizon, such that "the future has come to be discounted into the present" (Harvey, 1989, p. 291). When we begin to let go of the modernist belief in the importance of progress where the focus is on the future, the busyness and pace of the present is preoccupying. For the postmodernist, "a present geared to accelerated innovation is beginning to devour the future" (Nowotony, 1994, p. 11).

Families live in a frenzied temporal climate. Many of the presenting problems in family therapy are ones that reflect the pervasiveness of time as a constraining, debilitating factor in the maintenance of vital family relationships. For example, parents who are having trouble "controlling" their teenage children rarely see them because their schedules don't correspond; the husband and wife who complain about not talking or not having sex both work at careers that leave them too tired and irritable to do either; or the single parent who abuses her child is exhausted as a result of working the double shift of provider and caregiver (Ritterman, 1995). Or as Ventura (1995) has questioned, is it surprising that couples have difficulty communicating or that one half of marriages end in divorce when they spend on average 20 minutes a day sharing time together?

Therapists are not exempt from the frenetic tempo of the lives of their clients, offering them "brief" therapy or medications as a way of offering quick, efficient, and cost-effective solutions to their problems. At the extreme, a New York therapy firm offers "mobile therapy" for angst-ridden executives whose already bloated schedules push them to get "therapy on the run" (Wylie, 1995, p. 11). While on the way to the airport or between meetings, these therapy sessions champion the values of speed and efficiency, and in so doing, bring the therapist into collusion with the accelerated staccato of our cultural rhythm.

One of the major forces in the acceleration family of time has been the strong increase in the number of women who work outside the home. When both partners work in the paid labor force, time becomes a more scarce commodity. When couples return to the household after a day of working full-time, they may walk into a temporal explosion where the "future, present and past are all congealed in one frantic extended episode of fragmented time segments" (Ritterman, 1995, p. 49). Specifically,

The housekeeper makes a run for it, the kids start quarreling for her attention, her fax machine sends urgent messages, her business phone line is usually ringing, the dinner is still packaged and cold in the refrigerator and freezer. While she rushes around the kitchen, still in her high heels, punching microwave buttons, throwing plates and silverware at the table, a portable phone nestled in her shoulder, she's also worrying about the conference that didn't go so well that morning, wondering if she and the kids have clean clothes for tomorrow and whether she has time to do a load of laundry before bed. (p. 49)

The escalation of pace in our culture has, ironically, resulted in a longing for the past. Nostalgia has become a major force in the marketplace where people are not so interested in the details of history but rather look for a "commodified and instantaneous heritage" (Urry, 1994, p. 138) that can be readily purchased as a historical artifact, an antique, or even as a good reproduction that exudes the feel of the past. The rise of nostalgia has resulted in "an increased aesthetic sensibility for old places, crafts, houses and countryside so that almost everything that is old is thought to be valuable, whether it is an old master or a cake tin" (Urry, 1994, pp. 138-139). Not only has there been a draw to the commodities of the past, but there is a nostalgia for families of the past. Although the golden age of the extended family who lived simply and honestly is a wishful artifact of mythical proportions (Coontz, 1992), there is, nevertheless, a desire to return to a time when roles and responsibilities were clear and straightforward. Our current tendency to put on pace in our current family life goes hand in hand with more complicated roles and timetables. By contrast, the families of the past offer a sanitized and uncomplicated point of reference for how we would like things to be. Like William Goode's classical extended family of Western nostalgia, these were large supportive networks embedded in a rich tradition of family values and experiences where family members knew their place. In this nostalgic view of the past, family togetherness was made possible by a rudimentary schedule that seemed to allow for meals together, shared leisure, and time to be family. The nostalgic yearnings for this fictive past serves as further evidence for the acceleration of family life.

Underlying the perception of increasing time scarcity in families is the reality that parents are spending less time with their children. The "home-time" structure of family life is being transformed by the growing diversity of work schedules: Mothers are spending less time with their children than in the past because of their work; fathers are spending less time with their children because of separation and divorce; and mothers, fathers, and children of intact families are spending less time together because parents are working different hours or days (Presser, 1989). Moreover, the culturally valued association of speed with the quantitative time of the marketplace has come into direct conflict with the nonprofit, inefficient use of time for caregiving and nurturance. As this suggests, the structure of family time is undergoing a transformation that has consequences for family members in all types of families.

Although the dominant theme is one of increasing time scarcity, there is an emerging paradox between the perceived shortage of time due to acceleration and the deceleration of the aging process that is associated with increased longevity (Pasero, 1994). As life expectancy increases, there is an accompanying expectation that there be a growing intensity and variety of experiences in each phase of life. Hence, there is an overall deceleration of time due to the aging process during which we can expect to have more time and a simultaneous acceleration and compression within that time of many life experiences (Pasero, 1994).

The acceleration of time in our culture gives rise to a new politics of time. Although the politics of the globe has traditionally focused on the creation and defense of spatial or geographical boundaries, we are entering an era where the politics of temporality is taking its place next to the politics of territory (Rifkin, 1987). Pockets of resistance have begun to surface in response to the increasing need for speed and efficiency. These are the "time heretics" of our day who argue that we need to bring time back into union with nature, which provides for a more tolerable pace and tempo for human living (Rifkin, 1987). This call to a different temporal pace undergirds the environmental movement, the holistic health movement, and the economic democracy movement (Rifkin, 1987). Thus far, however, it appears that families have not joined in this chorus to revolt against the accelerated time frame. If anything, families appear to be putting on pace to keep up.

## Summary

Grand narrative views of history, which are characteristic of a modernist perspective, have played an important role in our understanding of the way that families have changed over time. According to this model, family change is determined by social structural developments. As a result, the emphasis has been on understanding the way that families are affected by major world events such as the onset of capitalism, the factory system, world wars, depressions, or the prosperity of the 1950s. Although grand narrative views of history are still popular today, they are limited by the fact that they are dominant stories that emphasize singular constructions of reality. Subjugated in the process are the multiple experiences and the divergent constructions that characterize the creation of history at any moment in time.

Dynamic models of history place an emphasis on the way that families are "intertwined" with their history. In distinction from grand narrative views, which emphasize the unidirectional impact of world events on family experience, dynamic models of history explore the way that families are both the producers and recipients of history. Hence, as Elder (1974) demonstrated in his analysis of children of the Depression, all families were not affected in the same way. Rather, families varied in their response depending on their age, resources, and problem-solving ability. In this regard, families are conceptualized as active, adaptive, problem-solving units rather than passive recipients of historical forces. When cast in this way, we can gain a better understanding of how families have adapted and changed in response to various social conditions. As a result, changes such as more variant patterns of individual development, a shrinking family life cycle, or changes in fertility rates, are a function of the interplay between family adaptation and structural changes.

Modernist themes are slowly giving way to postmodernist conceptualizations of families and time. Modernist ideas are rooted in a belief about the importance of progress. Progress is mechanistic, unilinear, and driven by the precise measure of the clock. Families have been active participants in the modernist march of progress, first playing the role of productive contributors and then adding to that their role as the primary consumption unit. With speed and efficiency as the key values, families had to sharpen their skills of being organized, efficient, and punctual.

When we let go of modernist and grand narrative views of family history and focus instead on the postmodern view, we are left with an image of the family bobbing in a maelstrom of flux, change, and diversity. Time is at once globalized, and therefore common to all, and yet disembedded and foreign. The traditional affinity between time and space has begun to break down as global communications become more sophisticated and accessible. Families live at the abrasive meeting point of a progressive but nostalgic tradition and the multiple contingencies of a demanding present that is expressed through television, consumerism, and the constraints of work and the calendar. The postmodern turn is resulting in both a new set of opportunities and a new set of pressures for families. On the one hand, the disembeddedness of time from space provides the opportunity for broadened consumerism and access to global information; on the other hand, the increasing number of technological distractions and demands make it more difficult to maintain the family as a "secure mooring." Overall, there is a heightened anxiety about time that arises from the vigilance to the multiple demands of "world time."

The increasing diversification of temporal forms is central to the postmodern view. The increasing acceptance of multiple types of culture, lifestyles, families, and working patterns has meant that there is a growing pluralization of time use. Technologies such as personal phones and beepers have normalized the expectation of constant availability and interruption, resulting in an experience of time that is fragmented, contradictory, plural, and variable. As men, women, and children in families work out the challenge of meeting their individual work commitments, they are increasingly seeking solutions that allow for the customization of schedules. "Flextime" and "off-scheduling" have become part of our cultural discourse. Such terminology is indicative of the challenges associated with the destandardization of temporal forms.

Of critical importance for understanding the postmodern view of time is the idea that the world is accelerating rapidly. With the constant newness of forms and the high-speed production of consumer goods, impatience, instantaneity, and temporariness have come to color the experience of everyday life. Families are uneasily pulling on the throttle of time where the pace of their lives leaves little time for the shared experience of being a family. With the growing diversity of schedules and the quickening of the pace, mothers, fathers, and children are spending less time together. The increasing pace of life has given rise to an emerging "crisis" mentality with respect to time, accompanied by a yearning for a simpler and slower past. The challenge for families is to be highly adaptable and fast moving in response to these demands while maintaining a sense of family that guards against the sensory overloading of postmodern culture.

For many families, this is indeed a daunting challenge. With the majority of wives now working in the paid labor force, family members reconverge on the family home carrying with them the frenzied pace of their individual routines. Of course, it doesn't stop there. Although it is nice to think of the home as the safe haven where calm can be restored, it is typically the place where other demands and negotiations for time are presented. Housework, homework, classes, games, caregiving responsibilities, and meetings result in a new form of family work: the strategic organization of many schedules to keep pace with the accelerating culture.

A postmodern analysis of time provides the broad cultural context for examining the way that families experience time. In the next chapter, the focus shifts to an analysis of the ways that families socially construct time within these cultural parameters.

# Note

1. Giddens makes the distinction between postmodernism and postmodernity: Whereas postmodernism is best left to the arts—literature, painting, and architecture—postmodernity has to do with social developments. As a result of this distinction, I will use the term *postmodernity*.

# 3

## The Social Construction
## of Time in Families

A social constructionist perspective on time begins with the notion that our understanding of time is shaped by our cultural experience of time. In other words, time can be understood by examining the way that people experience the passage of time through their social and organizational behavior. What are the ways that they experience events and actions through time? What are the definitions that they bring to the passage of events and the relationships between changing events? What are the images and metaphors that they use to conceptualize time? A social constructionist position on time embraces the idea that time is "neither objectively given as 'real' time nor subjectively inaccessible to others as 'lived' time, but rather is constructed as cultural object and internalized as a part of self" (Rutz, 1992, p. 3). From a social constructionist perspective, time does not consist of standard units but, rather, "moments of time are conceived of as qualitatively uneven" where "some are critical; others routine" (Lyman & Scott, 1970, p. 212). In this regard, a social constructionist view of time is consistent with a postmodern view: Instead of externalized, standard forms of clock time, there is an emphasis on the diversity of temporal forms through social definition.

A social constructionist view of time is in contrast to the Kantian idea that time is a *prior* condition of our minds that affects our experience of the world. As Whitrow (1988) has indicated, an *a priori* view of time did not explain how different human societies come to think of time differently and afford it varying levels of significance. Rather than a prior condition, our concept of time is a *consequence* of our experience of the world that reflects the power of the human mind "to construct the idea of time from our awareness of certain features characterizing the data of our experience" (Whitrow, 1988, p. 186). Our ideas of time are mental constructs that are both created and learned through symbols, rules, and the need for synchronized activity (Elias, 1992).

As a socially constituted reality, time finds its shape in the interpretive domain that lies between the subjective definitions of the self and the objectively available cues that are available in the situation. Time, as a construction, is constituted through the interaction of individual and social phenomena. From this perspective, time must be viewed as a phenomenon that is both uniquely but intersubjectively experienced. In this regard, time "is the language of the mind, informing our behaviour and defining our personality . . . [it] is the instrument that makes possible group interaction and the creation of culture" (Rifkin, 1987, p. 1).

As a social construction, time is both subjective and social. A number of phenomenologists have emphasized the social nature of subjective time experience. Husserl (1964), for example, referred to the temporal as the field of occurrence. Bergson (1965) emphasized the perceived and lived experience of time through the concept of *la durée*. For Merleau-Ponty (1962), time is an experience of succession where the past and the future are aspects of subjective experience that exist only in the present. Within each of these perspectives, subjective time is tied to the duration of experience. This is "consciential time" (Gonseth, 1972, p. 51) where the experience of duration is marked in reference to "exterior realities" (p. 57).

At the root of the social constructionist view of time is the link between time and activity. William James (1890/1952) emphasized this link when he identified the relationship between the perceptions of duration and the events that take place in an interval. For George Herbert Mead (1932), time and society are understandable through the emergent actions of individual actors. In contrast to Durkheim's view of time as an external force whereby individuals operate within an existing framework of time, Mead focused on a theory of action whereby activity is seen as the emergence of events that constitute a present with a past and future horizon. The emphasis on "emergence" suggests that experience itself is a time-creating activity where the past, present, and future are created out of intentionality. In contrast to a linear view of time, past, present, and future are not points on a line but are contingencies that are always fluctuating in accordance with lived experience in the moment.

Schutz (1962) elaborated on this relationship by emphasizing that all action is an ongoing process that involves continual reference to the past and the future. Any anticipated action involves "projecting into the future" to "visualize the state of affairs" that will result (p. 68). Projections of the future, however, are based "upon my knowledge of the previously performed acts which are typically similar to the prescribed one" (p. 69). The symbolic field within which we experience the world does not have rigid temporal boundaries around what constitutes the present, the past, or the future. We manipulate symbolic representations of temporal reality in a way that is always mixing prior contexts of meaning with present experiences and future plans. Furthermore, plans for action are also coordinated intersubjectively. Activity and plans for activity are grounded in a shared time consciousness.

To think of time as socially constructed activity is to focus on its "situated" aspects. Consistent with the symbolic interactionist notion that identity is situated insofar as self-definition is contingent on social location (Stone, 1981), the meaning and definition of time is situated in a context, a point of reference, and a set of emergent interactive dynamics. Hence, whether time is perceived to be running fast or slow, whether it is constraining or not evident will be shaped by the characteristics of the actors (age, gender, personality, social position), their reasons for interaction (coincidence, competition, pleasure), and their unfolding definitions and meanings of the situation (interesting or boring, worthwhile or waste of time, "when will this end?"). From this perspective, time enters the interactive flow as a reference point that reflects the orientations and interests of those involved and as a tool for definition of the situation in terms of pace, duration, value, and cadence.

Through the assignment of meaning to time in social situations we create meanings that shape the identities of the individuals involved and give direction to the course of the interaction. Our sense of identity is "time dependent" (Russell, 1992, p. 152). Identity exists in a temporal dimension that is ongoingly constructed and coordinated. In this vein, that Strauss (1965) emphasized Mead's ideas about the negotiated temporal order. Individual actors bring to an interaction preferences about activity rates and time allocations in order to arrive at a *negotiated* temporal order in which they adjust their activity patterns to coordinate with one another.

Feelings play an important part in the way that time is negotiated and ordered in interaction (Shaw, 1994). For example, feelings that are associated with punctuality are reflective of how the relationship is defined and experienced. Hence, being on time gives rise to respect or trust. Conversely, being kept waiting can foster feelings of distress through loss of control, helplessness, anger, fantasies of calamities, and possibly even deep-rooted fears of abandonment (Shaw, 1994). Although most people tend to excuse lateness with comments such as "It's OK," this usually masks a seething rage or spiraling imaginings that something truly awful had happened (Shaw, 1994, p. 84).

## The Meaning of Temporal Awareness in Families

Reflexivity, or the work of paying attention to our experience, is at the root of our awareness of time. Commenting on the ideas of George Herbert Mead, Maines (1987) makes the claim that temporality is by its very nature reflexive, insofar as it is "constructive and structuring as well as reconstructive and mythical" (p. 307). Being conscious of the past, present, and future is part of lived experience and is fundamental to our experience of change and growth. Although we tend to think of the past, present, and future as linear in nature, they are, in the lived experience of time, considerably more disjointed.

As Husserl (1964) has pointed out, they are contingencies whose horizons are continually fluctuating around the constitutive concerns of the momentary present. In this regard, temporal awareness is always located in the present. Memory is not the random appearance or retrieval of events emerging out of the fog of the past but rather is the product of present concerns projected into the past (Hendricks & Peters, 1986). Although the relation between the present and the past is never well-defined, to be remembered, events must be relevant to some ongoing project.

Given the anchoring position of the present, the awareness of time within families is shaped by the intersection of many temporalities. The family is at the crossroads of several time dimensions, including the life cycles of each of its members, the work paths of husband and wife, and the family life cycle itself (Pronovost, 1989).

In terms of individual life cycles, aging is in itself the process of having some awareness of our lived time. According to Hendricks and Peters (1986), aging is both continuous and episodic. Our awareness of age arises in our understanding of change:

> To the extent that we are aware of some personal development or change during our "lived time" we perceived time stretching out behind us, and accordingly, we evaluate ourselves in terms of the magnitude of change we apprehend. It is through this assessment of "elapsed change" that we acquire some sense of our personal rates of experience and create the basis for age identification. (p. 672)

Within families, members have a different awareness of time depending on their development stage. For example, whereas school-aged children experience the long, seemingly endless days of summer, parents wonder why there are not enough hours in the day to complete all the work that must be done.

In terms of the work lives of husbands and wives, temporal awareness is gendered. Despite dramatic changes in labor force participation, women's work outside of the family is usually subject to family constraints (Pronovost, 1989). As this suggests, a woman's awareness of time is usually more tethered to family needs and concerns (see Chapter 7).

Finally, the stage of the family life cycle also plays a major role in the awareness of time. The meaning, the pace, and the quality of time varies depending on whether the family is childless, has a crying infant in the middle of the night, has school-aged children who are enrolled in several after school programs, has adolescent children who persistently test curfews, or has launched children into their own temporal worlds. Of course, these temporal experiences within families are even more diverse in light of the many kinds of families that exist. Hence, the farm family will have a different awareness of time from the dual-earner family, in the same way that the single-parent family will have a different experience than the stepfamily.

## The Development of Temporal Awareness

The family is usually the primary forum for the child's construction of a world of meaning. Specifically, within this forum, children learn an awareness of time and begin to understand the way that time shapes and structures the course of their lives. The family, then, constitutes "the first temporal horizon for children" (Pronovost, 1989, p. 47).

There is a considerable literature within psychology that examines the way that children develop an awareness of time. As Piaget (1970) argued, this is a process whereby "time must be *constructed* into a unique schema by operations, and moreover, by the same groupings and groups as enters into the construction of logical and arithmetical forms" (p. 274). For Piaget, there were three developmental stages in the developmental comprehension of time. Using a set of experiments that are based on the child's observations of how objects move, Piaget focused on the concepts of "seriation" and "succession" as the first steps in the comprehension of time. In Piaget's work, children around the age of 6 were able to accurately comprehend notions of "before" and "after." This step is followed by the comprehension of concepts of "simultaneity" and "duration" around the ages of 7 and 8. In stage three, which begins around the age of 8, children develop a real understanding of time and its measurement through the concept of "reversibility." Reversibility refers to the ability to retrace time, both forward and backward, which is a necessary construct of the logical rational think ng style that is linked to memory and the concomitants of identity (Edlund, 1987).

Other prominent theorists, such as Erikson, have argued that the infant's world is filled with recurrent temporal rhythms that involve sensations of mounting tension, delay, and finally satisfaction (Cottle & Klineberg, 1974). More recent research studies indicate that even within the first 6 months of life, infants can distinguish among different rhythmic structures, silence intervals in different sound groupings, and differences in the timing of various visual cues (Friedman, 1990). Moreover, there is other research that suggests that Piaget's ideas may have obscured some of the competence about time that young children do possess in early childhood. This research supports the idea that children between 3 and 5 years of age demonstrate a knowledge of sequence and a corresponding causal relation; are able to distinguish between the past, present, and future; show a comprehension of the daily ordering of activities; and by the age of 5, are usually able to infer the relative duration of two events based on starting and stopping times (Friedman, 1990). Furthermore, there is evidence to suggest that infants show an ability to regulate action in time and to process temporal information in terms of succession and duration (Pouthas, Droit, & Jacquet, 1993).

During middle childhood and adolescence, there are two trends in the development of temporal knowledge (Friedman, 1990). One is the increase in the number and scale of temporal structures, which includes an increasing comprehension of calendars, schedules, and history. During middle childhood, children shift from conditioned responses to cognitively regulated behaviors that incorporate time (Pouthas et al., 1993). Children learn the rules of time and are able to temporally regulate their actions and behaviors. This involves the potential to conceive of time in quantitative terms and to be able to count and measure it as part of incorporating time into their day-to-day behaviors (Pouthas et al., 1993). The second trend is an increase in the uniformity of time as something that is measurable and relatively unaffected by changes in clocks, time zones, or scales of measurement. As this discussion suggests, time is socially constructed in developmental terms. Children learn the meanings of time as their cognitive abilities allow.

Digital technology has had an important impact on the way that children learn about clock time and their ability to incorporate clock time into their day-to-day experience. The digital clock has made time telling easier because it has removed some of the logical difficulties presented by the two-handed clock face (Elkind, 1981). On a traditional clock face, the three can represent two different measures of time: one being 3 o'clock, the other 15 minutes past the hour. By contrast, on a digital clock, each unit of seconds, minutes, and hours has its own place. The result for the child is that the logical difficulty of sorting out big-hand/little-hand representations is eliminated, such that the child can read the numbers directly from the clock (Elkind, 1981). Although digital clocks do not speed up their cognitive development, they do make clock time more accessible at an earlier age.

In contrast to some of the more psychological explanations for how people develop a temporal awareness, Elias (1992) emphasizes that the individual does not invent the concept of time on his own. One learns both the concept and the social institution of time from childhood on by learning self-constraint that is compatible with the institutional context of time. There is a temporal socialization whereby children learn to be punctual, organized, and coordinated in their activities in order to fit into and contribute to an orderly culture. Similar to Berger and Luckmann's (1966) idea of internalization, Elias (1992) speaks of a temporal socialization as a process of self-constraint whereby there is a "conversion of the external compulsion coming from the social institution of time into a pattern of self-constraint embracing the whole life of the individual" (p. 11). This conversion results in a "temporal conscience" that is in turn expressed through our common language of time. The clock, for example, transmits messages, and, in turn, it serves as a basis for regulating behavior within a group (Elias, 1992). It serves as the basis by which we establish a discourse of speed, promptness, and duration.

## Time and Identity

As the preceding discussion suggests, temporal awareness is an elementary dimension of socialization. As such, the developing experience of time plays an important role in shaping identity. In addition to learning the basics of succession, reversibility or the temporal constraint of the clock, individuals develop a biography through the establishment of their own time line. The developing self can be conceptualized as a series of "timemarkers" and "turning points" that serve as "comparative anchor points" for both "shaping the past and influencing the present" (Charmez, 1991, pp. 1-2). The "sociological calendar" is a device that focuses on the key themes and dates that organize temporal experience. Instead of emphasizing the standard units of clock time or calendar time, the units of the sociological calendar reflect "the rhythm and change of pressing issues and pace-setting activities as they occur in the lives of individuals" (Hendricks & Peters, 1986). As such, it is a useful analytical tool for examining the way that people at various stages of the life cycle conceive of the passage of time.

Anticipation is a key temporal aspect in the social construction of identity. The core of development is creating a conception of the self within a social framework in both its lived and as yet unlived portions (Cottle & Klineberg, 1974, p. 3). This is the anticipation of the personal future that involves, on the one hand, being able to imagine events that have no concrete reality, and on the other hand, being able to "confer a sense of reality on them by attributing them to the realm of the possible" (Cottle & Klineberg, 1974, p. 4). The father who continues to work hard based on the anxiety that he may not be able to provide for his children's education is one example of the way that the future shapes present behavior (Cottle & Klineberg, 1974). Remembering is an important companion to anticipating in the construction of self: "Self-awareness implies a knowledge not only of where a person is now, but also of where he was in the past and where he expects to be in the future" (p. 9). Identity is a process of bridging the past, present, and future. Specifically, it involves assimilating recollections and reconstructions of the past with present events and creating images of the future that also confer meaning on present events. From this perspective all individual action is both retrospective and prospective.

In the same way that time shapes individual identity, it is also central to the formulation and revision of family identity. If we think of families as having a collective identity, then that identity at any moment can be understood with reference to both the composite of their individual and shared recollections and with reference to their anticipated future together. It is to these shared orientations toward time in families that the emphasis now shifts.

## Orientations Toward Time in Families

Orientations toward time are concerned with the temporal horizons of the past, present, and the future. Specifically, orienting has to do with selecting, directing, and maintaining attitudes toward the past, present, and future (Kantor & Lehr, 1976). Orienting is concerned with the reference points in time that a family uses to conduct its affairs. Past orienting involves living in the past or a preoccupation with the history or tradition of the family. Families organize their experience of time through the process of remembering, reexperiencing, or reenacting (Silverstone, 1993). Present orientation has to do with the here and now—with what is being currently experienced. It focuses on the present experiences as the justification for action. The future orientation is concerned with the prediction or "divination" of the future. It is the stereotypical middle-class trait that emphasizes anticipation, imagining, or planning ahead (Silverstone, 1993). This temporal orientation is expressed in many ways in families through patterns of consumption, friendship ties, or contacts with extended family.

In their classic work on the psychosocial dynamics of family systems, Hess and Handel (1959) emphasize the importance of temporal orientation for understanding the family's "psychological mobility." The Clarks, for example, focus on a future as a way of avoiding the psychological and economic misfortunes of the past. They seek to "surmount the childhood which still opposes them from within" and to build for themselves a "secure, stable family with a dependable income, respectable children and moral behaviour" (p. 20). By contrast, the Lansons are a family whose lives are a continuous blend of the past, present, and future. Preference is not given to any particular temporal orientation but, instead, "any special claims upon time are relinquished; there are no 'good old days,' nor will the future return miraculous dividends" (p. 95). Rather, commitment to the past, present, or future is painted over with a "neutral shade" that provides the basis for a temporal continuity between the attachments of their family of origin and their experiences and plans as a family of procreation.

These temporal orientations within families are profoundly influenced by the dominant temporal orientations of the broader culture (Silverstone, 1993). Rather than extremes of either families' shaping their temporal orientation in isolation or being unidirectionally dominated by the public culture, families can be seen as mediating the dominant temporalities of the public domain with and through their own temporal agendas (Silverstone, 1993). Furthermore, information and communication technologies are involved increasingly in that mediation. Television, in particular, plays a key role in the way that families monitor and participate in the temporal structure of the public domain. Television is a medium that fosters an orientation to the present: It is used to "monitor and survey the present, to manage anxiety and to provide us with enough current information (from news) or gossip (from soap operas) to enable us to integrate ourselves into the flux of everyday experience" (Silverstone, 1993, p. 299).

Families may have a dominant orientation to the past, present, or future, but they are also challenged to continuously reconcile the various demands imposed by each of these orientations. "Integration" is the mechanism by which families organize the experience of the past, present, and future (Kantor & Lehr, 1976). The notion that individuals and families are always bridging time (i.e., the past, the present, and the future) suggests that linear metaphors of time do not adequately account for experience of time in families. Although it is often assumed that the past is fixed and immutable, Berger (1963) has argued that "within our own consciousness, the past is malleable and flexible, constantly changing as our recollection reinterprets and re-explains what has happened" (p. 57). Einstein took the lead in natural science in getting rid of singular, unidirectional linear conceptualizations of time. In his general theory of relativity, Einstein demonstrated that there are as many times as there are frames of reference. In this regard, time is relative and not absolute: It is imposed on events and activities by the observer and is not intrinsic to nature itself. Although families can be seen on a developmental course of linear time, it is important to look at the ways that families experience a multiplicity of times depending on their frame of reference. As Gurvitch (1964) has pointed out, the past, the present, and the future are sometimes projected into one another, sometimes dominant over one another, and sometimes reduced to one another.

In a similar way, Reiss (1981) makes reference to the experience of "fusion in time" whereby the family repeats ritualistic family behavior. Time is fused when the family "reexperiences a crucial aspect of its past as if that past were present" (Reiss, 1981, p. 238). Death anniversaries, for example, can resurrect grief in a way that the past is relived according to the same schedule of events as the actual experience. This can be especially pronounced in the case of unexpected deaths that arise from suicide, violence, or accident. These deaths are more likely to result in an experience of reliving the past with a sense of regret (Lopata, 1986). Sudden death of a loved one leaves all of the grief and reconstruction of the self to the period following the death (Charmez, 1980). There is no preparation and no opportunity to make realignments prior to the death. This can result in a sense of unfinished business where survivors express regrets over "what could have been" or the time wasted because it had not been spent in a more enjoyable manner (Lopata, 1986).

Remembering and celebrating the circumstances of the past plays an important role in the maintenance of family paradigms. Family paradigms, which are composed of the family's persistent attitudes and assumptions about the social and physical world, are shaped through individual member's memories of the family's history, myths, heroes, values, and secrets (Reiss, 1981). From this perspective, family behavior can be seen to have a "memorial function" (Reiss, 1981). Through interaction, a family shapes and modulates information from outside the family; it has a capacity to store information over time and, on the basis of these, can objectify its beliefs about itself (Reiss, 1981). The memorial function of families serves as a framework for the enactment of the family paradigm in the everyday world.

Although memories may serve as an important mechanism for the emergence of individual identity, individual memory is also an aspect of group memory. Families, for example, have their own peculiar memories whereby they reconstruct the past following a logic of their own (Halbwachs, 1992). The similarity of memories within families is a reflection of their communal traditions, interests, thoughts, and secrets. These collective memories are not simply images of the past; they represent the "attitude of the group" insofar as they define its nature, qualities, and weaknesses (Halbwachs, 1992, p. 59). In this regard, family memories are always being imbued with new meanings. A family memory does not appear as an event that we experienced in the past, but "we compose it anew and introduce elements borrowed from several periods which preceded or followed the scene in question" (Halbwachs, 1992, p. 61). For example, when families celebrate the entrance of a new member to the family through birth, adoption, or marriage, the family might bring forward reflections or impressions regarding the circumstances of the event. Not only do the memories involve the retrieval and reconstruction of the celebrated event, they serve as an opportunity for family members to ruminate on the significance or meaning that the person has for them (Halbwachs, 1992, p. 71).

It has been argued, however, that the present is the crucial frame of reference for understanding the past. The past does not "recur," nor is it "preserved"—rather, it is reconstructed on the basis of the present conditions (Halbwachs, 1992). Although there is a tendency to think of the past as final and irrevocable, it is as "hypothetical as the future" (G. H. Mead cited in Maines, Sugrue, & Katovich, 1983, p. 161). The fact that historians are constantly rewriting history is a function of the fact that "historical time is reconstructed according of the criteria of present societies and groups" (Gurvitch, 1964, p. 35). "Collective memories" are formed within a variety of milieus, including family, religion, and social class, and these serve as an interpretive framework (Halbwachs, 1992). From this perspective, memories play an important role in the formation and preservation of identity. There is a "continual relationship" with memories that are reproduced in successive periods of our lives. Memories lose the form and appearance that they once had because we force them into the framework of the present. Nevertheless, identity is continuously reformed on the basis of the continuity that arises in the process of reconstructing past memories in the present moment. As Schutz (1964) has indicated, we cannot repeat experience: We grow older, novel experiences emerge continuously within our stream of thought, and previous experiences are "permanently receiving additional interpretive meanings" (pp. 114-115). As a result, "an experience of the

past can never be reinstated in another present exactly as it was"
(p. 115).

There is evidence that temporal orientation changes with the aging
process. Early research indicated that there is a general speedup of
time as an individual ages. As individuals age, time as registered by the
clock and calendar appears to pass ever more rapidly (Whitrow,
1988). This has been variously attributed to the fear of approaching
death, the amount of elapsed time experience, and the increasing
volume of experience encountered by the adult mind (Hendricks &
Hendricks, 1976, p. 34). This is consistent with other psychological
research that indicates that intervals filled with activity will pass more
rapidly than unfilled temporal intervals (Hendricks & Hendricks,
1976). More recent research refutes the linear conceptualization of a
developmental speedup and, instead, demonstrates that middle-aged
people, when compared to the young and the old, are most likely to
report that time has passed more quickly (Flaherty & Meer, 1994).
This is referred to as an experience of "temporal compression" where
the past is perceived as having "flown by." This is attributed to the
greater density of routine activity in middle age associated with
the responsibilities of marriage, parenthood, and work. It is consistent
with other research that reports that middle-aged adults (aged 35-
54) are most likely to report feeling rushed in their everyday lives
(Robinson, 1990).

In a review of time orientation in the gerontology literature, Seltzer
and Hendricks (1986) point out that with aging, futurity declines and
retrospection increases. Indeed, key concepts in the human development literature such as Neugarten's (1973b) "interiority" during the
latter part of middle adulthood or Butler's (1963) "life review" in old
age are essentially retrospective activities. Erikson's (1963) notion of
"ego integrity" is based on an acceptance of the way that one has lived
life in the past. The perception of a shrinking future seems to direct
attention to the fullness of the past. The process of life review involves
recounting aspects of one's life in the past and relating them to present
experience. It can be the opportunity to resolve past conflicts and to
take pride in past accomplishments and contributions to others. It can
also serve as the story thread that links the generations by relating the
memories and experiences of prior generations to the younger generations who will carry the stories into the future. When the life review

is part of the experience of dying, men and women appear to focus on different concerns. Although men appear to worry most about their ability to die with dignity, women worry about their unfulfilled obligations to the loved ones they are leaving behind (Lopata, 1986).

Health plays an important role in the management of temporal orientation. Efforts during early and middle adulthood to adopt and maintain a healthy lifestyle through exercise and proper diet are in some respects investments in the future. Investments in fitness are based on a belief that extra effort now can make the "reservoir of future time" even more pleasant than would otherwise be expected (Rakowski, 1986, p. 732). In later life, the assessment of one's reservoir of future time may be more tentative due to the increasing likelihood of illness or physical limitation for oneself and through the anxieties produced by health problems seen among age peers (Rakowski, 1986).

The onset of chronic illness has an important impact on the experience of the future. It involves anticipating the trajectory of the illness and the probable treatment paths; an assessment of future potentials and limitations; adapting to the continuity of self-image through past, present, and future; and adjustments to future ambiguities and uncertainties (Rakowski, 1986). When the future is doubtful or filled with unwelcome prospects, there may be a tendency toward what Cottle and Klineberg (1974) have referred to as "antepression." This is an avoidance in thinking about the future because of the limited or negative possibilities that exist in the future. The events of an illness can also serve as markers for the construction of a chronology that gives the self a sense of form and meaning and that can stand as "the history of a transformed self" (Charmez, 1991, p. 3). Anniversaries of key events and important diagnoses are markers that are not merely reconstructions after the events but are active constructions that mark events while immersed in the illness and that serve to measure the next hurdle. As such, they are ongoing constructions in the present. Although timemarkers are external and shared, "identifying moments" are existential experiences that are filled with new self-images that spark new realizations about the self and divulge to others what to think (Charmez, 1991, p. 5). In turn, these identifying moments can become significant events that "freeze and enlarge a moment in time" in a way that shakes the assumed self and can precipitate a turning point or reconstruction of the self. Furthermore, these remembered events of the past are relived and reexperienced in a way that the past story foretells the future self: "By telling and retelling, they develop, solidify, and reify a stance on the event, on themselves in the event, and on their future selves" (Charmez, 1991, p. 11).

## Working With Temporal Orientation in Families: Family Therapy

Families do not live time in the same way. One way of conceptualizing these differences is to think of family time experience as occurring on a continuum ranging from "rigid" transactions to "chaotic" transactions (Ausloos, 1986). For families with rigid transactions, time is arrested and characterized by no change, immobility, and a fusion of the past and future with no prospects of change in the future. Families with chaotic transitions are characterized by incessant but impermanent changes and the absence of stable and trustworthy rules. For therapists, understanding "where the time game lies" plays a crucial role for opening up possibilities for change within the family system (Ausloos, 1986). Specifically it may mean "mobilizing time" by stirring up crises to get out of rigid patterns, or by slowing down time by introducing a notion of duration to escape chaos (Ausloos, 1986). Other approaches in therapy involve working specifically with the past and the future.

### WORKING WITH THE PAST

In family therapy, families revisit, reexperience, and quite often restory the past events of their lives to sort out their present conflicts and to construct invitations to a different future. Taking control of time in this way is an inherently political process. First, it touches on family paradigms that can gravitate toward extreme positions such as "What is done is done and cannot be undone" (which is a position of powerlessness over the events of the past) to a position of reconstructing the past in a way that allows the individual to take control over or take responsibility for events that have occurred. Similar to this,

Gergen and Gergen (1984) refer to "progressive" and "regressive" forms of narrative (p. 176). Individuals can either progressively feel control over and shape their personal stories in a way that is deemed incremental (progressive), or they must contend with their relative inability to control the events of their lives and evaluate their experience of time as a decrement (regressive). Reversing time can be a mechanism for taking control over events and behavior.

The integration of pasts, presents, and futures serves as the basis on which White and Epston (1990) outline the narrative approach to family therapy. Consistent with the social constructionist idea that all behavior is ascribed meaning, they argue that time plays an important role in the way that these meanings are interpreted. Specifically, although a piece of behavior occurs in time in such a way that it no longer exists in the present by the time it is attended to, the meaning that is ascribed to the behavior survives across time. They go on to suggest that people in their lives seek to create a coherent account of themselves and the world around them "by arranging their experience of events in sequences across time" (p. 10). Specifically, the self-narrative involves connecting in lineal sequence the experiences of events in the past and present and those that are predicted to occur in the future. Narrative accounts allow the individual to see life events as systematically and coherently connected (Gergen & Gergen, 1984). This is the "storying of experience"—it gives order to daily lives and serves as the basis for the interpretation of future experiences. All stories, according to White and Epston, have a beginning (history), a middle (present), and an ending (future). In keeping with this, the interpretation of current events is as much future shaped as it is past determined (p. 10). Furthermore, individuals are always "immersed" in narrative insofar as they are continuously "recounting and reassessing the meanings of our past actions, anticipating the outcome of our future projects, situating ourselves at the intersection of several stories not yet completed" (Brooks, 1984, p. 3).

The structuring of a narrative is also a selective process whereby people "prune" from experience those events that do not fit with the dominant evolving stories—as a result, a good part of experience goes unstoried. In living our lives, then, our stories are full of gaps. However, in telling the story, some of these gaps must be filled in by "performing the story." People are "reauthoring their lives" insofar as they enter into them, take them over, and make them their own (White & Epston, 1990, p. 13). In this regard, Kvale (1977) refers to remembering as a search for meaning that involves an imaginative reconstruction of past events. Therapy then is a "context for the re-authoring of lives and relationships" (White & Epston, 1990, p. 17). Persons can tell their stories, "perform" their stories, arrive at new outcomes to their stories, ascribe new meaning to their stories, perform alternative stories, elaborate stories, and perhaps most important, separate themselves from their stories so that they can experience a sense of personal agency. By "breaking from the performance of their stories, they experience a capacity to intervene in their own lives and relationships" (White & Epston, 1990, p. 17).

Part of this process involves opening spaces for the "subjugated knowledges" (White & Epston, 1990, p. 32). Whereas the dominant stories are "problem-saturated" stories of family life, the subjugated stories are previously neglected but vital aspects of lived experience. This is an "archaeological endeavor" whereby people are invited to investigate their family and community archives as well as any historical documents that would have a bearing on their current practices. More simply, therapy involves questions that "historicize" alternative knowledges by casting attention on how conclusions have been reached with respect to capabilities of persons and relationships (White & Epston, 1990, p. 21). These are the basis for a discussion of "new destinations and futures" (p. 21). They suggest the use of "future-oriented, backward-looking questions" that request "persons to imagine themselves arriving at some valued destination in life and then to look back at the present to determine which of those steps they are taking are most relevant or important to achieving that destination" (p. 22). "Re-authoring" of stories through therapeutic means is way of arriving at new meanings of past events. By plotting alternative stories of one's past, people arrive at "unique redescriptions" of themselves and their relationships, which in turn can serve as an opportunity to "revision" their relationships with themselves and others.

Although it is tempting to think of narratives as the product of an individual's reflections and experiences, it is important to acknowledge that narratives are essentially "communal products" that arise out of social interaction (Gergen & Gergen, 1984, p. 174). Even

self-narratives or autobiographical accounts are not independent constructions, for the individual is limited to a vocabulary and a narrative
form that is comprehensible within the cultural milieu. Furthermore,
the actions that follow personal narratives are subject to evaluation
insofar as people can find the narratives to be credible or misleading.
Because narratives are realized in the public arena, they are susceptible
to evaluation and sanctioning (Gergen & Gergen, 1984, p. 185). In
this respect, narratives are open to be negotiated and revised. Although the person giving the narrative may be the central protagonist,
others are required to play supporting roles in the narrative construction. In this regard, there is an interdependence of constructed narrative that involves a negotiation of meaning between the self and the
supporting cast who are required to sustain the credibility of the
narrative. Furthermore, we typically think that people have a single
life story, but it appears that there is usually more than one story to
tell (Gergen & Gergen, 1984). Specifically, people are able to adopt
multiple perspectives and focus on particular events as a way of
embellishing and justifying the selected narrative.

WORKING WITH THE FUTURE

   Although we often think of the past as that which is restoried, the
future is also amenable to reconstruction. Anticipatory grief and
"rehearsals for widowhood" (Neugarten, 1973a) occur when people
must deal with the impending death of a loved one or see their friends
going through the experience of death and loss. On this basis, they
begin to project a different future for themselves. Lopata (1986), in
her studies of Chicago widows, suggests that grief ties together the
past and the future: "Grief work requires a reconstruction of the past
to fit the present and the creation of a new future as a substitute for
the future blocked by death" (p. 700). Hence, in addition to reviewing
and reliving the past as it was experienced prior to the death of a
spouse, grief involves the creation of a new future that involves
entering into new roles and rearranging priorities in the absence of
her identity as a wife. As this suggests, time is not experienced by
widows in linear and unidirectional modes but in a more variable
manner that is shaped from the vantage point of the present (Lopata,
1986). Furthermore, the indeterminacy of the timing of widowhood

is such that there may be little opportunity to create in a meaningful way the shape of the future.

People also use the future as a way of shaping current activities. An expected life history is a way of structuring a personalized future that involves carrying out specific roles, engaging in planned activities, and projecting the quality of future life (Seltzer & Troll, 1986). The expected life history can then precipitate present actions that serve to either bring about or prevent expected futures. The available family roles, positions and traditions play an important role in determining the way that these personalized futures are set up. For example, positions such as the family "kinkeeper," historian, or moneymaker are family expectations that can be incorporated into expected life histories (Seltzer & Troll, 1986). History too plays a role in the way that expected futures are constructed. Women today, for example, have different expected life histories from their own mothers and grandmothers because of different job options, pressures, and goals. Expected life histories involve alignments in the present as a result of an attentiveness to the future. It is a framework of projected events and circumstances that reflexively influences the present. In this regard, expectations concerning time of marriage, plans for children, or occupational achievements shape current actions in a way so as to bring about the particular timetables for the particular events (Seltzer & Troll, 1986).

Restorying past events or using the future as a mirror to reflect back changes that are necessary in the present are both models that go beyond linear conceptions of time. There is a reflexive dynamic whereby the past and the future are domains of experience (actual or projected) that can be visited and manipulated as a way of designing or recasting the present. There is also a circularity in the experience of time that is introduced by virtue of replaying and rehearsing events in the past and the future.

The emphasis on narrative and expected life histories reflects a further erosion of the dominance of the objective clock time associated with modernity. Giddens (1991) suggested that objective time is slowly giving way to individualized subjective temporalities where individuals create their own individualized time-of-life narratives. This focus on personal narrative is in keeping with the postmodern turn. One manifestation of the increased importance of the personal narrative has been in the increased importance of therapy as a "methodology for life-planning [which] represents the way in which the temporal lifespan is separated from traditional structures, moral and other concerns" (Urry, 1994, p. 145). Therapy is the opportunity for "privatized reflexivity" that involves "continuous self-observation and monitoring" (Urry, 1994, p. 144). From this perspective, therapy individualizes and privatizes time, and from this perspective, temporal experience within families constitutes an ongoing project of social construction.

## Summary

A social constructionist view, with its emphasis on emergent meanings, is well suited to the task of analyzing and understanding the increasing diversification of forms associated with postmodernity. A social constructionist view places emphasis on time as an ongoing project of activity. As a construction, time is subjective and social because it involves both the idiosyncratic perspective of the individual and the shared, intersubjective meanings of time that are necessary for aligned interaction. Hence, individual experiences of pace and duration are continuously being reconciled with the schedules and deadlines of the social situation. Interpretation mediates the subjective meanings and objectively available cues so that individual courses of action can be aligned with the constraining effect of broader temporal frameworks. Symbols, in the form of clocks, calendars, daily schedules, and vocabularies of time, serve as the mechanisms that make these interpretive processes possible. Furthermore, symbols are the basis for the creation and negotiation of shared meanings of time. The meaning of time is established in the situation when individual actors coordinate their definitions of when they come together, for how long, and with what kind of tempo.

Within families, time is an ongoing project of changing meanings and negotiations. Not only do individual family members have to reconcile their individual time orientations with the external world, but they must do it with each other. Hence, the coordination of schedules, finding time to be alone and together, or finding alignments in terms of the pace of their lives, involve a continuing process of defining for themselves and each other their meanings and expectations around time. Although daily routines can become habitual and taken for granted, there are still daily negotiations around time that arise in the course of defining the immediate situation. Examples include, "When will you be home tonight?" "Can you be home after school for the kids?" or "I am going to have to leave early in the morning."

Given the importance of changing meanings of time, temporal awareness is central to the social constructionist position. Because definitions of time occur in the emerging present, our awareness of time is always located in the present. Being conscious of the past, present, and future is part of lived experience. The way that past events are defined or interpreted will change according to present concerns. As a result, past family events are interpreted and imbued with the meanings of the present. Similarly, future goals and expectations within families are continually fluctuating according to the changing circumstances of the present. At any given time, temporal awareness is shaped by the complex intersection of many temporalities, including the life cycles of each family member, the work paths of husbands and wives and the stage of the family life cycle.

The family is the primary forum where the sociocultural meanings of time are learned. It is within the family that children learn temporal routines, how to order events, and how to abide by temporal norms and rules. Time plays a central role in the socialization of children to be social beings. Time is not a private, subjective creation of the individual. Rather, the meaning of time arises out of the process of learning self-constraint in relation to a time-ordered culture. Through this process, children learn the essential survival skills of punctuality, organization, and coordination.

Socializing children to be attentive to time is central to the formulation of both individual and family identity. Through the development of temporal awareness, children learn how to manage time in interaction by being attentive to the intricacies of sequencing, sharing, or ending an interactive episode. In addition, children develop a biography through the establishment of their own time line that is marked by key anchor points and transitions. Time is also central to the formulation of family identity. Families have a "memorial function" that arises through their capacity to store information over time about their history, their myths, values, secrets, and hopes for the future. Through these accumulated and shared meanings, families formulate a set of beliefs about who they are.

In the same way that historians rewrite history on the basis of new information arising in the present, families, too, rewrite their collective past and shared future as circumstances change. In this regard, collective memories in families are not so much preserved as they are reproduced within ever-changing present contexts. On this basis, social constructionist and narrative approaches to therapy provide an opportunity for families to revisit and possibly restory the past events of their lives. This approach offers an invitation to families to intervene in their own lives by returning to the past to reauthor their lives and relationships. Specifically, by seizing control over the way that stories have been ordered in time, families can arrive at new outcomes to their stories, ascribe new meaning to their stories, perform alternative stories, and separate themselves from their stories so that they can break free of the tyrannizing effects of old storylines. Families are also able to reconstruct the future. The sudden death of a loved one or the unanticipated onset of chronic illness or disability precipitates a dramatic restructuring of the anticipated future horizon. Therapy can also serve as a useful tool for individuals to realize a personalized future where plans and goals serve as the basis for redesigning the present. In this regard, the present is the site for the ongoing construction and reconstruction of time in families.

To speak of "family time" is to refer to an important cultural symbol in our culture. Family time is a socially constructed notion that carries with it a host of meanings and interpretations. In the next chapter, there is an examination of this important, albeit obscure notion of "family time."

# 4

## Time Together

### *The Social Construction of Family Time*

### The Social Meanings of Family Time

"Family time" is now a central part of Western discourse when referring to family experience. Many images can be conjured up for family time. Some of these are traditional with nostalgic hues: the family vacation, meals together, the family working together, attendance at religious functions, or time together on special occasions, feasts, or holidays. Others are more contemporary and reflect an escalated pace of life in families: time together in the car on the way to dropping off members for their individual activities, discussions around the microwave as individual dinners are being warmed up, or a serial discussion that occurs during the commercials. Although it obviously encompasses a wide spectrum of activities, family time in its traditional form is most readily conjured up. Family time has a strong flavor of sentimentality that is rooted in notions of togetherness, intensive interaction, and pride.

Historical evidence, however, suggests that the expectation that time spent in the family should be the main source of fulfillment was not traditional in the 18th and 19th centuries (Coontz, 1992). Occasions such as Thanksgiving and Christmas were more focused on attending parties and dances than in celebrating family solidarity (Coontz, 1992). It wasn't until the 20th century that family time took on importance as the site of festivity, celebration, and emotional intensity. For many families, the nostalgic images of family time may continue to be important idealizations that guide their behavior. These images may also be at the root of tremendous disappointment when important family occasions of togetherness do not go well—the times when drunkenness, harsh words, or family tensions override the expected "glow" of well-being that is expected of family time together.

For other families, time together is more often a sporadic coincidence that may go unnoticed due to being caught in the "insidious cycle of work and spend" (Schor, 1991, p. 107). Family time can be like the pit stop of the racing world where depleted energy resources are replenished in the name of "get up and go." Family time is more like the coincidental sharing of space and time that arises from the intersection of busy lives. Given the family's outward orientation whereby individual members spend a good portion of their time involved in unconnected worlds and interests, family time can be seen as a "distraction from other pursuits" (Ventura, 1995). For still other families, where violence and conflict tend to prevail, family time may be something to be actively avoided. Hence, although the discourse of family time reflects an ideology of togetherness, it can mean many things: It may be a family goal associated with values and beliefs about what it means to be a good family; it can be a set of actions that varies according to how deliberate and conscious they are about spending time together; and it can be intensively interactive to extremely evasive in the nature of the activity that constitutes it.

Family time is colored by some of the ideological debates that are carried out with respect to the family itself. In the same way that families of the past have been romanticized and idealized, so too has family time. As Shaw (1992) has pointed out, family leisure is typically portrayed in the media as "occasions that are consistently happy, mutually enjoyable and beneficial" for the whole family. The dominant view of family leisure reflects the romanticized version of family life and is captured in the modified adage "the family that plays together, stays together" (Shaw, 1992). Citing a variety of parenting and women's magazines, Shaw points to an emphasis that is placed on the importance of families spending "quality" time together, strategies for how to make outings fun for all concerned, the overall importance of family togetherness as a value, and how spending time with children can help them overcome psychosomatic illnesses and enhance positive psychological development (Shaw, 1992). This is the hegemonic view of family time that emphasizes only the positive aspects and, as a result, is reified as part of the pro-family ideology (Shaw, 1992). From this view, family time does not typically include portrayals of the negative aspects or outcomes of family activities, nor does it typically include nontraditional families.

Although the notions of togetherness and positive family experience are attractive ideas insofar as they fit with some of our nostalgic yearnings, they tend to mask some of the underlying conflicts, contradictions, or inequalities with respect to the experience of family time. Rubin (1976), for example, in asking participants about the good things they remembered growing up in a working-class family, found that most people worked very hard at trying to put a positive spin on their childhood stories of family time. However, most often her question was met with a "series of halting attempts to enumerate the 'good' memories" with the result being that the conversation usually "limped to an uncomfortable end" as memories of pain and deprivation took over (p. 47). Other research has shown that shared family activities can be both a source of both cohesion and conflict (Orthner & Mancini, 1990). Blended families have an experience of family time that can bring together both the nontraditional and conflictual aspects of family time. Winton (1995) describes the experience of family time in a blended family:

> Marriage into a stepfamily is sometimes described as having a honeymoon in a crowd. The parents feel that they are being drawn and quartered by family members' demands for time. First of all, the parent must spend time with the new spouse in order to establish a new marital relation. Then the parents' biological children expect time alone with their parent, in a nostalgic attempt to maintain the former single-parent household. These biological children want time together with their

biological parent as the old single-parent unit, and each child also wants time alone with his or her biological parent, time that does not have to be shared with siblings. Each parent must, in addition, spend time with his or her new stepchildren, both together and individually, in order to establish a unique relationship with each of them. And the parents must spend time with the entire stepfamily as a unit, with all members together so that they can establish the sense of a new family unit. There is just not enough time to devote to all these diverse permutations. (pp. 172-173)

Family time, then, needs to be seen as a full spectrum of possibilities ranging from the positive view that casts it as the opportunity for togetherness and the more negative end of the continuum where time together is constraining and filled with competing interests.

Positive constructions of family time also gloss over the different experience of family time for men and women. Shaw (1992), in her research on gender differences in the experience of family time, discovered that men and women have very different constructions of the meanings of family time. The "gendered" division of family leisure that she found indicates that men and women define family time very differently in terms of the degree to which it is considered work or leisure. Whereas men are more likely to define family time as leisure, women were more likely to define family time as work or a combination of work and leisure activity. Although there is a tendency to view family time as a monolithic construction, the meanings of family time are not necessarily shared or intersubjective within the family but are contingent on individual definitions of the situation. Shaw (1992) demonstrates how definitions of family time are different for men and women, but one could also hypothesize that definitions of family time would be different for adults and children. Children's experiences and definitions of family time have received little attention in the research literature. Family meal times have also been cast as traditionally positive experiences. Yet as Vuchinich (1987) has demonstrated with his observational work on family meal times, dinners together are an important opportunity for the expression of family conflict. In an examination of 64 audio- and videotaped family dinners, that ranged from 15 minutes to more than an hour, there was an average of 3.3 conflict episodes per dinner. The topics of these conflicts were diverse and included food, money, future plans, sexual behavior, and drugs. Interestingly, there was a roughly even split between parents and children with regard to the initiation of family conflicts with parents beginning 48% and children initiating 52% (Vuchinich, 1987).

The meaning of family time in our current cultural context must also be attentive to the changing values associated with privacy and autonomy. Although families are always faced with striking a balance between too much cohesion (enmeshment) and too much individual autonomy (chaotic), they are influenced by the prevailing values of the time. In the well-known book *Habits of the Heart,* concern is expressed that "individualism may have grown cancerous" in America (Bellah, Madsen, Sullivan, Swidler, & Tipton, 1985, p. vii). In comparison to de Toucqueville's 19th-century study, which pointed to the family as a defense against individualism, it appears now that "individualism is in the family as well as outside of the family" (Bellah et al., 1985, p. 90). Staying single, remaining child free, small families, and the freedom to divorce all point to a growing individualism within the family (Bellah et al., 1985). This has been referred to as an "integration crisis" where parents are off on their own working long hours and children are left unsupervised or in the care of others (Winton, 1995). The implication of this growing individualism is that family time may be increasingly viewed as a product of individualistic uses of time rather than a cohesive, shared phenomenon.

## Family Time as a Boundaried Experience

Family time and work time have traditionally been viewed as highly boundaried experiences. Family time becomes meaningful only when we think of it as time that is carved out from the rest of day-to-day experience. In this regard, family time is understandable only insofar as it is separate from other kinds of time. The separation of "work" and "family" during the onset of industrial capitalism played a key role in bracketing family time as different from work time. Prior to capitalism, families were not different from the economy because they carried out a full range of "natural" functions that included reproduction, care of the sick, the maintenance of personal property, and the basic forms of material production necessary to sustain life (Zaretsky, 1976). In this regard, the family was the basic economic unit in society. There was no division between production and consumption (Toffler,

1980). Capitalism divided material production organized as wage labor from the forms of production that were taking place in the family. For Zaretsky (1976) this split in productive activity resulted in a host of profound divisions between the economy and the family, the outer world of personal labor and the inner world of personal feeling, or quite simply between "work" and "life." The net impact of these divisions was that family became "the major space in society in which the individual self could be valued 'for itself' " (Zaretsky, 1976, p. 31). It is precisely within this "major space" that family time took on a set of meanings that made it private, controlled, and personal. The emergence of family time as a private experience gives rise to the need for family members to negotiate "protected time" that reduces the interfering noise from outside the family system (Broderick, 1988, p. 86).

The emergence of family time, as a socially constructed concept, is similar in some ways to the emergence of the notion of "spare time." Spare time emerged in the 19th century as part of the industrial revolution, where the Victorian work ethic held out spare time as a reward for hard work (Whitrow, 1988, p. 162). Although spare time was promised, in reality workers were often so exhausted and had so few options for recreation that they did little but try to recuperate from the demands of work. Holidays, feasts, and celebrations also play an important role in punctuating everyday reality with special family time. On the basis of Durkheim's ideas about solidarity, Pasero (1994) contends that holidays and feasts play an important role in the cohesion of groups by highlighting the common experience and beliefs shared by a collection of people. Families come together to experience this extraordinary time in the form of anniversaries, religious celebrations, births, deaths, and marriages. Ritual represents a moment of "antitemporality" where time is frozen or reversed in the world of the sacred (Silverstone, 1993). These events, however, were different from our contemporary views of family time. Although it has developed into an experience that is viewed as highly privatized, in the 19th century, family time was typically a much more public experience involving the participation of many families and many members of the community.

Although Durkheim's view emphasizes the common experience of this kind of time, it is critical to emphasize that family celebrations are quite often the occasions for the expression of tensions and conflicts. For example, beneath the veneer of the happy wedding celebration may be a seething antagonism or a protective anxiety that is expressed in private conversations about whether the new spouse is "good enough." Furthermore, gender plays an important role in understanding how individuals within families may have dramatically different experiences of these important celebrations. Bella (1987, cited in Henderson & Allen, 1991), for example, examined the role that women have in the production of a Christmas celebration. Although Christmas is usually thought of as a time for family togetherness and mutual enjoyment, Bella described the physical and emotional work that a woman invests in Christmas as social convener, cook, shopper for food and gifts, organizer of Christmas cards, gift wrapper, decorator, and baker. In addition, she is expected to attend spouse's and children's Christmas parties and create a peaceful atmosphere in which people are made to feel welcome and cared for.

The boundaries between work time and family time are still strong, but technology has opened a hole in the fence. For example, in the film *Hook,* Robin Williams plays the role of the father who takes his children to England for a holiday visit with his aging grandmother. Shortly after arriving, he gets a call on his cellular phone as the children play noisily in the background. It is a work call concerning, in his words, "the deal of lifetime." Partway through the call, he stops and screams at the children to be quiet. A conflict with his wife ensues and she throws the cellular phone out the window. The viewer is left with the interpretation that it is the father, and not the noisy children, who is guilty of a transgression: The father has violated the sanctity of family time by allowing work time to intrude. The cellular phone is the technological wedge that has allowed the public world of work to penetrate the private and boundaried world of family time. Studies that have examined the relationship between employment and family roles suggests that persons who are involved in highly salient, time-demanding occupations tend to have the greatest difficulty segregating work time from family time (Key & Sanik, 1990). Like the experience of the father in *Hook,* boundaries between work time and family time are difficult to maintain when family time is dominated by highly demanding occupations.

In light of the growing plurality in postmodern society, one of the traditional distinctions between "work time" and Sundays as a day of rest, has also started to break down. Rooted in a Christian tradition, Sundays were reserved for rest, worship, leisure, and family togetherness. The day was marked by different activities and "Sunday best" clothing (Pasero, 1994, p. 185). In the 1840s, the Sabbatarian movement agitated for the suspension of labor and commerce, by law, on the Sabbath (O'Malley, 1990). In reaction to the tyranny of the industrial clock, they sought to preserve one day of the week that should properly be spent at home in the name of spiritual and physical renewal (O'Malley, 1990). Although similar debates about the sanctity of Sunday time continue to simmer in contemporary society, the conventional distinctiveness of Sundays has broken down as a result of a confluence of forces. Debates about the appropriateness of Sunday shopping tend to focus the issues here. These typically include the plurality of religious beliefs that are present in multicultural Western societies that do not have the same interpretations of Sunday. It also includes what has been referred to as the colonization of time (Melbin, 1978). This involves the extension of working hours into all hours of the night and into the available times of the weekends, which, in turn, results in an escalating demand for services at any time. Although Sundays and holidays still represent extraordinary time patterns for many people, it is now a matter of choice rather than an unequivocal community standard. The diverse interests for leisure time has had the effect of homogenizing leisure time insofar as it has reduced the number of days that are special or reserved for assembly, recuperation, or celebration (Pasero, 1994).

One of the traditional ways that the family and work time boundaries are exercised in everyday life is through the distinction between the work week and the weekend where there are 5 days for work and two for play. However, a recent analysis of the rhythm of family time across the week, based on the General Social Survey conducted by Statistics Canada in 1986, suggests that this kind of distinction is too simple (Zuzanek & Smale, 1992). Rather, they argue that we need to go beyond the workday-weekend dichotomy when trying to understand the rhythm of the week and rather look at a number of unique behavioral patterns associated with the days of the week. For example,

Saturdays and Sundays differ significantly: Saturdays are used for domestic work, shopping, and some leisure, and Sundays are used for rest, outings, family contacts, and child care (Zuzanek & Smale, 1992). Tuesday appears to be the day with the highest number of work hours (Zuzanek & Smale, 1992). Other research indicates that Mondays and Fridays have behavioral patterns that make them distinct from other work days (Zerubavel, 1985). Monday, for example, has high rates of absenteeism and higher rates of emergency calls to hospitals, whereas Fridays, because of the proximity to the weekend, tend to have the lowest reported levels of paid work (Zerubavel, 1985). However, subsequent research reports that there is a gender difference for the pattern of paid work on Fridays: Men work fewer hours on Fridays and women work slightly more hours than on other workdays (Zuzanek & Smale, 1992).

Vacations are culturally viewed as a temporal oasis away from the rigid schedules and demands of the everyday work world, yet they can often mirror the frantic pace of everyday life. For some families, every holiday begins with an intensive discussion of the day's itinerary with negotiations and trade-offs about what they can cram into the time that they have available. Erkel (1995) has referred to this as "relaxation achievement." Other highly structured holidays, such as organized tours or long-distance traveling, often maintain or intensify the daily pace of people's lives. With family vacations, there is also a question about the degree to which vacations represent any kind of significant change for many women. According to Henderson and Allen (1991), vacations are not necessarily leisure for women unless they go alone because they tend to be an extension of the normal domestic and child care responsibilities and are often not a time free from tensions and conflicts.

The increased variation and desynchronization of people's times in a postmodern culture also has profound implications for the experience of family meal times. "Grazing" has taken on increased significance in the way that family members manage their food consumption (Urry, 1994). Instead of coming together for fixed meal times in the same place, family members grab what they can when their schedule allows. Solitary eating by parents is most likely to occur during the week when the "opportunity costs" of arranging shared meal times and the constraints of paid employment are at their highest levels (Bryant & Wang, 1990). When eating alone, the amount of time given to eating is much less than when the meal is shared. Furthermore, shared meal times are charged with extra meaning insofar as the time together takes on social significance that goes beyond physical and nutritional value (Bryant & Wang, 1990).

Space within the household also plays an important role in shaping the way temporal boundaries are constructed and maintained within families. The experience of time for families within the household "cannot be divorced from both the material and symbolic organization of space" (Silverstone, 1993, p. 287). Activities in time take place in space. Even having a home, or a space that can be called home, has a lot to do with apprehending time and normalizing activity. To have a home of one's own is to control one's own time to a greater degree than someone who does not (Rutz, 1992). The homeless, for example, are dependent on the time schedules of the shelters and food banks and must submit to these schedules to survive. With no home space, they have little control over the daily organization of their time.

Within households, domestic space gives rise to issues of time that are associated with privacy, ownership, and sharing. For example, as literacy grew in importance in England in the late 19th century, well-to-do families would often come together in a common space (usually the parlor or the drawing room) to read a book aloud. Because there was often only one good lamp in the house, the family was required to share time and space around the light needed for this activity (Horna, 1992). By contrast, leisure today has become more private and fragmented, with the consequence that individual family members seek out space and time for their own pursuits.

Domestic space is typically gendered in the home. Although women have may have relinquished *exclusive* claim to kitchen space, it is still more frequently associated with *her* space. As a result, she exercises more entitlement regarding how time is structured in that space. Similarly, the workshop in the basement is still a sacred space for men, allowing them temporal control over its use. Separate spaces precipitate few conflicts about time, for little negotiation is required with respect to when the space is to be used. Common spaces within the household, such as the "family room," are more likely to trigger temporal conflicts. On a Saturday morning, a parent gravitates to a favorite chair with coffee, newspaper, and a desire for quiet solitude, while children occupy the couch with the blare of morning cartoons. Although space is the arena in which the conflict is set, it is the competition for the space *at the same time* that is at the root of the conflict. From this perspective, time and space must be seen as fully confounded. In light of this, family members also erect temporal boundaries, as well as spatial ones to regulate access to one another (Silverstone, 1993).

## Technology and Family Time

Technology, in its myriad forms, is destined to have a profound impact on the organization and experience of family time. As Toffler (1980) predicted, computers are on the track of transforming the home into the "electronic cottage" with the effect of reintegrating work and family time. The Internet, fax machines, cellular phones, and television also allow for the transcendence of space and, in so doing, give rise to an image of the family as a node in an ever-expanding electronic network. Technology is no longer something that is restricted to the workplace but is everywhere, including one's house and, as is the case with the increasingly popular mobile personal telephone, on one's body (Nowotony, 1994). One commentator has argued that if we wish to understand family time, we need to understand "family-plus-media" (Ventura, 1995, p. 29). Specifically, the "media has moved in with the family and has become one of its core components" (p. 29).

Television, in particular, is a technology that affects family experience by breaking down the boundaries between public and private domains. The television is the window on the outside world that becomes the focus of the family gaze. It is the mechanism that allows the violence, sentimentality, and commercialism of the public sphere to pour into the family living room. Television "extends our senses into distant places so that we can experience what is happening all over the world" (Elkind, 1981, p. 71). Although this has implications for all members of the family, for children it means that they grow up fast. Television makes adult stories and ideas accessible to children in a way that hurries them to grow up quickly (Elkind, 1981). For example, sex and violence are routinely depicted on television and expose children to adult experiences and concerns that may hurry them into experiences not open to them before or for which they may be developmentally unprepared (Elkind, 1981).

There is a considerable literature that has examined the impact of television viewing on the experience of family time. It is estimated that families spend approximately 40% of their private lives with television (Ventura, 1995). As Kubey (1990) has argued in his review of some of the early scholarship on the relationship between TV and the family, the emphasis was placed on the pacifying effects of the medium. According to Kubey (1990), example, Urie Bronfrenbrenner focused on how TV "freezes everybody," Eleanor Maccoby emphasized the quiet absorption and the "parallel" sociality of family members when the TV is on, and Herbert Marcuse suggested that families become passive and one-dimensional in the face of the TV influence. In contrast to these views that emphasize the negative impact of TV, more recent research directs us to consider that television viewing is linked to more frequent and positive family interactions. For example, a study of young adolescent viewers found that heavy viewers tend to spend more time with their families and feel better with their families than do light viewers (Larson, Kubey, & Colletti, 1989). Similarly, in a study of adult family activities, Kubey (1990) reports that respondents who watched more television also spent more time with their families than light viewers. In addition, contrary to the commonly held belief that communication is nonexistent when the television is being viewed, the researcher found that talking coincided with 21% of television viewing occasions occurring in the family (Kubey, 1990). This compared with 36% for all other non-TV familial activities, representing a 40% reduction in family talking when the television is watched. Although this represents a significant drop in talking when the TV is on, it is a dramatically different picture from families sitting together "frozen" and gazing in a parallel fashion.

Television broadcasting has the capacity to provide a fundamental temporal structuring of everyday life insofar as families structure their waking hours around the rhythms of television programming (Silverstone, 1993, p. 294). On the one hand, individual family members may schedule family activities around favorite programs. A homemaker who schedules chores around daytime soaps or a husband who schedules weekends around sports broadcasts have an important influence on the nature of family interaction (Ventura, 1995). Families may have less shared experience together save for the experience of interacting with an array of "imaginary" people from the set who "command loyalty and have influence" (Ventura, 1995, p. 29). As this suggests, the experience of family time is quite often more saliently affected by the presence of fictitious characters on the screen than real characters next to them on the couch.

On the other hand, television is sometimes one of the few ritualized occasions when family can congregate together and meet in time and space (Silverstone, 1993). The television can bring families together, but there is still a sense that the machine has produced passive togetherness rather than active togetherness (Burton, 1992). Although there is a good deal of talking that goes on when families are watching TV together, heavier viewers were more likely to spend more time passively with one another than lighter viewers (Kubey, 1990). This greater passivity of heavy viewers also had a spillover effect into non-TV familial activities, where they tended to be less activated then their light viewing counterparts (Kubey, 1990).

Video cassette recorders (VCRs) mean that television shows can be recorded and played at one's own convenience, which can also in-fluence the amount of shared family time. From one perspective, VCRs free the family from the rigidity of the broadcast schedule and allow individual members to record their own programs and watch them on their own time, which can subvert the family time of shared television viewing. At the same time, however, the greater control that is introduced with the use of VCRs allows families to schedule times of togetherness that are convenient for all members. This desire and ability (because of technology) to seize control over family time may be part of a more general trend toward "cocooning," where the family seeks insulation and avoidance, peace and protection, and coziness and control (Popcorn, 1991).

Although there is little research that examines the extent to which families are cocooning more now than in the past, there are projections that suggest that technology plays a key role in the return of families to the home (Burton, 1992). Technology appears to be encouraging the cocooning trend in two spheres: recreation and work. Machines such as VCRs, compact discs, home computers, and home exercise machines allow and encourage the expenditure of recreational time in the home. Similarly, electronic mail, phone mail, fax machines, and computer networks create an opportunity for the home to be the center of production. Time is saved in transportation to and from work and there is a temporal efficiency that results from the absence of social distractions within the workplace. However, information technologies are double-edged in the amount of control that they allow. Although faxes and computers allow for the instantaneous delivery of messages, thereby allowing for the control of time, they at the same time create the opportunity for one's own time to be compromised and interrupted in return. Overall, computers are not only the basis for redefining schedules and accessibility, but they are also altering our fundamental conceptions of time. Not only is our immediate urban environment a "sleepless Gorgon" (Toffler, 1980), but we are also part of a larger virtual environment where the Internet pulses 24 hours a day with an endless array of information and opportunities.

Although definitions of home-based work vary considerably, it is estimated that 8% to 23% of the population is engaged in paid work done in or from the home (Pratt, cited in Winter, Puspitawati, Heck, & Stafford, 1993). It has been suggested that home-based work may be an effective way to balance the demands of work and family (Voydanoff, 1988), but the boundaries between income-generating activities and household production or leisure activities can be a problem. Reviewing the research in this area, Winter et al. (1993) pointed out that work time at home is frequently interrupted by children, household chores, or telephone calls; that work done at home lacks credibility as "real work"; and that there is considerable overlap between work activity, household production, and leisure.


## Measurement of Family Time


Given the range of conceptual meanings that are associated with family time, there are a number of difficulties that one encounters when trying to measure family time. One approach is to simply measure the amount of time that all members of any family are together. This measure, though focusing on copresence in the house-hold at any given point, gives little insight into the way that time is experienced and the degree to which any of the activities that are carried out during that time are shared. A more detailed picture of family time emerges from studies that measure various time allocations in families. These measures examine family time in terms of categories such as housework, recreation time, mealtimes, sleeping, personal care, or shopping. Although these categories give a more refined picture of family time by measuring how long families are together for a particular activity, they do not do an adequate job of assessing the degree to which family members are sharing participation in any of these activities. In fact, as Shaw (1992) has pointed out, family members are quite often engaged in qualitatively different activities during these times. For example, during family meal times, wives are more likely to be cooking or cleaning up while children and fathers are eating (Shaw, 1992). Similarly, family time with children is more likely to be experienced as work or a combination of work and leisure for women and leisure for men (Shaw, 1992).

Studies of parental involvement with children have also grappled with the thorny issue of how to measure time. For example, in a review of fathers' involvement with children, Pleck (in press) identified a dizzying array of time measures: father's total time with one child or more than one child; solo time with the child or with the mother present; emotional, caregiving, leisure, and playtime with a child; or interactive time and parallel activity time. Although these many categories of time refer to some of the possible configurations of family time within the parent-child dyad, the categories get even more complex when trying to understand the experience of family time for all members of the family.

Furthermore, "leisure time" itself is a problematic term. Although freedom of choice is usually the prerequisite for any definition of leisure, it also involves many other components that include intrinsic motivation, freedom of choice, enjoyment, relaxation, role interactions, personal involvement, and self-expression (Henderson & Allen, 1991; Shaw, 1985). Family leisure may also include individual, shared, or parallel activities (Orthner, 1976). Leisure time can also be classified as informal, scheduled, constrained, or preferred (Kelly, 1983). As a result, the measurement of leisure time must in some way reflect the multidimensional nature of the experience. In addition, the meaning of leisure must be attentive to the attitudes and perceptions associated with particular situations (Shaw, 1985).

Other researchers have challenged the compartmentalization of lived experience into the categories of work, family, and leisure (Henderson & Dialeschki, 1991). For example, the boundaries between work and leisure are often blurry for some women who believe that their domestic work and their personal leisure are one and the same (Henderson & Dialeschki, 1991). There is even some question as to whether time is even relevant to the issue of leisure, for leisure can be defined as a quality of experience rather than a period of time (de Grazia, 1964). However, lack of time is the major barrier to leisure for both men and women, and as a result, it is necessary to consider the opportunity to spend time in situations that are experienced as leisure (Shaw, 1991). There are also many classifications of leisure that have been used in which distinctions are made between domestic and nondomestic leisure (Firestone & Shelton, 1994; Gloor, 1992), free time and leisure time (de Grazia, 1964; Shaw, 1988, 1991), and among active, passive, and social entertainment and TV leisure (Altergott & McCreedy, 1993).

As this range of conceptualizations suggests, there are numerous challenges associated with the measurement of family time. The first of these is to address the complex, multidimensional nature of the family time experience. In distinction from the traditional image of the family gathering in the parlor to read around the lamp, contemporary family time must be examined in a more fractured manner. This involves an attentiveness to marriage time, parent-child time, parent-to-parent time, or extended family time. The second of these challenges is to go beyond the traditional, imposed categorizations that have been used in the measurement of family time (leisure time, work time, free time, family time) and to examine the meanings of family time from the perspectives of the experiencing members. In this regard, W. I. Thomas's famous dictum about "defining situations as real" is instructive for this analysis insofar as family time that is defined as real is real in its consequences. Qualitative research can play an important role in the development of a grounded theory of family time that is based on the emergent definitions and meanings of individual family members. Using this approach, one could expect different constructions of the family time experience from the perspective of children, parents, and grandparents; women and men; and people living in different kinds of families.

## Summary

The meaning of family time has been shaped by a variety of historical forces. Capitalism, religious beliefs, technology, and changing patterns of labor force participation have both given rise to family time as a highly boundaried experience and contributed to its demise in the postmodern era. Although our current interpretations of family time tend to coalesce around notions of family togetherness and solidarity, this has not always been the case. In the 19th century, for example, community togetherness during key celebrations was viewed as a much more important source of fulfillment than spending time alone in families. However, in response to the fast pace of technology and the dramatic increase of women in the paid labor force, family time has been idealized as the private still point in an otherwise frenzied life pattern. In some ways, this hegemonic view of family time is a modernist belief because it emphasizes the distinction between the public world of productive work and the private world of personal feeling where family time is held out as the reward for successful productivity. Whereas a modernist view neatly dichotomizes work and family time into distinct and uniform domains, a postmodern perspective calls out for an analysis of the diverse experiences of family time. This includes portrayals of the negative aspects or outcomes of family time together and an analysis of the different ways that family time is experienced by nontraditional families. A postmodern view of family time also calls out for an analysis of the underlying conflicts and inequalities with respect to the experience of family time. In this regard, adults, children, women, and men make different contributions to family time, play different roles, and as a result, have different social constructions of the experience of family time.

Although the idea of private family time continues to be salient as a cultural ideal, a variety of forces make the realization of this goal difficult. One of these forces is the expansion of commerce into all days of the week, which has resulted in the deterioration of the distinction between work time and sanctioned days of rest. For example, with the growing pluralization of cultural practices within North America, what were once hegemonic Christian ideas about Sundays as a day of rest have begun to break down. The effect is that many families no longer have culturally prescribed days for togetherness. Similarly, on a day-to-day basis, family members typically disperse into their own temporal routines that have varying degrees of overlap. For these families, it is difficult to have fixed and shared meal times, which have traditionally been one of the focal points for the experience of family time.

Technology plays a major role in reshaping the meaning of family time. Devices such as personal phones and home computers have made the boundary between work time and family time much more permeable than it ever was. By opening a "hole in the fence" of private family time, technology keeps families in a state of interruption. At the same time, the availability of technology within the home also appears to be playing a role in keeping the family closer to home. The increasing availability of VCRs, compact discs, home computers, and home exercise machines means an increase in the opportunities for leisure at home. Similarly, electronic mail, phone mail, fax machines, and computer networks create an opportunity for family members to do their paid work at home. Television, too, with its expanding band of cable channels, continues to draw families into the home for time together. Although stereotyped notions suggest that families sit passively gazing at the tube, research indicates that a good deal of family interaction does occur as they sit around the electronic hearth. With the proliferation of technological devices within the home, it appears that families are at the crossroads of two very different tracks: one that provides them with many new opportunities for shared activity within the home and another that easily distracts them into the solitary world of technology that demands their undivided attention.

The growing diversification in the meanings and experiences of family time has meant that it has become increasingly difficult to measure what family time is. Although quantitative measures of family time can provide some indication of the availability of family members, it says little about the nature of the engagement among family members. Categorizations such as family time, free time, and leisure time put a sharper point on the meaning of time spent within the home but still leave a large number of unanswered questions about the experience and meaning of family time. Qualitative research, focusing on perceptions and changing meanings, is needed to come to a better understanding of the day-to-day experience of family time.

Underlying the challenge of finding shared family time is the degree to which families are able to control time in their lives. It is to this issue that the discussion now turns.

# 5

# Controlling Family Time

The idea that family time can be controlled rests on the assumption that, like productive time, family time is broken down into a set of quantifiable, objectified units that can be socially controlled. Whereas industrialization separated work time and free time, in our postmodern culture, time has been fragmented into many domains that are shaped by the forces of globalization, consumerism, the mass media, and the daily dispersion of individual family members into their own routines. Nevertheless, clocks and schedules objectify all aspects of time, and as a result, time is subject to control through relations of power.

At the most fundamental level, individuals seek to gain some level of control over their daily experience of time and their own passage of time. As a child, I was always impressed by my father's valiant efforts to "make good time" when traveling to our holiday destination. Although some might argue that this was simply a cover for speeding, it can also be seen as winning against time. By making good time, my father was somehow able to not only gain control over time but to beat time insofar as he traveled the distance in space faster than what is expected for that time. Many other metaphors reveal this personal competition that we have with time—"I am really pressed for time," or "I am up against a deadline"—where we are in a race to condense a certain amount of activity into a period of time. Of course, in the moral economy of time, we are considered good managers of our time if we successfully meet deadlines; if we miss the deadline, we are not well organized or are considered poor budgeters of our time.

Faced with their ultimate transience and finitude of existence, human beings have sought to take control over the time aspects of their living conditions. Through the use of symbolic language, technologies, and institutions, human beings have sought to control the decline of their bodies, the synchronization of collective action, and the structure of daily activities both in the present and in the future (Adam, 1990). In this sense, it is the individual in a struggle or a race against time, as if time were "out there" as a relentless and finite hourglass. In the words of John Dewey, "time is the tooth that gnaws, it is the great destroyer, we are born only to die and every day brings us one day nearer death" (Dewey, 1957, p. 141). From a psychoanalytical perspective, there is a close link between time and the frustrations imposed by authority figures that is rooted in the individual's ultimate impotence in the face of mortality (Arlow, 1989). This impotence in relation to time has also been interpreted as the "the chief means whereby reality subdues pleasure and is, therefore, forever resented" (Shaw, 1994, p. 91). And in light of the escalating pace in our lives, "time is devoured erratically by an army of ant-like interruptions swarming over the minutes and hours of our lives" (Ritterman, 1995, p. 51).

Biology is perhaps the greatest foil in our efforts to control time. For example, women who have delayed childbearing or who experience a fertility problem often speak of the ticking of their own "biological clocks" (Daly, 1988). Faced with this inevitable, yet ambiguous parameter, they adopt a variety of strategies to control the passage of time. They intensify their efforts to get pregnant in anticipation of this loss of control over their reproductive time. They employ metaphors of hope ("Well, not this month") that hint at their ultimate victory over their biological deadline. Ironically, well-wishing friends suggest that they gain the upper hand on the passage of time by "taking some time off to relax." In the end, however, they are as impotent in their efforts to control time as they are in their efforts to change the natural processes of reproduction.

Individuals who are faced with a terminal illness must also contend with new challenges associated with the control over time. Ironically, in the process of ultimately surrendering their control over time to death, they often seize the future to maximize the time they have left. Matocha (1992), for example, made reference in her research to how persons with AIDS and their caregivers are deliberate about controlling their future. With a sense of abandon about the future, one caregiver said this:

> You always wanted to go to Europe. You always wanted to go on a cruise. But you think of pensions and retirements and IRAs and all that crap. All that's of absolutely no concern. Right now my taxes and personal finances are so screwed up like you would not believe. I could care less. It doesn't bother me one bit. We're going on a cruise in January.

Similarly, people who experience chronic illnesses must be much more deliberate in the way that they structure time. Strauss (1975) has referred to this as "reordering time" to accommodate the symptoms or consequences of a chronic illness. For example, people with colitis, diabetes, or emphysema engage in an ongoing process of "temporal juggling" in response to changes in symptomatology, regimen, or life style (Strauss, 1975, p. 46).

Although individuals seek to control the passage of time, biology serves to limit this control. In addition to the constraining effects of illness and disease, humans must contend with the biological rhythms of the body. Like all living organisms, human beings experience the rhythm of their own circadian clocks, which regulate a variety of behavioral and physiological rhythms. These are associated with 24-hour cycles of temperature and light and include sleep-wake cycles, feeding cycles, body temperature cycles, and a variety of hormonal and metabolic oscillations (Friedman, 1990). These natural body rhythms have implications for a variety of cognitive and motor performances, with the early morning hours (i.e., 4:00 a.m.) being the low point for most of these performance tasks (Friedman, 1990). There is little surprise, then, that studies of shift workers show higher levels of insomnia and gastrointestinal upset as a result of the "desynchronization of their circadian systems" (Edlund, 1987).

Most human beings have been able to control their time by developing routines that allow them to sleep through these circadian low points. However, it appears that there has been an increasing tendency over the years to spread wakeful activity throughout the 24-hour day (Melbin, 1978). This is the "colonization" of time whereby circadian rhythms are subjugated to a 24-hour clock that is characterized by generic, interchangeable hours of the day (Melbin, 1978). Paralleling the occupation of space, the colonization of time refers to the filling of previously unoccupied time with people and activities. Specifically, it is the expansion of time use from the typically well-used hours of the day into the adjacent predawn and postnightfall times (Melbin, 1978). Based on a variety of data sources, evidence is provided for significant nighttime expansion: dramatic increases in 24-hour radio and television broadcasting, increases in shift work in the manufacturing sector, and a proliferation of service-oriented industries catering to all manner of consumer needs (Melbin, 1978). For example, 24-hour restaurants and shopping facilities, continuous hospital services, and global telecommunications that bridge time zones are all examples of "incessant" activity. The creation of shift work was probably the key force in industrialized society for the colonization of time. As Marx recognized, multiple shifting reduces the overall cost of owning production facilities by increasing the yield that comes from them (Melbin, 1978). The more recent introduction of bank machines provides for continuous access to money. The Internet is always on and it too holds promise for unlimited consumerism. The overall effect is that both production and consumerism can proceed without interruption. Although this allows families who work weekends or shifts to shop when it is convenient, it has the overall effect of solidly entrenching families in unrelenting consumptive activity. Consumption is an intrusion of market priorities into the home in a way that transforms the nonutilitarian bonds of family into the contractual relationships of the public commercial sphere (Elshtain, 1982).

The colonization of time is like an imperial force that penetrates ever more deeply into our indigenous temporal rhythms. When the lights of the world are always on, individuals face the challenge of attending to their own temporal rhythms in the face of a perpetually active commercial and technological global community. At the root of this challenge is a question about how individuals and families are able to control time.

To understand time as an instrument of power or a vehicle of control, it is necessary to begin with a discussion of the underlying premises. First, time is associated with power by virtue of the values that are assigned to time. Second, these values are present in the cultural norms that we have about time. Third, time is accessible to control when it is objectified.

## Time as Value

To understand time as value is to examine the way that evaluative meanings are attached to time. Any decisions that are made about the allocation of time—whether it be to floss your teeth, work the week-end, or play Legos on the floor—implicitly involve grafting meaning or assigning value to the activity. Is it time that is "well spent" or a "waste of time"? Or is there some percolating ambivalence about whether it is "worthwhile"? It is the nature of the activity that invokes questions and assessments about the value and importance of time allocation and expenditure. Activities serve as "points of reference" (Pronovost, 1989, p. 11) for distinguishing different kinds of social time and for evaluating their relative importance.

The value of time can be understood through change and waiting. An appreciation of change is contingent on a retrospective tracing of changes in activity. In this regard, change is temporally contingent— we can understand transformation of behavior or activity only by reference to an earlier and different state of being. Change, too, then becomes the focal point for assessing the value of time. Change can be seen as small or dramatic, for the better or for the worse, or fast or slow. So too with waiting. When we wait for something, we are willing to sacrifice one kind of activity to engage in another, more worthwhile activity. According to the principles of supply and demand, someone who desires a valued service must often wait until others, who also demand the service, are accommodated. The server, who represents the system's control over the valued resource, is in a position to control the time of others through waiting. In this regard, waiting is patterned by the distribution of power in a social system (Schwartz, 1975). As a general rule, the higher the power and status, the more others' access must be controlled. Waiting, then, gives insight into the value of time. Waiting time is typically viewed as a "cost of activities foregone" (Schwartz, 1975, p. 17). Equally, however, waiting can be seen as the cost of anticipated activity, where the value to be received is at least equivalent to the costs incurred in waiting.

The value of time associated with activities cannot be understood in isolation from the context in which those activities occur. Families live in a world of accelerated time demands that inflates the value of time. As time becomes more scarce, "its value increases and there is more competition to acquire it" (Lewis & Weigert, 1981, p. 454). Parents crave to "spend more time with their children" or spouses "juggle their schedules" to have some time off together. In this regard, activities that occur rarely or are "otherwise rationed" derive their positive valences (Lawton, Moss, & Fulcomer, 1987, p. 174).

The experience of scarce time is not a *natural* occurrence but is the product of individual *role bargains* that are constructed within a sociocultural environment that is perceived by the individual to place multiple, and often conflicting, demands on their time and energy (Marks, 1977). With multiple demands on time and the continual pressure of making choices about time, there is a "high consciousness of the value of time" in the culture (Rezsohazy, cited in Pronovost, 1989, p. 28). The dictum of "no time to lose" resonates throughout our everyday lives.

THE MORAL IMPORTANCE OF WORK

Arising out of the dust of the speedup in work and family life is a *moral economy of time.* The moral economy of time champions speed and efficiency and condemns a wasteful, laissez-faire approach to time. There is a limited amount of time available and individuals are expected to make "good use" of it (Telles, 1980). Of course, the moral standard of "making good use of time" is symptomatic of the hegemonic positioning of "work time" in our culture. Work time is the occasion for productive activity that supports the Western reward economy of status, material gain, and wealth. In Western culture, work time holds the key to how society is organized, and as a result, leisure and family time fall into the shadows of its dominance.

The way that we give priority to work time is not a new phenomenon. Ever since Adam and Eve were told to abandon their perpetual picnic in paradise, work has been a central theme in the Judeo-Christian tradition. In the 13th century, the Benedictine monks believed that work *was* prayer and that wasting time offended God (O'Malley, 1990). Max Weber's (1958) *The Protestant Ethic and the Spirit of Capitalism* is based on the Calvinist view of predestination whereby individuals are called by God to salvation. The way that one could demonstrate this calling was through hard and faithful work in the name of God. This resulted in the confounding of morality and labor discipline that was central to the development of capitalist economic organization. In ascetic Protestantism, work was virtuous with the result being that "waste of time is thus the first and in principle the deadliest of sins" (Weber, 1958, p. 157). Commenting on the Puritan works of Richard Baxter in the late 1600s, Weber (1958) goes on to suggest that "loss of time through sociability, idle talk, luxury, even more sleep than is necessary for health, six to at most eight hours, is worthy of absolute moral condemnation" (pp. 157-158). In the 19th century, time shifted from being a phenomenon rooted in God and nature to one that was embodied in the clocked machines of industrial society, which established new patterns for self-discipline and social order (O'Malley, 1990).

TECHNOLOGY AND THE VALUE OF TIME

Technology has heightened our expectations of time: We continuously search for ways to increase the efficiency of time to condense more activity into various periods of time. Although our lives may be filled with devices that are designed to save time, the saved time is usually filled with new chores or tasks that leave people with a feeling of "not satisfaction but a frustrated sense of continual interruption" (Ventura, 1995, p. 23). With the invention of washing machines and microwave ovens, domestic activities such as hand washing laundry and preparing a wood stove for cooking were considered, in retrospect, as slow and laborious. Where once these activities took hours of onerous work, they now take a few minutes to set up and allow the participants to put the time to some other good use while the machine does the work.

Despite these efforts to be more efficient with time, the reality is that the amount of time that is devoted to housework has stayed constant with respect to some jobs and has increased with respect to others (laundry, consumer activities, child care) (Burton, 1992; Eichler, 1988). Technology has "industrialized" housework and, in the process, has driven up the standards of cleanliness in the home (Eichler, 1988). It appears that the "drudgery of old fashioned labour has given way to more diffuse and time consuming activities" (Forman, 1989, p. 3). Not only has the nature of the activities associated with housework changed, so too have the temporal values imposed on those activities changed. Although the nature of housework activities has become more diverse due to technology, some have observed that it has not increased the pleasantness of the work, made it more interesting, or improved the self-worth of the housewife (Bose, Bereano, & Malloy, 1984). Furthermore, others have argued that technology has redistributed household work by putting more of the burden on the mother over time (Cowan, 1983) and has made household work more isolated because it transforms what were once group activities into solitary activities (e.g., the dishwasher requires one person to load it, whereas doing the dishes by hand involved a washer and one or more dryers) (Burton, 1992).

THE EXPANDING WORK ETHIC

Finding the "balance" among daily time demands has become a necessary survival skill in a complex social environment. Contrary to predictions in the 1950s and 1960s that called for a broad social adaptation due to the expansion of leisure time (because of automation), there in fact appears to be an increased emphasis on the importance of work—both in the home and the marketplace (Schor, 1991). According to national time use surveys, there was an overall increase, for men and women, in the number of hours worked at home and in the marketplace. Work time in particular has been increasing in the last 20 years for both men and women, those in the working class as well as professionals and across all marital statuses and income groups (Schor, 1991). Moonlighting was more prevalent in the late 1980s than in the previous three decades (Schor, 1991). Both men and women experienced a greater "time-squeeze" due to the decline in leisure time between 1969 and 1989 (Leete & Schor, 1994).

This expanding work ethic is not restricted to adults. Studies of adolescents and work indicate that between 1947 and 1980, there was a 65% increase in the labor force participation of school-enrolled 16- and 17-year-old boys and a 240% increase among girls of the same age (Greenberger, 1988). Although this is a cross-class phenomenon, those in the middle classes are more likely to be working than those from less affluent families (Greenberger, 1988). Indeed, Whites are more likely to be employed than Blacks or Latinos, and youth from the suburbs are more likely to work than those from the inner city. Historically, the meaning of children's work has changed dramatically: Whereas once children's work was motivated primarily by their family's financial need, their work now serves chiefly their own needs for increased consumer spending and the consumption of luxury goods. It appears that adolescents have also entered into the "insidious cycle of work and spend" (Schor, 1991, p. 107).

The net result of this "time-squeeze" is a worsening time famine within families and a corresponding elevation in the value of family time. A middle-class participant in McMahon's (1995) study of motherhood expresses the everyday meaning of time famine when asked about "the worst things of being a parent":

> I feel like we've absolutely no time to do anything. . . . Because we both work . . . we feel that we want to be with the children when we have a free moment. And the other thing is just time for yourself. Even little trivial things . . . like you have a shower in the morning and you race out of that. Once in a while—to file your nails—you just don't have time for yourself. (p. 208)

Schor (1991) reports that 8 of 10 American workers would be willing to trade off some income for more time with their family.

It is no surprise, then, that when couples present themselves for therapy, one of the more common underlying concerns is that they have little time for one another or their lives are somehow out of synchrony. Temporally, their lives are out of control. One of the common therapeutic prescriptions is to try to "shoehorn" a "little more quality time into a time frame that is already bursting at the seams" (Ritterman, 1995, p. 49). Although the rearrangement of work schedules or the renegotiation of child care responsibilities may temporarily open some time spaces in the relationship, it is mechanical and does nothing to change the underlying values associated with time, which will carry through in their urgent and demanding way. The result is that nothing has changed their "inner sense of time," with the implication that the created time will be "perfunctory, duty bound without any vital current of compassion or empathy" (Ritterman, 1995, p. 49). Time management strategies ironically heighten the need for temporal efficiency rather than ameliorating the strain that arises from it. Rather than trying to make the family more efficient by modifying the productive routines, what may be required is for the family to become nonfunctional in some way that would allow for the inefficient use of time—time that could be used without a purpose or task attached so that they could just be with one another (Ritterman, 1995). For some families, this might mean learning how to slow down or learning to *"tolerate* slowness" in a climate that is normally fast paced and goal oriented. Ultimately, it means changing the balance of control by learning to be in time rather than propelled along by time.

## HUMAN CAPITAL AND THE INVESTMENT OF TIME

The concept of "human capital" also provides insight into the meaning of time as value. Human capital refers to the bundle of skills and knowledge that an individual expends in productive activity (Bryant, 1992). Unlike the use of physical and financial capital that tends to depreciate with use, the use of human capital through experience makes it grow larger and raises the productivity of time (Bryant, 1992). For example, in the same way that individuals gain experience in paid employment, they gain experience in household activities, such as child care or space and time management. The result is that this experience "augments the individual's human capital and raises the individual's productivity in those activities" (Bryant, 1992, p. 398). For example, the transition to parenthood can be stressful because it requires the development of a wide range of new skills and organizational schemes. Over time, and with the birth of additional children, parents typically develop many efficiencies that allow them to carry out the additional complex tasks associated with more than one child and increasingly sophisticated demands. Their investment of time in parenting results in the growth of their own human capital. Although there are many economically based productive activities in families, there are also psychosocial productive activities in families. Individual commitments in time within families can result in a variety of noneconomic productive outcomes, including communication skills, management of resources, and the ability to solve marital and family problems (Dollahite & Rommel, 1993). Within families, the expenditure of time on various caregiving and household activities results in the growth of human capital. As human capital grows as a result of more family and household experience, there is the potential for that accumulated human capital to have "carryover" value in other activities. Although some skills and knowledge are specific to the operation of a particular household, others can be generalized across activities of experience. For example, laundry and child care may be experiences that are limited to the household, whereas other experiences, such as budgeting, scheduling, negotiation, or conflict management, have the potential to increase the market productivity of family members.

The investment of time in children by parents plays a key role in the production of children's human capital (Bryant, 1992). In fact, the development of human capital in individual family members has been identified as a critical function of families (Dollahite & Rommel, 1993). The investment of time by parents in their children involves foregoing current expenditures of time and money in order to facilitate their children's acquisition of knowledge, skills, and credentials for future benefit. However, the increased number of women in the paid labor force, the growing demand for day care, and the rise in single-parent families resulting from divorce has meant that time use with children has become an increasingly political matter. It is political because it involves questions of responsibility associated with parental time use. For example, questions of time priorities, values, and commitments arise in dual-earner families where both partners are unavailable for significant parts of the child's day. When children are entrusted to day care providers, questions arise for parents and policymakers alike about whether the state should subsidize the development of human capital among children. Other political questions arise with respect to parental leave and flextime, which allow parents more flexibility in the way that they shape their time investments in their children. The development of children's human capital invoke critical time use questions that are directly concerned with values and priorities.

The concept of human capital has also been expanded to encompass investments of time in family relationships (Dollahite & Rommel, 1993). Relationships are generated, maintained, and improved through the investment of shared time and activity in families. This has been conceptualized to reflect both the development of marital capital through an investment of time in dates, shared hobbies, enrichment programs, or even therapy and the development of family capital through family vacations, parent-child activities, or parent education classes. In all of these activities, time is the central component of the capital investment. There are many dimensions to the time that is available to be invested in marital and family capital, including the quantity and the quality of the time available at various stages of the family life cycle, decisions about the allocation of time to marital versus family capital development, and inequities between men and women with respect to the investment of time in both marital and family capital development (Dollahite & Rommel, 1993).

There is some research that has examined relationship satisfaction on the basis of how couples use their leisure time. Consistent with the idea that an investment in leisure time together will result in the development of marital capital and overall satisfaction, a study of 251 married individuals from a nonclinical sample reported that spending leisure time together is significantly related to spousal satisfaction (Smith, Snyder, Trull, & Monsma, 1988). In addition, engagement in individual pursuits and interaction with others to the exclusion of one's spouse was particularly predictive of marital distress. Although this applied to both husbands and wives, it was particularly important for wives, for whom there was a significantly stronger relationship between nonshared leisure activities and marital distress (Smith et al., 1988).

Sex is another important aspect of investing time in the name of marital capital. For many families, however, where both husband and wife are working outside of the home, investing in the sexual aspects

of the marriage is very difficult. This is especially challenging among
working-class families where space restrictions or limited resources
with which to buy time and privacy restrict the opportunity for sexual
expression. In her study of working-class families, Rubin (1994)
reported a great deal of dissatisfaction among dual earner couples
because there was little time for sex. Although both felt unhappy about
the lack of investment in the sexual aspects of their relationship, there
were "his" and "hers" versions of the story:

> Between times, he's busy calculating how much time has passed: "it's
> been over two weeks"; nursing his wounds: "I don't want to have to beg
> her"; feeling deprived and angry: "I don't know why I got married." . . .
> She too is preoccupied with sex, not with thoughts of pleasure but with
> figuring out how much time she has, as she puts it, "he walks around
> with his mouth stuck out. I know I'm in real big trouble if I don't do it
> once a week. So I make sure I do, even if I don't want to." (pp. 99-100)

Whether time is viewed as efficiency, as priorities, or as a form of
human capital, its essence is determined by *value*. Time is a measure
of worth, importance, and utility, and as a result, it is subject to efforts
of preservation, investment, and control. As is the case with all forms
of value, there are both personal meanings and cultural prescriptions
that shape how they are expressed. In this regard, the control of time
is shaped not only by the personal assignment of value but by cultural
time norms.

## Time Norms

The way that family members talk about time serves as an important
window on their beliefs, commitments, and priorities. Language is not
simply a kind of behavior in social life but the basis on which the
"order of things" is created, sustained, and resisted (L. Miller, 1993).
In this regard, discourse carries with it a set of meanings that reflect
cultural ideologies, personal values, and relations of power. The
language of time among family members is a function of both public
and private values: public insofar as family allocations of time are
shaped by their participation in a variety of other temporal domains
(e.g., work, school, day care) and private insofar as they exercise some

level of discretion over the assignment of their time within the home. As Zerubavel (1987, p. 353) has argued, the language of time is used strategically and manipulatively at both the microsocial level of interpersonal relations and the macrosocial level of societal politics. "Spending time with the family" is an important part of the social discourse that reflects both the ideological expectation that they spend time together and the variation in the importance given to family time by individual family members.

The discourse of family time is manifested in the presence of time norms that provide insight into the standards, rules, and limits of time use. Time expectations, similar to any other kind of social expectations, are embedded in social structures and individual actions. In this regard, time is part of the familiar background for what constitutes the normal and which gives meaning and direction to actions (Zerubavel, 1979). In families, there are normal limits for the allocation of time to various activities. Standards of cleanliness require a commitment of time: whether that is keeping the grass at a certain height or keeping a certain shine on the kitchen floor. Parents make decisions about time spent with their children on the basis of changing community standards for how men and women should allocate time to home and work. Whereas 30 years ago women were expected to be at home with their growing children, now there is a growing unease among women for being out of the workforce for too long. In addition, there are norms that are manifested in relation to gender activities and roles, division of labor, how leisure hours are to be spent, punctuality, and activities related to integration (being together for meals or holidays). For example, when parents insist that their children do their homework before going out to play, they are appealing to the generalized time norm of "work before play," which dictates a temporal order to their action.

IMPLICIT TIME CODES

The meanings that time has in our culture are often hidden by their taken-for-granted nature. In other words, they are so embedded in the mundaneness of our everyday life worlds that they are difficult to see. Routine activities appear to take no time, for it is only the vivid instant, the important event or the exciting period that leaves the impression of time or duration (de Grazia, 1962, p. 319). Cross-cultural lenses can play a useful part in contrasting the values currently associated with time in our own culture. For example, whereas punctuality in North America means that you must arrive within minutes of the appointed hour to be "on time," in Brazil, one usually has the flexibility of an hour or two before being considered late (Levine, 1988). The pace of activities also serves as an important window on the cultural values associated with time. For example, urban dwellers have a faster pace of life than do rural dwellers. For urbanites, this can be attributed to the "stimulation overload" of the city that requires a more hurried movement between activities or an escalation in the value of time due to more competing demands and resulting in a more hurried pace of life (Levine, 1988). Urban street people may be an exception to this, for they tend to live their lives by "what's happening" rather than by the fast pace of the clock (Horton, 1967). Comparisons of ethnic groups within a larger culture can also offer some insight into the variations in the meaning of time. Hareven (1982) points to the different time norms for family transitions that exist when one compares "Irish family time," "French-Canadian family time," or "Native American family time." For example, each of these ethnic cultures have different temporal norms and practices about when childbearing and rearing should begin and end.

Many family time norms are implicit or consensual and serve as effective instruments of temporal control (Rutz, 1992). A good example of the presence of implicit codes occurs within the politics of parenting where the implicit message of "you could spend more time with the kids" is given to husbands by their wives. This can be expressed as an exasperation at the apparent inability of their husbands to take the initiative to do something with the children to more subtle clues about the number of hours worked or the number of evenings devoted to meetings. Questions of whether time is used "appropriately" implies that there is an accountability to time use that is expected but not explicit. Hence, when boredom sets in for children at the end of summer holidays, parents have been known to snap at their children "Why don't you do something?!" suggesting that they put their time to better use. In this regard, time is open to the dynamics of power and control. It can become the property of others "to be appropriated in the projects of others rather than allocated efficiently from the standpoint of the possessive individual" (Rutz, 1992, p. 5). The saying "my time is not my own" is one obvious indicator of this idea of external control.

Surprise is usually an indication that a time norm has been violated. Surprise serves as evidence of prior expectations that events will occur within a certain order, rate, or duration (Zerubavel, 1981). These taken-for-granted expectations are part of the regularity of social life. Hence, when a teenage son cleans up his room at twice the speed he usually does, this may not only cause surprise but may arouse suspicion at the significance of this unusual behavior. Similarly, when an aging mother comes to visit one of her children after a long period of separation, the child may be very aware of how slowed down she has become and how frequently she needs to rest. When father comes home early from work, the response may be "What are you doing here?" Abrupt changes, irregularities, or disruptions in "normal" temporal routines cast expectations for how events are supposed to transpire into sharp relief. As these expectations indicate, temporal regularity and routine predictability of behavior are important values in and of themselves. When there are temporal irregularities, there must be some way to reorient the situation and to "temporally anchor" it (Zerubavel, 1982, p. 129) to a new situation. In other words, there is a call to "account" for the break from the expected.

TIME NORMS AS THE
BASIS FOR CONFLICT

Roth (1963) argues that time norms are the basis for time-related conflicts. When norms are violated, there is argument, sanction, and efforts to change or influence. For example, when Mom must unexpectedly work all weekend, there may be cries of protest from family members who were expecting a trip to the swimming pool. In the face of such a temporal irregularity, considerable energy may be expended in trying to realign the normative violation. This may involve an appeal to the norm that "You're not supposed to work weekends, Mom!" Alternately, the parent's violation of the time norm can be sanctioned by the child's deliverance of generous doses of guilt: "You promised to take us this weekend!"

Although conflicts may arise over the violation of a shared time norm, there are also instances when there is conflict as a result of the discordant nature of time norms. Cultural assumptions about the nature of temporal order are multiple and often discordant (Moore, 1963). The lack of clear temporal norms, or conflicting temporal norms, results in a tension of temporal coordination. The classic example of this is the conflicting expectation that women who have young children are supposed to maintain their full-time caregiving responsibilities as mothers while at the same time working outside of the home as contributors to the family income. In some instances, this gave rise to the short-lived cultural hero "super mom" who managed the impossible temporal coordination of work, family, and her own individual needs for rest and leisure. In many other instances, however, it simply resulted in work overload where the impossible demands precipitated a letting go of some aspect of these competing temporal demands.

The discordant nature of time norms is rooted in the multiplicity of values attached to time that is determined by the social position of individual actors, the characteristics of the immediate situation, and their place in the social structure. As Gurvitch (1964) has pointed out, social activity occurs within divergent and often contradictory manifestations of social time with the result being that society imposes a hierarchical organization on these multiple manifestations of time. Hence, we can think of the dominant time standards of middle-class, industrial culture, where promptness and working long hours are exalted and rewarded. Those who either choose, or are unable, to participate fully in this "standard" time are tagged with labels that reflect their subjugated position. Hence, the family receiving welfare or the unemployed are attributed with a sense of time that is personally lazy and publicly dysfunctional to the stability of the political and economic order.

## SOCIAL CLASS AND
## DISCORDANT TIME NORMS

Social class, then, is one of the key ways that discordant time norms are expressed and experienced in the culture. Research has indicated that our time culture is deeply differentiated by social class whereby the more educated are more concerned about keeping track of and controlling their time and the less educated have a more fatalistic position of powerlessness in relation to time (LeShan, 1957; Pronovost, 1989; Rifkin, 1987; Rubin, 1976). Within the subculture of poverty, there is a strong present-time orientation with a strong sense of resignation and fatalism about the future (Cottle & Klineberg, 1974). For people living under the conditions of poverty, it is difficult to imagine the future when there is a preoccupation with daily survival. As a 32-year-old working-class man expressed it in Rubin's (1976) study, the future just doesn't get much attention:

> There was no demand on any of us for any goal. You see, my father wasn't an educated man. He was taken out of school when he was nine, and him not having an education, it kept him from seeing a lot of hopes for his kids . . . like going to college was never discussed. It never occurred to me to think about it. That was something other kids—rich kids—did. (pp. 37-38)

Rubin (1976) concluded that it is the inability to control the future that most sharply distinguishes the working class from the more privileged classes.

There are also differences in time norms and philosophies among the classes. In the middle class, people *occupy positions* and *pursue careers,* which puts them on the track of the "perpetually unattained" (Henry, 1949, cited in Cottle & Klineberg, 1974). Future horizons are more highly valued than the present. For the working class, however, the future is not as highly valued, for they have jobs that proceed on a flat level (Cottle & Klineberg, 1974). These class differences are also apparent among women's accounts of life stages and biographical time. When discussing motherhood, middle-class women were more likely to talk about biological age than working-class women (McMahon, 1995). A future orientation was more evident among middle-class women, who were more likely to express concerns about being too old to have children, whereas working-class women focused on wanting to be young with their children in the present (McMahon, 1995). At the other extreme are those in upper-class occupations that Veblen (1899/1934), in his classic work, referred to as the "leisure class." Consisting of nobles, priests, and stars in government, war, religion, or sports, the leisure class has as a fundamental goal the "nonproductive consumption of time" (p. 34). This is rooted in a sense of the "unworthiness" of productive work and is intended as a demonstration of their pecuniary ability to afford a life of idleness (Veblen, 1899/1934).

Although the evidence points strongly to a fatalistic, present orientation among the working class, care must be used not to overstate the case. The unemployed, street corner population is stereotypically presented as living in an irrational present sense of time, yet there are still dreams and fantasies about the future (Horton, 1967). Here there is an important distinction between fantasy and a realistic future orientation. For those who are anchored in the world of the street, a different future is usually a fantasy because people do not have the knowledge, means, or will to realize their dreams. As Horton (1967) expressed it, "minority groups survive in the present, but their survival is nourished by a dream of the future" (p. 9).

Within families, social class also plays an important role in the amount of control that can be exercised over the use of time. For example, one study found that men in high-status jobs experienced a drop in strain and overload in the summer months because they had the autonomy to reduce the number of hours they spent at work in the summer to accommodate increased family demands (Crouter, Hawkins, & Hostetler, 1992). By contrast, for those in lower prestige jobs, overload and strain remain constant or increase in the summer months. Jobs with less prestige are jobs with less autonomy, and as a result, there is not the same freedom to become involved as parents. In keeping with this, fathers in low-prestige jobs increased their concern about spending time with their families during the summer months.

On the basis of these social class differences, we may also project that men and women will experience discordant time values. For example, given the ghettoization of women's work into service type jobs, women are more likely to proceed "on a flat level" in comparison to men's jobs that have a more prominent future horizon. Indeed, recent work has begun to differentiate meanings of time according to gender, where women's time is seen to have a unique set of phenomenological characteristics (Forman, 1989) and to be more susceptible to the strains of work and family (Hochschild,

1989). In this light, the diverse valuations of time within society serve as an important point of departure for understanding the political economy of temporal relations among individuals, groups, and organizations.

## The Objectification of Time

Although values and norms are critical for understanding the way that time is controlled, the objectification of time is most critical for understanding the way that time is controlled and susceptible to the forces of power. Clocks, calendars, schedules, and various normative codes (appropriations of "when" or "how long") serve to objectify time and thereby make it accessible to control through relations of power (Rutz, 1992). Corporate and bureaucratic organizations depend on a rigid, standardized temporal order that provides the basis for synchronized and highly orchestrated activities. Members of these organizations are therefore prone to the control that is exercised by these institutional timetables and deadlines. Whether it is the sound of buzzers and bells at the school, the start of the shift at the factory, or the executive meeting "first thing in the morning," organizations cannot function well without compliance to the temporal order.

### THE CLOCK AND
### NEW RULES OF TIME

The creation of the clock is the key for understanding the objectification and control of time. The first mechanical clocks were developed in the thirteenth century in medieval monasteries, where the strict regulation of time was needed to help maintain the discipline of monastic life (Whitrow, 1988). Over the course of the fourteenth century, mechanical clocks became more numerous in European churches. Clocks then moved from the church steeple to the town belfry and, in so doing, moved time into the secular world (Boorstin, 1983). They served as public machines that became the center of community life: The toll of the town clock brought citizens together to defend, celebrate, or mourn (Boorstin, 1983). The adoption of the uniform hour of 60 minutes came to dominate the schedule of everyday life.

The clock represents the departure of time from the properties of nature (movement of the sun, seasons, and tides) to the realm of human construction. As a result, it became the means by which time came to be controlled. It served as the basis for the creation of new rules and temporal structures. For example, following from its introduction through the Church, canons, or rules of prayer, were established for certain hours in the day. As early as the 14th century, the 60-minute hour replaced the day as the fundamental unit of labor time in the textile industry (Whitrow, 1988). Furthermore, the introduction of the clock represented another patriarchal force in history. As the metaphor "Father Time" suggests, the clock reinforced the tradition of "male dominion over time" (Forman, 1989, p. 4).

With the rise of the money economy in the 14th century, the value of time began to rise (Whitrow, 1988). Prior to this, power was concentrated primarily in the unchanging ownership of land, with the consequence that the control of time was not relevant to the maintenance of power. With the increased circulation of money, however, time came to be associated with commercial value, for the activities used to generate money or profit could now be weighed in terms of how much time it took to ready a product for sale. Furthermore, the rise in the use of money in commercial transactions in the medieval period pushed merchants to follow a more predictable measure of time for the orderly conduct of business (Le Goff, 1980).

## TIME AS A COMMODITY

One of the key ways that time is objectified is through the tendency to treat it as a commodified form. Modern industrial society is based on an "economy of time" (Giddens, 1987, p. 150). Marx spoke about the historical transformation of time through the emergence of capitalism. Labor power, and time itself, became a commodity through the factory system. The clock was a precise measure of activity. It made possible "a temporal environment that is spatial, quantitative, fast paced, efficient and predictable" (Neustadter, 1992, p. 380). The result was that the measure of a man's worth was focused on performance where quantity of work conducted superseded the quality of the work. Personality was separated from the "reified, mechanically objectified 'performance' of the worker" with the consequence that "time sheds its qualitative, variable flowing nature; it freezes into an exactly delimited, quantifiable continuum filled with quantifiable 'things' " (Lukacs (1922/1971, p. 90). The economy ultimately reduces itself to an economy of time, for "money measures value, but if we ask what constitutes value in the first instance, we find it impossible to define value without saying something about how the time of social labour is allocated" (Harvey, 1989, p. 227). This "economic-utilitarian" view of time (Zerubavel, 1981, p. 59) laid the foundation for our current propensity to view time in its objectified form: in quantitative terms as something that can be segmented, counted, measured and as a result, controlled. Through its objectification, time is related to power: Through labor, those who control the instruments of time control labor power. Following from this, "representations of time become ideologies that legitimize the exercise of power" (Rutz, 1992, p. 8).

On the basis of the Marxist idea that labor is commodified under the capitalist system, time spent in work is readily translated into a commodified form that is measured by "40-hour weeks," "overtime," or "maternity leave." As a commodity, time is subject to production, discipline, and choices of exchange. The metaphor "time is money" is the dominant way that we conceptualize time in our industrialized culture, for "it is the kind of thing that can be spent, wasted, budgeted, invested wisely or poorly, saved or squandered" (Lakoff & Johnson, 1980). In the industrial-bureaucratic Western world, the wasting of time is an economic crime, for it is a waste or a loss of a scarce resource (Tiryakian, 1978). For Marx, moments are the "elements of profit" insofar as the control over the labor time of others is the basis by which capitalists appropriate profit as their own (Harvey, 1989). In this regard, time is the essential element in the measure of productivity (Bryant, 1992).

In our culture, we measure our work and our value by the "hour" in a way that people who are paid $6.50 an hour are treated differently, and often treat themselves differently, from people paid $100 an hour (Ventura, 1995). This monetary valuing of time reflects issues of class and self-worth that lie at the core of family well-being. There is little wonder why housewives, who do the work without a wage, question their own self-worth. Similarly, ongoing disparities in the money that is paid to women and men are indicative of the way that women's time has traditionally been undervalued in Western culture. The continuing, and apparently growing, need of men and women to gain status and self-esteem through paid work is testimony to the hegemonic nature of "time is money" in our culture.

Although time can be seen as a commodity with varying degrees of value associated with it, it is not as simple as saying that time is money, for as Moore (1963) points out, time is not money for the un-employed, the very rich who need not work, or those who "have a lot of time on their hands." In this regard, it is like a "currency" that fluctuates with the forces of supply and demand: "The less time that we have, the more precious it becomes" (Adam, 1990, p. 114). Unlike money, however, which can be transferred directly and without respect of person, time is tied to individuals and the context of their lives (Nowotony, 1994). In this regard, time is a commodity that is *possessed* by the individual (Telles, 1980). However, as time for personal use becomes more scarce, there is a growing urgency to gain control over the disposition of that time. And indeed, it appears that for many families, time has become more scarce and more precious as both men and women work more and feel the growing intensification of time. The feeling of possessing time is a function of autonomy, control, and status.

As a possession, time is a symbol of status and responsibility, such that the degree of control that persons have over their time is an indication of their status (Hall, 1983). As this suggests, there is a stratification of time that is associated with the status of the actor. Hence, a doctor's time is more important than a patient's and a parent's time is more important than a child's. Writing about the domestic economy in the 1840s, Catherine Beecher emphasized the importance of economizing time. As the factory system was gaining momentum in North America, so too was time increasing in value. Although the accumulation of material goods was a measure of success for men, time was identified as women's only real property, insofar as material property typically belonged to men (O'Malley, 1990).

Clock time is further objectified when it is stripped of its contextual meanings. The French Revolution played a key role in neutralizing and secularizing the calendar (de Grazia, 1962). Prior to this, there were well over 100 days in the year devoted to the saints, which meant that people were not allowed to work but were to feast or fast according to the custom of that day. When Protestantism refused to recognize the saints, customary feast days were stripped of their significance so that days became interchangeable like standard parts. When work time is divided into standardized, homogeneous units of minutes and hours, there is no longer any way to take account of the specific needs and conditions of the individual or the culture. According to Adam (1990, p. 112), the calculation of "man-hours," like the standardized clock units on which it is based, is "an invariable, standardized measure that can be applied universally regardless of context." In this regard, time in productive work is stripped of its subjective purpose and meaning. It is objectified as a commodity with exchange value. In its commodified form, time is "disconnected from the materiality of experience" and comes to be perceived as "objective time, because, like money, it is expressed in a universal and public mode" as a standard measure (Giddens, 1981, p. 131). As a reified, abstract measure, time is the medium of exchange that is central to the calculation of efficiency and profit (Adam, 1993).

Perhaps the most significant step in the evolution of clocks and the objectification of time occurred with the adoption of a world standard of time. In response to economic progress arising from the development of railroads, machine-based industry, and emerging global trade patterns in the second half of the 19th century, there was a call for a universal time reckoning system. In 1884, the International Meridian Conference voted to standardize world time with Greenwich as the zero meridian (Rifkin, 1987). This was the final decontextualization of time whereby the new global "temporal imperialism" came to dominate local timekeeping systems that were tied to traditional rhythms and practices (Rifkin, 1987). Clocks, and the commodification of time, served not only to change cultural practices and the meaning of time but to establish structures of dominance.

## Commodification and the
## Control of Family Time

In the family literature, the dominant emphasis has been on the way that time is allocated to various activities associated with work and family. With the dramatic movement of women into the paid labor force in recent decades, the primary emphasis has been on counting the number of hours that men and women commit to their paid and unpaid work activities. Underlying these studies is an assumption about the commodified nature of time. Time is a reified, abstract measure that is counted, quantified, and subsequently used as a basis for comparing the paid and unpaid work of men and women.

Home economics literature from the early part of the 19th century emphasized the value of time and punctuality for the proper management of the home. In an examination of home advice manuals from the 1830s, O'Malley (1990) points to the messages that encourage young brides to treat time like money and to ensure that in their housework "they gather up fragments of time as well as materials" (p. 42). Emphasis in these manuals was also placed on the value of punctuality and rising at regular hours, all of which would "secure regular and precise habits at home and in public life" (p. 43). As this historical documentation suggests, the importance of the clock in the public domain of industrialized work was being mirrored in the private domain of the household. Furthermore, the women readers of these advice manuals "could use the clock to systematize the small hierarchical machinery of the home, in turn preparing their families for regulation in the larger machinery of the public work place" (O'Malley, 1990, p. 44).

Our current thinking about time in families continues to reflect a tension between the mechanistic demands of society and the habits of home life. Language such as "time demands on families" or "time famine" within families suggest that there is an ever-shrinking allotment of time to the day-to-day experience of family living. Underlying these notions is the idea that families are in competition with many social institutions for the precious commodity of time. As Rubin (1994) concludes in her study of working class families, this is especially the case in families with two working parents for whom

time has become their most precious commodity—time to attend to the necessary tasks of family life; time to nurture the relationships between wife and husband, between parents and children; time for oneself, time for others; time for solitude, time for social life. Today more than ever before, family life has become impoverished for want of time, adding another threat to the already fragile bonds that hold families together. (pp. 245-246)

From one perspective, the apparent decrease in the amount of time that families have for various activities may be a function of the evolution of Western industrialized societies, which have become more differentiated and specialized (Parsons & Bales, 1955). In this light, inasmuch as other institutions have taken on some of the specialized functions that were once part of the family domain (e.g., day care, education), families do not need as much time to fulfill the responsibilities of care, education, or nurturance as they once did. Furthermore, advances in technology have meant the wide-scale use of major appliances and easy access to a variety of power sources so that modern appliances are now used in almost all household productive activities—doing laundry, preparing food, cleaning house, washing dishes. In addition, goods and services previously produced within the household are now available for purchase, including ready-to-use products that are purchased outside the home and consumed within the family (e.g., ordering in fast food) or products that are consumed outside the household (i.e., going to a restaurant).

All of these technological advances were intended to be time-saving devices—leaving the family with more time than ever. However, the expected gain in time for families has not materialized because of rising standards of personal and household cleanliness that require continued high investments of time (Burton, 1992). When these trends are coupled with the increase in the number of hours that family members commit to paid work in North America over the last couple of decades (Schor, 1991), the result is that families continue to vie for time, and continue to strive for ways to make more time for themselves.

One of the ways that families can be viewed as having control over their time is to examine which aspects of family experience and household production require the participation of family members and which are amenable to substitution from the marketplace. As families feel more stretched for time, coupled with the proliferation of services available for purchase, there is an opportunity for families to control their time by delegating tasks and services to helpers outside the family. Buying time in families by substituting purchased services has been conceptualized in a number of ways in theories having to do with family resource management. For example, Foa and Foa (1980), in their resource exchange theory, contend that families are able to exchange some resources and not others. Beutler and Owen (1980) make the distinction between inseparable and separable household production. Inseparable household production concerns those activities that have pure use value and that must, therefore, be carried out by family members. Therefore, making the family's favorite recipes or baking that special coffee cake are activities that cannot be substituted with similar services from the marketplace. Similarly, various forms of caregiving that involve expressions of love or an acquaintanceship with the recipient's habits and preferences cannot be substituted with market services. By contrast, separable household production refers to those activities that can be delegated to an outside helper, which enables the family to use the time for other activities. Hiring a housekeeper, having a nurse check in on an aging parent, or sending a child to day care are ways that family members can buy time for themselves. However, the availability of goods and services on the market does not guarantee accessibility for all who might wish to take advantage of them, nor do they replace the meanings and or the quality of things that are produced within the home.

Several studies have examined the extent to which families have responded to the acceleration of time by trying to buy time with money through the purchase of goods and services that provide efficiency and convenience. Although the expectation is that dual-earner families will more regularly seek to buy time through the market purchase of goods and services, there is remarkably little difference between single-earner and dual-earner families (Rubin & Riney, 1994). Studies have found that family income, not the wife's employment status, was the key to whether the family purchases time-saving appliances, equipment, or services (Nickols & Fox, 1983; Rubin & Riney, 1994; Strober & Weinberg, 1980). Furthermore, as the education level of employed women rises, so too does the value of their time and its opportunity cost. As a result, as a wife's time becomes more expensive according to education level, there is a greater tendency to turn toward the marketplace to purchase time-saving devices or services (Rubin & Riney, 1994). Market research that looks at the food consumption patterns of families where both spouses are in the paid labor force concluded that these families spend significantly more money on meals away from home (Darian & Tucci, 1992). However, rather than a time-saving strategy in families, this may be in part attributable to the fact that wives are more likely to purchase breakfast or lunch at work (Rubin & Riney, 1994).

Insight into the way that families make decisions about the exchange or delegation of time resources to others also means being attentive to social class and family type. For example, working-class families quite often do not have the resources to "buy time within the home." Middle-class families are in a better position to use discretionary income to purchase day care or food prepared outside the home. Some families seek to maintain stability over time by compensating for short-term deficiencies in family time with a higher commitment to household time when demands have lessened in the future (Olson, Ponzetti, & Olson, 1989). This is like borrowing time on credit with an accompanying danger that the "less demanding future" never materializes. The circumplex model of family types (Olson, Sprenkle, & Russell, 1979) can also be used as a basis for understanding differences in family time use. For example, disengaged families (low in cohesion) may consider all resources exchangeable with the result that they have very little interdependence, whereas families who are enmeshed (high cohesion) tend to expect that all resources are provided by family members (Olson et al., 1989).

Families are in a perpetual state of tension between the preservation of time for themselves required to meet their internal needs for relationship, household activity, rest, and physical nurturance and the external demands that are imposed by virtue of their participation in a variety of social institutions. The degree to which they are able to manage this tension in their favor is contingent on many factors, including the stage of the family life cycle, the structure of the family, patterns of paid employment within the family, and the socioeconomic context of which they are a part. Control over family time is concerned with the management of this tension. In light of the increasing scarcity of family time, especially in dual-earner families (Kingston & Nock, 1987), some researchers have questioned whether there is a "bottom line." Is there a minimal level of family time that is necessary to maintain the family as a unit, such that if the family were to drop below this line for a given period of time that the family structure and stability would be threatened (Olson et al., 1989)? Although most family dysfunctions are not typically attributed to families who have fallen below this time threshold, there is little doubt about the importance of a critical mass of time for basic family functioning.

## Summary

The idea that family time can be controlled rests on several assumptions. First, there is a multiplicity of values that are attached to time. These are shaped by history, culture, experience, social class, normative expectation, gender, and family tradition. Individuals stand in a unique relationship to time, depending on their biography, location, status, and specific social situation. At this level, individuals are involved in an ongoing effort to control their own passage of time. Mortality, illness, and their own circadian rhythms serve as ongoing challenges in the effort to control time. Second, time is alienated from experience as an object for negotiation, exchange, and control. As a reified commodity, time is possessed in varying degrees by the individual. Participation in organizational structures involves an exchange of time that is open to exploitation and control by those who hold power. People whose time is valued at the minimum wage have must less control over time than corporate executives whose salaries give them a great deal of discretion over their time use. By virtue of the fact that families participate in many other organizations, family time is broken down into a set of quantifiable, objectified units that can be socially controlled. Third, time in its reified form is finite and limited. It is inherently scarce, and like all scarce commodities, it "acquires meaning relative to one's position in the stratification system and one's resultant ability to control it" (Lewis & Weigert, 1981, p. 447). For many families, however, accountability to the temporal demands of work seem to supersede their sense of being able to control time.

Technology has also heightened the expectations for production and efficiency, with the result that women and men work harder and attempt to squeeze more activity into the time that is available. The overall result is a perception of a shortage of time that is often noticed in the family domain. In some ways, this marks the ultimate success of the commodification of time wherein productive work is paramount and all other activity is secondary or residual. As Schor (1991) has convincingly argued in *The Overworked American,* our culture is increasingly work oriented and appears to be moving ever closer to the full commodification of time. Nevertheless, many people are willing to trade less pay for more time that they can call their own (Schor, 1991). Ultimately, the control over time comes down to a question about the allocation of priorities for how time is to be used. Contrary to the strong work ethic in North America, cultural attitudes in countries such as Germany discourage overworking and tend to view it as a sign of weakness. Within this kind of cultural context, control over individual time is highly valued. Fundamental questions, therefore, arise with respect to the link between values and time: What is the relative importance of health and lifestyle, material acquisition, and the satisfaction that can be expected from family, work, and leisure? Questions of time priorities very quickly become questions of values.

As the external demands on family time become more intense, the synchronization of many timetables within families becomes more problematic and conflictual. Although individual family members exercise different levels of control over time by virtue of their social positions, power over time within families is systemic insofar as all members participate in its distribution, management, and use, which can result in a web of contradictory interests and compromises (Ausloos, 1986). The manner in which time is controlled within families rests on an analysis of the "interlacing" of values, norms, objectifications, and dynamics of power that are associated with time. From this perspective, it is possible to examine both the conflict that arises when different meanings and values are assigned to time and the power that is exercised in the effort to control whose preferences and priorities for time use will take precedence.

Time is a medium of exchange both within families and between families and the various organizations that they participate in. In the face of escalating time demands, families are faced with a relentless series of decisions about how to allocate, share, or preserve the time that they have available to them. These are economic problems insofar as they involve establishing priorities for goals, balancing needs and available time resources, and planning for the allocation of time as a resource (Rettig, 1988). At the center of these decisions are questions about who has the power to decide, whether cooperation or conflict is the norm and whether the individual or group concerns take precedence. In addition, "the power to decide" may increasingly involve decisions not to get involved in activities that offer limited rewards. This could mean not doing them at all or, in cases where the activity is necessary, delegating responsibility to those who can commit the time. The proliferation of housecleaning services in the last decade is one example of the power to delegate.

Time is one of the media that are used by a family to gain control over itself or its environment. In the chapters which follow, the control of time is explored on several levels. First, there is an exploration of the dynamics of temporal control between families and society. In Chapter 6, there is an analysis of how families seek to control their time in the face of structural, ideological and cultural constraints. Second, the control of time is concerned with the negotiation among and between family members for the way that decisions about time are made. These intrafamilial dynamics of time are explored along two axes: gender and generation. Men and women stand in a different relationship to time and as a result have different entitlements to, and power over, the time that is available to them. The dynamics of temporal control between men and women in families is explored in Chapter 7. Power over time is also organized along generational lines in families. The dynamics of temporal control between generations of parents and children will be the focus of Chapter 8.

# 6

# The Politics of Time
# Between Families and Society

To speak of controlling time is to speak about the politics of time. A politics of time is primarily concerned with the interpersonal and systemic dynamics of power as it comes to bear on time. The politics of time is ubiquitous, for no one can ever escape the "pincers of time" and "each moment of life creates a play between the restraints and opportunities jointly offered by time" (D. F. Miller, 1993, p. 193). Families living in time compression are tyrannized by the escalating demands of a tightly scheduled clock culture and seduced by the burgeoning need for time efficiency. Caught at the nexus between a public world that is speeding along on information superhighways and their own private desire to preserve the family as a rest stop, family members look for new and more efficient ways to protect, control and manage their time.

With the escalating sense of time scarcity, there are more conflicts—both within families and between families and the social order of which they are a part—about time control, allocation, and entitlement. This is consistent with the postmodernist emphasis on the accelerated pace of change and the constant newness of forms that accompanies it (Cheal, 1993). For families, this means examining time in light of increasing diversity and disorder in family structure and in relation to the accompanying ambivalence and indecision that exists with respect to relationships and gender arrangements. Whereas life-long relationships were once the norm with respect to marriage, now, many more contingencies give rise to new forms of negotiation over time in the formation and sustenance of family relationships. In light of these many new forms, there are many questions about who has power and control over the patterning of family time.

When high-profile politicians or executives resign unexpectedly from their positions of power, the reason that is frequently given is that "they wish to spend more time with their families." Pierre Trudeau, a former prime minister of Canada, cited that very reason when he resigned his position as leader of the country in 1979. Although there were obviously many factors unrelated to family that came into play when he made that decision, giving this as the main reason ensured that it would be uncontested in the public domain. Who would dare suggest that "spending more time with the family" was less worthy than running the country?

As this example suggests, "spending time with the family" is a highly cherished value in our culture. Ideologically, it represents a set of beliefs about the primary importance of good parenting and family togetherness as the foundation for a stable society. To invest time in the family is to invest in the next generation so as to ensure a solid future for society. However, on the level of individual actions, the realization of these lofty goals is considerably more problematic. Pierre Trudeau returned to politics several months after his resignation. In sharp contrast to the rhetoric of his resignation, his decision to return to his commitment to public life is an example of some of the difficulties that arise in maintaining that investment of time in families. We believe that it is important to spend time with our families, but in practice, it seems that there are always a variety of demands that take precedence and therefore interfere with the realization of this ideal.

Understanding the disparity between the ideology of spending time with the family and the behavioral commitment to actually spend that time with the family rests in an analysis of the nexus between the individual experience of family time and the temporal order of which families are a part. In this regard, the experience of time is an experience of conflict, where there is ongoing agitation between individual desires for using time and the imposition of temporal demands and restrictions from the broader sociocultural order. To understand the politics of time, it is necessary to understand the conflicts between the individual and society:

> Time represents a central dimension of power which manifests itself in the systems of time that dictate priorities and speeds, beginning and end, content and form of the activities to be performed in time. In the beginning, it was the priests who, in almost all societies, established the prevailing systems of time in accordance with those of the supernatural order, and separated sacred times from profane. Today, the systems of time are chiefly fixed by the market and the state. (Nowotony, 1994, p. 105)

## The Temporal Politics of Family in Society

The emptiness of a suburban street during "working hours" is a strong symbol for the daily participation of all family members in an external temporal order. Daily routines are no longer shaped by the crow of the rooster and a home-based time order but are now determined by the chorus of several different clock radios alerting individual members to their separate routines. The morning ritual is now a ritual of dispersion where everyone works to ready themselves for presentation to the outside world and in a closely timed set of movements work toward "getting there on time." "Being ready" and "getting there on time" are marks of success for a repeated and often stressfully demanding routine that gets people to where they are supposed to be "on time." The result is that families live fragmented lives, with each member responding to an individualized schedule: Young children are placed in day care routines, older children go to school, parents are in their respective jobs. Ironically, although mothers have entered into the paid labor force to relieve financial stress, they too often discover that time takes its place next to money as a source of strain, tension, and conflict (Rubin, 1994).

What do these routines tell us about the temporal politics of families in society? They suggest that families are working within and against a temporal structure that is perceived to be externally based. As a result, the masters of time are perceived as the school, the employer and all other events that arise to impose various temporal demands on the family. As Adam (1990) reminds us too, even people who are at home most of the time cannot extricate themselves from the institutional timetables imposed on other members of the family, for they, too, are constrained by the schedule of those working outside the home, school hours of children, and the opening hours of various amenities. For example, an old couple who rarely leave the home may still organize their day on the basis of external time structures, such as the arrival of the mail or their meals on wheels. For other families, the timing of activities is structured around the institutional timetables of schools, work schedules, public transport, and the accessibility of public amenities. The magnitude of external temporal demands can easily become invasive. One commentator described his experience in this way:

> We allowed the outside time pressure of school and work to invade our home and completely absorb what used to be savoured as family time. We were all unintentionally but routinely sending one another messages that time spent with one another—down time, slow time spent listening, talking, and being with the people that we loved most, was actually less important than the fast time imposed by our external obligations. (Ritterman, 1995, p. 46)

The temporal politics of families in society is concerned with the dynamics of control over time between the family and the socially structured temporal order of which they are a part. The objectification of time in these various organizations undergirds the control that is exercised over family time. In an effort to elaborate this theme, I will examine the structure and organization of time in society, the temporal order of families, and the synchronization of public and private temporal orders, and finally, I will look at the dynamics of control that exist between the structure of time in families and the broader temporal order of which they are a part.

## The Temporal Order of Society

Time as structure is concerned with the way that time is organized and synchronized within a culture. As such, it is social time insofar as it is shared, normative, and referential. Although the individual is an active agent who continuously defines and experiences time, the experience exists within a framework that facilitates, constrains, and shapes the kinds of options that are available. This framework represents the "rhythm of collective life" (Sorokin & Merton, 1937) that is both constituted by individual actors and that serves in turn to organize their actions. According to Durkheim (1915), there is a shared understanding of time in society that is based on the collective consciousness of its members. In modern urban culture, the timing and coordination of activities is essential. As Simmel (1950) indicated, the "relationships and affairs of the typical metropolitan are so varied and complex that without the strictest punctuality in promises and services the whole structure would break down into an inextricable chaos" (p. 412). The schedule and the calendar are the central mechanisms that organize time so that it can be collectively experienced.

The social organization of time in our culture has been referred to as the "sociotemporal order" (Zerubavel, 1982). This is an endogenous approach to time that rests on social conventions. It is external to the individual and is endowed with "coercive power, which is felt mostly when one attempts to resist it" (Zerubavel, 1982, p. 129). The implication is that people rarely try to resist this order and, instead, take it for granted and use it as a basis for ordering social activities (Zerubavel, 1982). The sociotemporal order is manifested through the schedule and imposes itself as an agency of social control. A structural view of time is a reified view of time where time is external to the individual, an object, a quantity to be accumulated or wasted. From this perspective, objective clock time has become a "coercive concept" (Hendricks & Hendricks, 1976, p. 14). Time is coercive and an agent of control because it is firmly embedded in our normative structure. For Hall (1983), North American time is structured functionally and is used to control the flow of work, activities, and involvement with others. Organizations have hours of operation that prescribe when individuals participate in them.

Calendars and schedules are two forms of time that serve to control everyday action. Calendars, with holy days, seasonal markings, political holidays, and financial reference points "express the essential politics of the culture" at a macro level (Rifkin, 1987, p. 85). Social calendars both reflect and maintain the rhythms of social life (Hagestad, 1986). As a result, the individual sense of time is inextricably linked to the culture in which the individual is embedded. More potent, however, in the control that is exerted over our day-to-day lives is the schedule. Schedules are "the weapons of temporal control within bureaucracies and formal organizations of all kinds" (Rutz, 1992, p. 5). Time that is scheduled is time that is associated with productivity (Rifkin, 1987, p. 95). As instruments of efficiency, schedules routinize and confine activity by delimiting goals and are used for the purpose of discipline and surveillance (Rutz, 1992).

Organizational schedules are so deeply ingrained in our day-to-day experience that they have become part of the moral fiber of society. Punctuality is the moral mechanism that maintains the orderly adherence to rigid time structures. Being on time is "part of the ethics of everyday life, a matter of manners and courtesy" such that people tend to be very "rigid and defensive" about their own and other people's timekeeping behavior (Shaw, 1994, pp. 79-80). Indeed, time is "contractual" insofar as being late has consequences for the other (anger) and the self (being considered unreliable) (Shaw, 1994, p. 94). From this perspective, being on time is concerned not simply with the rules of punctuality but with the underlying anxieties that arise in the effort to adhere to these rules. Furthermore, in keeping with the rigid principles of the structural perspective, punctuality is "about fixity, not flexibility" (Shaw, 1994, p. 80). Punctuality is "synchronized behaviour bolstered by a moral system" (Shaw, 1994, p. 81). Calendars, schedules, and the ethics of punctuality serve as the basis of our social order.

## The Temporal Order of Families

Time serves as one of the central dimensions along which families organize their lives. To live in a family is to be located in a generation, a family history, and a set of daily routines and schedules that provide the structural framework for the organization of experience. On one level, there are family routines that consist of awakening hours, mealtimes, and curfews. At another level, there are family "benchmarks" (Roth, 1963) such as birthdays or anniversaries that flag the family's calendar. These are the nexus points of the family's "collective memory" where members share in the retrieval of realities that they have come to know through intimate experience (Halbwachs, 1992, p. 71).

The temporal ordering of family experience straddles the intersection of public and private domains. Although families operate on the basis of constructed daily and weekly routines, these are shaped by both their internal needs for rest, food, leisure, and intimacy and the external forces of work, school, and the temporal structure of the marketplace. As such, the structured order of domestic time is the product of "detailed struggle and negotiation—a domestic politics" that is "fragile, ephemeral, gendered and often a source of conflict" (Silverstone, 1993, p. 287). Two concepts are of particular importance for understanding the temporal order of family time: clocking and synchronization.

## CLOCKING

Schedules and clocking behaviors lie at the root of the temporal organization of the family. Scheduling includes "sequencing" or the placement of activities in a relative temporal order, and "timetagging," which is concerned with the duration of an activity that is tagged with starting and ending points (Avery & Stafford, 1991). Both of these mental processes are required in the construction of a household activity plan. Schedules in families encompass both the consciously planned activities and the more repetitive and routine aspects of family behavior.

Kantor and Lehr (1976) talked about clocking in families as the "regulation" of sequence, frequency, duration, and pace of immediately experienced events. Whereas orienting is concerned with perspectives on calendar time, clocking is concerned with the daily cycles of time. In this regard, the key emphasis is on schedules and routines. For example, clocking involves giving attention to when and how much TV is watched, the timing and duration of telephone calls to relatives, or the expectations for the timing and pace of meal times (Broderick, 1988). Clocking phenomena are among the most immediate, poignant, and observable influences on family behavior: "Every experience is affected in one way or another by the way in which the family regulates its members' clocking—if people are out of phase with one another, they may not even be able to be home together at the same time, much less make love or fight with one another" (Kantor & Lehr, 1976, p. 82).

There is tremendous variation in the clocking behaviors of families (Reiss, 1981). Some families structure their experience of time into a clear, linear sequence of events with unambiguous boundaries so that mealtime, cleanup time, or bedtime are clearly sequenced and predictable. For other families, the order may be clear but the timing is less regulated. So although cleanup may follow mealtime, there is more uncertainty about when these events will occur. Families also differ in the speed at which they carry out their family routines. For some, there is a constant rush where activity is jammed into a short a time as possible; for others, time is slow, activities are unrushed, and schedules are kept light.

Clocking also reveals priorities in the family. If clocking is the organization and management of time around the household, then it reveals what the family considers most important (Kantor & Lehr, 1976). Clocking and scheduling of events in families is directly related to how the family establishes and maintains priorities. "In a very immediate sense, the way in which a family clocks its movements determines its members' access to affect, power and meaning" (Kantor & Lehr, 1976, p. 85). For example, during infancy, the length of time it took mothers to respond to hunger cries was an indication of our access to nurturance. In families, there is an ever-present layer of similar clocking messages: "when to start and finish things, how fast to move, and even how much time to give to specific events" (Kantor & Lehr, 1976, p. 86). Operationally, clocking patterns reveal family priorities.

The notion of clocking has received very little attention in the empirical literature. With most of the emphasis on time allocations or how much time is spent in various family and household activities, we have only a limited understanding of how families experience pace, duration, or sequence. The regular recurring behaviors by which families carry out their daily routine can play a crucial role in the conservation of the family paradigm (Reiss, 1981). From this perspective, research that seeks to understand the clocking behaviors of families can provide insight into the "deep-seated and persistent attitude" about the family's social and physical world (Reiss, 1981, p. 226).

Families readily get into "time ruts" where habit and routine take over (Kantor & Lehr, 1976, p. 86). Although many routines such as chores or meals may go unchecked, other habitual patterns are called into question. Time ruts are exposed either through crisis or through the monitoring function of one or more of the family members. The crisis may be a crisis of boredom, where one of the members challenges the way things are done on a daily basis—such as when the family decides to go away for a weekend rather than carrying out the predictable set of chores. Sickness or fatigue are crises that also serve a monitoring function in families that give rise to a reevaluation of the normal course of events. Changing family composition can also have an impact on clocking behaviors within the family. For example, when adult children return to the "empty nest," one of the most common concerns expressed by parents was the disruptive effect of "time of coming and going" and the irregularity of mealtimes (Clemens & Axelson, 1985). Monitors in families help to restore perspective on the way that family routines are carried out. They also play an important role in the ongoing project of synchronization that occurs in families.

SYNCHRONIZING

Synchronizing is another important element of family organization. Synchronization has to do with the extent to which families share their daily routines through the creation and execution of shared temporal guidelines. This concept deals with the central question of "How much time do we want to spend together?" and "How do we make that possible?" In families where there is a high degree of synchronization, there appears to be "effortless collaboration," patterned routines, and the coordination of interests and agendas (Reiss, 1981, p. 236). In families where there is little synchronization, different routines are competing for time and space, there is disagreement about plans, and there is conflict instead of collaboration with respect to activities. In families such as these, individual members tend to live in a separate space and time with only marginal reference to the family group as a whole (Reiss, 1981).

Family rituals are one way that family behaviors are synchronized. Family rituals require coordinated action from family members each time they are performed (Reiss, 1981). Simple rituals such as coming together for dinner serve to keep the life plans of individual family members in lockstep with one another. Furthermore, it is not simply the shared ritual itself that gives the sense of synchrony in each other's lives, but it is the planning and the punctuality associated with the ritual that keeps family members entangled in each other's lives (Reiss, 1981). Day-to-day rituals become reified as part of their taken-for-granted world. Their routine nature is noticeable only when one enters into another family where the rituals and temporal patterns are of a different sort. As one example, when a child sleeps over at a friend's house, the differences in family routines are very noticeable: different ways of saying good night and going to be bed or different routines with respect to who eats breakfast with whom and when.

Families are more likely to be aware of synchronicity in the family when there are synchronizing problems. One of the ways that this occurs in families is when there are differences in "morningness" and "nightness" (Adams & Cromwell, 1978; Cromwell, Keeney, & Adams, 1976). When a morning person is married to a night owl, couples are more likely to be "out of phase" and experience more frequent and severe dyadic adjustments (Adams & Cromwell, 1978). This includes more conflict, criticism, and argument in the relationship. In light of this preliminary research, it appears that marital harmony varies directly with temporal synchrony and that this is an area worthy of further study (Adams, 1987). Of course, the addition of members to the family, whether through birth, adoption, or remarriage, simply increases the possibility that members will be out of phase with each other (Adams & Cromwell, 1978).

Key family transitions may invoke synchronizing difficulties. The birth of a baby, for example, can play havoc with the synchronizing patterns within a family. As Broderick (1988) has pointed out, the transition to parenthood is fraught with time disruptions: late-night feedings, urgent unscheduled needs, unanticipated illnesses, and negotiations with baby-sitters. Each of these experiences challenges couples to revamp their synchronization patterns and, in the process, seek to preserve time for each other or for themselves (Broderick, 1988). Other family transitions, such as the launching of a child or the retirement of one of the partners, can precipitate the construction of new synchronization patterns in the family.

Scheduling congruity theory has been proposed as one way of conceptualizing the degree of synchronization among family members with regard to their schedules (Avery & Stafford, 1991). The temporal organization of activities within a family falls along a continuum that ranges from "simple congruity," where there is minimal daily synchronization of activity and individual members seem to operate on schedules that are independent and parallel, to "complex congruity," where activity schedules are integrated into shared activities and resources. Many other factors have a bearing on the way that schedules are established in families, including who carries responsibility for the master activity schedule in the family, the frequency of communication with respect to individual schedules, and the degree of control that individuals have over their personal schedules (Avery & Stafford, 1991). Furthermore, there are also questions about the overall commitment to scheduling congruity in the family, with conflict or changes in family boundaries stemming from the arrival or departure of family members having a bearing on the willingness and need of members to integrate their schedules.

The diversity of family forms in our postmodern culture gives rise to a number of new challenges with respect to synchronization. In blended families for example, there is a need to reconcile two sets of habits, routines, and temporal norms about punctuality or time spent together. When the task of synchronization is generally challenging within a nuclear family, it can be exponentially so within blended families. So too with adoptive families. Given the move toward greater openness in adoptive relationships, where the birth parents are more likely to be involved in the adoptee's life, there are ongoing challenges associated with the coordination of visits or the management of birthdays. With the increase in variations in family styles and forms, synchronization becomes more difficult.

## The Synchronization of
## Public and Private Temporal Orders

In families, one of the key struggles for the control of time exists between the demands of work and the demands of home. For the employed, measured time embodies a simple relationship between their employer's use of their time and their "own" time (Thompson, 1967). As Adam (1990) has clearly outlined, "labour is exchanged for money in a mediated form and time is the medium through which labour is translated into its abstract exchange value" (p. 111). In the early stages of industrialization, work time dominated nonwork time. Long hours and the exploitive conditions in mines, factories, and shops meant that workers were usually exhausted, ill, or fatigued at the end of the day with little option but to forget or rest (Horna, 1992). Although there is now tremendous variation in the level of control exercised by employers (from punch-in time clocks to somewhat looser performance expectations), there is an underlying principle of exchange whereby the control over their personal time is given over to the company in exchange for wages and salary. As such, time is at the center of a power-dependency dynamic that is susceptible to various strategies of social control.

### TEMPORAL BOUNDARIES
### BETWEEN WORK AND HOME

Time serves as a segmenting principle that can segregate the public and private through temporal boundaries (Zerubavel, 1981). There is, however, a sense of the two temporal spheres serving as opposing attractants. For example, Moore (1963, p. 77) talked about the idea that the "modern family is a residual claimant on time" insofar as outside organizations take precedence in their claim on time (this is tied to Parson's notion of increased specialization). In contrast with this perspective, others have argued that families are notoriously "greedy institutions" (Coser, 1974). From this perspective, families are institutions that make "total claims on their members" to maintain loyalty and allegiance and to reduce the claims of competing roles on their time (Coser, 1974, p. 4). Families have been particularly greedy with respect to the time and commitment that is demanded from women. Women, despite changes in their participation in the paid labor force, are still expected to devote much of their time and energy to their families. Taken together, there is a contradiction that arises between the dual pressures whereby the family is both a residual claimant on time and a greedy institution that demands time allegiance from its members. As a residual claimant, the family shows a deference to the demands of the world of work, while at the same time it greedily demands of its members a commitment to the activity of family experience. This contradiction lies at the root of the ongoing challenge to balance work and family life.

Although most people are typically conscious of a sharp dichotomization between the world of their private life and the world of large public institutions, there is tremendous pluralization *within* these spheres (Berger et al., 1973). In keeping with the defining characteristics of postmodernity, the immense complexity of institutional life worlds means that there are many shapes and forms of temporal consciousness. For example, there is a tremendous difference between the experience of time in a church (calm, slow, intimate) and the experience of trying to find out some information from the Department of Immigration (frustrating, anonymous, and slow). Although both may be experienced as slow, one may be calming while the other is infuriating. The same pluralization occurs within the private sphere. Although the individual tries to maintain "an order of integrative and sustaining meanings" in a "home world" (Berger et al., 1973, p. 66), this too is a world that takes on a different meanings with the "intrusion" of neighbors or television. Children create shifts in the temporal structure of the private sphere when they move from being small and dependent to leaving home, only to return to the home as adults.

There are other variations in the nature of the boundaries between work and leisure. For example, those who have higher rank in organizations, professionals or individuals who are self-employed tend to have more control over their time (Pronovost, 1989; Telles, 1980) and, as a result, may be more likely to have blurred boundaries between work and leisure. By contrast, those who have little control over their time or have their work time under heavy surveillance (e.g., working in a bureaucracy or on a production line) are more likely to have very strong boundaries between work time and family time.

Furthermore, men and women, by virtue of their historically different relationship to paid and unpaid work, also have different levels of control over their time. When work is dichotomized into work and nonwork time, then men as breadwinners have traditionally had more of an entitlement to use nonwork time for leisure pursuits (Seymour, 1992). By contrast, women who work within the home do not have the "demarcation line" of paid and unpaid work and, as a consequence, are less able to define when domestic work ends and begins. Time is not as readily compartmentalized within the domestic sphere as it is when moving between the public and domestic sphere. The result is that "while males can demand their entitlement to personal leisure time, female time is viewed by women and other family members as a common household resource" (Seymour, 1992, p. 190). Even when women enter into the paid labor force, time in the home is often used for "catching up" with the domestic work that they were unable to do during that time.

## WORK AS A DOMINANT
## CLAIM ON FAMILY TIME

In the literature on the family-work interface, work structures are usually conceptualized as having a unidirectional impact on the experience of family life. Work is the "dominant obligation" with the consequence that even free time (after work) is "tethered" to the clock-bound nature of work (de Grazia, 1962, p. 326). Work is the "pivotal aspect of time in industrial societies" and therefore free time (or private time) comes to be seen as something "marginal" to the time spent at work (Pronovost, 1989, p. 26). Work organizations take precedence so that people (especially men) in Western cultures over-perform in occupations and underperform in other roles (Goode, 1960). Insofar as people have much less control over their work lives than over their family lives, their family lives tend to adjust to their work schedules rather than the reverse (Staines & Pleck, 1983, pp. 122-123). Not only do family members spend much of their time in work but with the specialization of modern society, they are engaged in many other organizational activities. Education, community involvements, consumption activity, and leisure all make claims on time that tend to take precedence over "family time." Furthermore, there is a sequential inevitability to the course of people's lives that gives predominance to work and a "linear life plan" (Best, 1978, p. 97). People find themselves "trapped unwillingly" in the "lockstep flow" of learning basic skills in youth, working in midlife when abilities and responsibilities are at their peak, and retiring in old age when responsibilities decline or are withdrawn (Best, 1978, p. 96).

The external claims on family time can result in competition and conflict as families attempt to coordinate and integrate a wide range of temporalities. This includes coordinating common family activities such as meals, housework, or leisure activities. A recent visit to a friend's home where there are five children, three of whom are teenagers, revealed the importance of the master board next to the telephone in the kitchen. This appeared to be an essential tool for managing transportation, providing meals, and ensuring care for the smaller children. For the parents, the board was the "control tower" that allowed them not only to monitor the activities of all the family members but to anticipate and address the regular conflicts that arise with respect to various time commitments. Arrivals and departures of individual members to games, meetings, dates, appointments, and various other activities requires the systematic management of time flow in the family to ensure that everyone gets to where they are supposed to be at the right time. Of course, the more members there are in the family and the higher their level of activity, the more difficult it is to coordinate these diverse temporalities. Furthermore, when the variety of family structures is taken into account (single parent, stepparent, same-sex partners), the potential for competing or conflicting claims to time is also heightened. For example, when there is joint custody, there are additional challenges associated with the regular transition from one parent's temporal order to another. Although there is little empirical evidence to indicate how prevalent the "control tower" phenomenon is, it does point to the heightened demand on families to have some kind of organizational instrumentation to monitor their daily temporal routines.

SCHEDULING ASYNCHRONIES

The dispersion of family members into their various responsibilities and involvements gives rise to a number of "public issues" of time (to use Mills's, 1959, terminology). As Lewis and Weigert (1981) have proposed, "the degree of difficulty of temporal synchronization is a positive exponential function of the number of timetables involved" (p. 453). The dramatic increase in the number of women in the paid labor force has been a powerful force in the escalating complexity of family timetables. There is a direct relationship between the complex temporal realities of parents' work schedules and the complexity of their child care needs (Presser, 1989). For example, dual-earner parents with preschoolers and school-aged children are acutely aware of the challenges associated with the synchronization (or asynchrony) between the day care schedule and their own work schedules. On the basis of a Canadian national study of parental work patterns and child care needs, less than one third of dual-earner couples with children younger than 13 worked a standard work week (Monday to Friday, between 8 a.m. and 6 p.m.) (Lero, Goelman, Pence, Brockman, & Nutall, 1992). The result is that the majority of dual-earner families require some form of care on a weekend day, during a fixed late day or night shift, or to accommodate an irregular work schedule that varied from day to day.

There is some research that indicates that atypical work schedules create more strain for individuals working in families than regular 9 to 5 schedules (Pleck & Staines, 1985; Voydanoff, 1988; Voydanoff & Kelly, 1984). In reviewing the literature on the impact of shift work on families, Hoffman (1987) concluded that although night shift work may increase the amount of time that fathers have with their preschool children, it diminishes the amount of time they have with their school-aged children. There was also evidence that afternoon shifts interfere even more with the parental role than night shifts do. Shift work also has a detrimental effect on marriages with reports that social life is diminished and that wives tend to resent the husband's obtrusive presence during the day (Hoffman, 1987).

It is telling that family day care is called "*day* care," for such care is typically offered during traditional daytime working hours (Presser, 1989). The challenge of synchronization has become particularly acute for women in light of the growth of service sector jobs for women that extend their hours into evenings, nights, and weekends (Presser, 1989). There are several implications for the lack of fit between increasingly diverse work schedules and formal day care services. One is that married fathers spend more time caring for their children when their wives are at work (Presser, 1989). In other words, diversified work schedules may provide two-parent families with the opportunity to schedule work hours so as to share child care (Lero et al., 1992). Second, parents are likely to use a number of care arrangements to cover their child care needs over the course of the week, including off-shifting between spouses; care by relatives, neighbors, or paid sitters; day care centers, half-day preschools, or before and after school programs; and latchkey or sibling care (Lero et al., 1992).

These problems of temporal synchronization are not just personal troubles but public issues of day care policy and employer restrictions on when and where hours are worked. Although many employers have policies that allow a certain amount of time to be taken for family reasons, there is still no circumventing the challenge of deciding which parent will stay home when one of the children wakes up sick. What comes to bear here is not only the public issue of whether either of the parents can take the time off to stay at home (according to the corporate policy) but a whole range of public attitudes about who should take the time off to be with the child. Within corporate culture, mothers continue to carry the brunt of the normative expectation that they be the one to be there for their child (Haas & Hwang, 1995). Several factors contribute to this: One is the nature of the paid work done by women, which continues to be segregated and undervalued, which means that time off is not as costly. Second, there is a lingering ideological belief that women have the primary responsibility for children and are ultimately more competent in caring for them (especially when the children are sick). Third, men who take time off from work for family obligations may be seen as suspect by friends, family, and neighbors (Shelton, 1992).

THE CHALLENGE OF
CONTINUOUS COVERAGE

With most women now working in the paid labor force, there is a challenge to ensure that there is "continuous coverage" of care of children in the home. This is borrowed from Zerubavel's (1979, p. 40) conceptualization of continuous coverage in the hospital setting, where it is considered a moral imperative that hospitals are always open and provide medical coverage on a continuous basis. As this suggests, it is not just a practical necessity but a "morally significant cultural phenomenon" (p. 41) that makes any suspension of medical coverage intolerable. So it is with contemporary families. LaRossa and LaRossa (1981) have made reference to the continuous coverage that is required of parents when they have an infant in the home. However, as children get older the problems of "continuity maintenance" (Zerubavel, 1979, p. 37) continue and may get even more difficult as children begin to participate in a variety of organizational structures.

Although both parents are now typically working in the paid labor force, there is a "moral imperative" that they continue to provide continuous care for their children. There has always been a moral indignation associated with children's self-care that serves as a testimony to the strength of this imperative. For example, the term *latchkey child* emerged during the Second World War, when fathers were off fighting and mothers were in the factories working for the war effort (Padilla & Landreth, 1989). At that time, latchkey children were referred to as the "problem adolescents-to-be in the 1950s" and the "maladjusted parents-to-be in the 1960s" (Zucker, 1944, cited in Padilla & Landreth, 1989, p. 446). The alleged negative effects of self-care persist in the media today even though there is limited empirical evidence about the developmental risks associated with it (Flynn & Rodman, 1989). Although some of the research indicated that children in self-care exhibit higher levels of fear than children in adult care settings (Long & Long, 1982), other research indicated no significant differences on school adjustment, self-esteem, or locus of control (Galambos & Garbarino, 1983; Rodman, Pratto, & Nelson, 1985). Despite this research, the popular assumption is that self-care is a problem with the implication that either mothers *should* provide this care or be responsible for the recruitment of other adult caregivers (Flynn & Rodman, 1989). Furthermore, the popular emphasis on the negative consequences of self-care can also be seen as part of the social construction of the latchkey problem as a basis for eliciting a government-sponsored program and policy response (Rodman, 1990). The provision of continuous coverage has become more challenging because of increases in the number of families where both parents work, increases in the number of separations and divorces leaving one parent to manage paid labor and child care, and the reduced availability of extended family members for child care responsibilities (Rodman, 1990).

In the same way that medical staff move in and out of the same role to provide ongoing care in the hospital setting, the parents' job is to provide continuous care by an endless recruitment of interchangeable caregivers. At this level, there is an "impersonalization of coverage"— whereby different caregivers can move in and out of the same role to provide ongoing care (Zerubavel, 1979, p. 43). Dual-earner families spend a great deal of their time designating interchangeable or "temporary" caregivers for before- and after-school time periods, day care, professional development days, and summer holidays. "Caregiver" becomes a category that is objectified and independent of the personality that temporarily moves in to occupy the position. It is a category that is institutionalized with many interchangeable actors— from teachers to coaches to lunch supervisors.

One of the greatest challenges for dual-earner families is the synchronization of work and school hours. Not only are daily working hours and school hours often out of step, but periodic school holidays and regular summer recesses often pose major synchronization challenges. This asynchrony is one of the reasons why many women seek employment on a part-time basis when their children reach school age (Hantrais, 1993). Some preschool programs, concerned with the amount of shuffling between caregivers that children experience in a day, have begun to experiment with the "seamless day." With this approach, children stay in one place and different caregivers are brought to them. In the effort to maintain this constant coverage, families now spend a higher proportion of their time in the activity of organizing their daily schedules (Hochschild, 1989). These are challenges of temporal synchronization and are the result of an overall "speed up of work and family life" (Hochschild, 1989, p. 9).

Women have traditionally taken responsibility for ensuring that there is continuous coverage within the home. This begins in infancy when mothers, more than fathers, tend to be the ones to provide the continuous coverage that babies require (LaRossa & LaRossa, 1981). Not only have women carried the brunt of the "speedup work," but when outside caregivers are needed, it is usually mothers who take responsibility for the recruitment of these caregivers (Hessing, 1993). Furthermore, this responsibility extends to the orchestration of other people in the family's network. Day care workers, teachers, sports coaches, and neighbors are all part of the network through which mothers orchestrate both continuing and emergent needs (Hessing, 1993). In this regard, mothers can be seen to "establish networks that extend and replace their own capabilities in meeting family needs" (Hessing, 1993, p. 51).

The structure of the family work day can be conceptualized as having two dimensions (Nock & Kingston, 1984). The first has to do with number of hours that a couple works outside of the home, which is an indication of their total commitment of hours to work. The other dimension concerns the scheduling of the work time of family members. When both partners work, there is less discretion over the time available, and as a result, scheduling becomes more complicated and difficult. If couples in dual-earner families have coordinated work days, there is no time lost to their time together. By contrast, when couples work different shifts, they experience "off-scheduling" that can have a detrimental impact on their potential time together (Nock & Kingston, 1984, p. 335). At the same time, however, off-shifting has the advantage of allowing one parent to be available for child care while the other is working. Off-scheduling is prevalent among dual-earner families, and in Canada, 62% of dual-earner couples with children work in off-shifted schedules (Lero et al., 1992).

The evidence suggests that some families deliberately off-schedule their work to minimize the reliance on outside caregivers. For example, in the Canadian national child care study, one sixth of dual-earner couples deliberately off-shifted their work schedule to provide child care from within the family (Lero et al., 1992). The most common reason given for off-shifting was that they considered it best for their children, but one third indicated financial reasons. Deliberate off-shifting was most likely to occur in families that had heavy child-rearing demands. Specifically, deliberate off-shifting was more likely to occur in families with preschool children (Lero et al., 1992; Nock & Kingston, 1984) or in dual-earner families with three or more children under the age of 13 (Lero et al., 1992). Although this is a strategy that allows for constant coverage within the home, it may also have the consequence of resulting in a strained family life with the parenting partners continuously playing a game of "Tag—You're It" to provide the care that is required (Dienhart, 1995). As Rubin (1994) has described it, off-shifting is an experience of family life in which there is little time for the marriage:

> Conversation is limited to the logistics that take place at shift-changing time when children and chores are handed off from one to the other. With children dancing around underfoot, the incoming parent gets a quick summary of the day's or night's events, a list of reminders about things to be done, perhaps about what's cooking in the pot on the stove. "Sometimes when I'm coming home and it's been a hard day, I think: Wouldn't it be wonderful if I could just sit down with Leon for half an hour and we could have a quiet beer together?" (p. 95)

The challenge of continuous coverage may be particularly difficult for single mothers. Although married mothers can usually turn to their spouses for child care assistance, single parents usually have a more binding child care time constraint that restricts the alteration of their time-use patterns (Douthitt, Zick, & McCullough, 1990). Whereas at one level, single parents can be seen to have more control over their time allocations because they do not have to negotiate with a spouse, they tend to be more limited in how they allocate their time because of budget and job constraints (Douthitt et al., 1990). Compared to married mothers, single mothers are more likely to work long hours (Lero et al., 1992; Presser, 1989). On other dimensions, however, the research points to different patterns in Canada and the United States. Canadian data suggest that there are no significant differences between the work patterns of single mothers and married mothers, with approximately two thirds of each working standard hours. On the basis of American data, single parents were more likely to work more than 5 days a week, nonday fixed or rotating shifts, and on weekends (Presser, 1989). The result of these scheduling issues is that single mothers more often have to rely on the informal care that can be provided by relatives (Presser, 1989). This too becomes increasingly difficult because of the increasing number of these women who are themselves working in similar types of jobs. Furthermore, although the assumption is often made that this kind of care is adequate because it is provided by relatives, little information exists with respect to the quality of this kind of caregiving and the implications that it may have for the developing child.

As this discussion suggests, family structure plays a key role in shaping the degree of control that family members have over their time. In a study of time use in three different kinds of families (dual-earner households, single-parent households, and full-time homemakers), McCullough and Zick (1992) found that women in single-parent households experienced the greatest time demands, averaging 11 hours per day in housework, paid work, and committed activities. By contrast, mothers in dual-earner households averaged 10 hours per day and full-time homemakers 9 hours per day in work activities. This is consistent with other research that pointed to the limited time resources of single-parent families, in which one adult carries the responsibility for the duties usually fulfilled by two adults (Hill, 1986). In reviewing the research on how women in single-parent households cope with these time pressures, McCullough and Zick (1992) reported that the most common strategy is to decrease the amount of time spent in household work and to reduce time spent in recreation and self-care. Furthermore, as Quinn and Allen (1989) pointed out, their low incomes may also compound the problem by limiting their choices on how to allocate their time to meet the many role demands that are placed on them.

## The Dynamics of Time Control
## Between Families and Society

For families, the increasing commitment of time to paid work has left them feeling impoverished in their experience of leisure and free time. Although this may be most acute in families where spouses work opposite schedules, it is also present in couples who work the same shift and who must then work tirelessly to meet the demands of home and children. In dual-earner families, there is a feeling that they have lost control over leisure time. Rubin (1994) reports these sentiments from a working-class, 28-year-old African American father of two:

With both of us working like we do, there's no time for anything. We got two little kids; I commute better than an hour each way on my job. Then we live here for half the rent because I take care of the place for the landlord . . . it takes time. I sometimes wonder what life's all about, because this sure ain't what I call living. We don't go any place; we don't do anything; Christ, we hardly have time to go to the toilet. (pp. 98-99)

Although organizational structures such as work can be seen to impose time constraints on their members, individual actors are not simply pawns in these power dynamics of time. Individual control of time can be viewed along a "humanistic-fatalistic dimension" whereby members either exercise a great deal of mastery and control over their time (humanistic) or enter into time commitments on the basis of obligation, compulsion, domination, or coercion (Lyman & Scott, 1970, p. 191). In a similar vein, Marks (1977) emphasized the role of "commitment" for an allocation of time that is based on the assessment of the importance of a performance or activity in relation to other activities. Zerubavel (1976) also addressed issues associated with the control of time, arguing that schedules contain three components: "a totally self determined part, a totally environmentally determined part and a socially negotiable part in between" (p. 91). Hence, although work and school structures are usually viewed as having control over the use of time, the individual stands in relation to these structures with varying degrees of autonomy. In this regard, choices around time allocation can be viewed as indications of "attitudinal conformity" insofar as dedications of time, as an exchangeable resource, can be viewed as conforming (or not) to the performance demands of the organization (Telles, 1980, p. 172). As this suggests, choosing to spend time fulfilling performance demands is a choice of compliance. Although work organizations have traditionally monitored this conformity, families appear now to be more vocal in the expression of their demands for the commitment of time to the family organization. Due in large part to the increased participation of women in the paid labor force, the unexamined conformity to the demands of paid work is giving way to the daily struggle of finding a balance of allegiance in the family-work interface. These ideas can serve as a useful lens for the analysis of various dynamics of time control in families. Specifically, they can serve as an important point of departure for questions about the nature of domination by external structures and the extent to which individual actors position themselves in terms of feeling that their time is discretionary or imposed.

CHANGING WORK POLICIES

Politically, work organizations have begun to develop family responsive policies that shift the "humanistic-fatalistic" balance toward more control of time for family members. In 1985, one out of eight wage and salary earners had jobs in which they could vary the hours in which their work began and ended (Presser, 1989). Nevertheless, "family friendly" flextime and shift work are still unavailable to the majority of workers (Hessing, 1993). Flexible scheduling, for example, allows men and women more discretion in the way that they set up their daily or weekly schedule so that they can avoid conflicts with family and household responsibilities (Christensen & Staines, 1990). In a study of employed caregivers, 85% indicated that the most important and helpful workplace program is to provide flexible work schedules (Scharlach, 1994). Opportunities for job sharing and permanent part-time work also provide flexibility while maintaining job security and avoiding loss of benefits (Kingston, 1990). The "compressed" work week preserves the total number of hours by reducing a 5-day schedule into a 3- or 4-day schedule with longer hours worked each day (Rothman & Marks, 1987). The research on the effectiveness of flextime work schedules suggests that there is no particular kind of schedule that is most effective but, rather, what is most critical is a policy that allows many flexibilities so that employees can adapt work schedules to emergencies and changing family needs (Neal, Chapman, Ingersoll-Dayton, & Emlen, 1993, p. 74).

Relatively little is known, however, about the impact of flexible work hours for the time parents spend with children or their satisfaction at home. Of the few studies that have been done, it appears that the introduction of a formal flextime program has little impact on the time that parents spend with their children (Presser, 1989). In a comparison study of two similar organizations where one went to a compressed shift schedule, there was an overall improvement in family satisfaction, but these satisfaction scores were not significantly higher than the control organization (Cunningham, 1989). Nevertheless, they do indicate a trend toward greater satisfaction with family as a result of more free and discretionary time that can improve the opportunity for effectively fulfilling family roles.

Safe and convenient child care services and the development of equitable parental leave policies also serve to give family members more autonomy in the management of their family-work balance. Although family responsive policies are available to both men and women, it is women who typically take advantage of these policies (Haas & Hwang, 1995). As a result, they might as well be called "women-responsive policies" (Shelton, 1992). The data on the number of fathers who take advantage of available parental leave are scant, yet it appears that relatively few fathers do take advantage of it (Presser, 1989). Even in Sweden, for example, where gender-equal social policies have been progressive in relation to other industrialized nations, men use less than one third of the days set aside to care for sick children, whereas women use almost all of them (Haas & Hwang, 1995).

Some evidence indicates that the percentage of women who took advantage of paid leave tripled in the 1960s and 1970s such that close to half of all employed mothers took paid leave during the first six weeks after childbirth (Shelton, 1992). Traditionally, this has been a function of women's greater commitment to, and responsibility for, the smooth running of the household and care of children. The consequence, however, is that although employer- or government-sponsored leave policies may allow women to better manage work and child care demands, they may inadvertently reinforce the gender gap in the way that these commitments are balanced (Shelton, 1992). At the same time, however, it appears that the increasing diversity of work times and flexibility of work schedules may be just the lever that is necessary to move fathers into spending more time with their children. As Presser (1989) argued, "The diversity of work schedules, by facilitating the dual employment of married couples with children, may be doing more to increase male participation in child care than ideological changes concerning children's needs for more fathering or women's needs for more role sharing" (p. 538).

There is some evidence to suggest that improvements in work time flexibility have been slowest in the professional occupations. For example, in law, medicine, accountancy, and banking, anything less than full-time status is not readily accommodated by large organizations (Hantrais, 1993). Where there has been greater flexibility offered, the result is two different professional streams for women: the slow stream for those who want to combine family and professional life, which gives greater flexibility but limits prospects, and the fast stream that requires total availability and commitment for those who want to progress in their careers more rapidly (Hantrais, 1993).

Other research has examined the potential of work reduction schemes to alleviate the time stresses associated with the synchronization of family and work schedules. In the Canadian National Labour Force Survey, approximately one third of the respondents expressed an interest in work reduction (Desaulniers & Theberge, 1992). Two family circumstances were of particular importance for explaining preferences for work reduction: household income and the presence of children under the age of 5 (Desaulniers & Theberge, 1992). With respect to household income, the desire to reduce the number of paid working hours, for both men and women, is contingent on the ability to afford a decrease in income. Although having a child under the age of 5 was related to an interest in work reduction for both women and men, the direction of the relationship was opposite. For women, the interest in work reduction increases with the presence of young children, whereas for men, interest declines when there are young children in the house. As these findings suggest, the desire for work reduction among women reflects the continuing importance of mothering in women's lives, and for men it reflects either the continuing importance of the provider role or the desire to escape from child care responsibilities (Desaulniers & Theberge, 1992).

When the reasons for wanting a work reduction were explored with men and women, other gender differences were evident. For women, the main reason for wanting to reduce their time in paid work was to fulfill their responsibilities and obligations outside their paid work. The meaning of a reduction in paid work for women appears to be a means for juggling domestic and paid work. For men, by contrast, the main reason given for reducing work time was to pursue leisure interests through sports, education, travel, and hobbies, followed by a desire to have more family time.

## Summary

Families live on the cusp between the internal time needs associated with intimacy and rejuvenation and the unrelenting external forces of a sociotemporal order that demands compliance and diligent attentiveness. Finding the balance between these forces is in itself a time-consuming activity that requires planning and resourcefulness. The family's daily rhythm of dispersion into the world of work and school is punctuated by the organizational beats of "arriving at work on time," or ensuring that the kids are picked up on time. The temporal politics of the family in society involves a day-to-day negotiation of time that is perceived to be externally based and controlled. As a result, institutionally based calendars, schedules, and daily working hours are seen as forces of temporal control with which families must contend. This tension between families and the world of work has existed for many years, but it has become most acute in the past couple of decades. In light of dramatic increases in the number of women and teenage children in the paid workforce, there appears to be an increasing imbalance between the family's ability to control time and the imposed schedules of a variety of institutions. Work imposes temporal demands on families and the hours of day care, schools, and commercial organizations must somehow be fit in.

Clocking and synchronization can serve as useful conceptual tools for exploring the way that families attempt to bring some order and control to their temporal worlds. Clocking in families focuses on the way that the rhythm of daily life is shaped by sequence, pace, and duration of experienced events. There is now a well-developed literature that deals with the amount of time that families allocate to various household activities, yet we have only a limited understanding of clocking behaviors. Although many families lament the speedup of their lives, there is limited empirical evidence that can provide insight into the mechanisms that maintain this pace and the effects that it has on all family members. More specifically, little is known about the systemic conditions that give rise to the "operating pace" of any given family. Because the way that families manage the clocking behaviors in their daily routine is related to the maintenance of who they are as a family, focusing attention on these clocking behaviors can provide insight into the family paradigm (Reiss, 1981).

In light of increasing diversity in family forms and increasing complexity in family work schedules, families are summoned to be increasingly adaptable in the way that they respond to temporal demands. These are problems of synchronization. Whereas at one time key family transitions such as marriage or parenthood precipitated a "crisis" of synchronizing new patterns and timetables, it appears that temporal synchronization has become an everyday challenge. With the dispersion of family members into different and fragmented temporal domains, it has become more difficult to coordinate drop-offs and pick-ups, mealtimes, and coverage within the home. When nonstandard schedules and nonstandard families are added to this equation, there is an exponential increase in the difficulty of providing synchronized care within families.

Although the challenges associated with clocking and synchronization are at one level private troubles to be worked out by families themselves, they are also problems that are increasingly being recognized in the public sphere of work. In recent years, corporate culture has begun to develop family-responsive policies to provide more flexibility and control for family members in their efforts to manage the synchronization of complex schedules. These programs are available to women and men, but women are typically the ones to take advantage of them. Similarly, women express a greater interest in work reduction schemes when their children are small. Both of these trends point to the fact that women continue to carry the primary responsibility for managing the delicate family-work balance when children are small.

As these ideas suggest, men and women have a very different experience of time. In the next chapter there is a discussion of how they experience time differently and how this has resulted in a micropolitics of time within the home.

# 7

# Gender Politics of Family Time

The acceleration of time and its accompanying scarcity has resulted in an inflation of the value of time. Not only has time become more precious, but it has become more contentious. This is especially the case in the gender politics of time. As both women and men struggle for a sense of balance in both public and private domains, issues of entitlement to personal time, commitment to work and family, and access to traditional privileges boil to the surface.

There are many conflicts that men and women experience over time. Power and control over time are rooted in the values that are assigned to time through family responsibilities, money, position, and status. As Coser (1974) pointed out some time ago, it is not a simple matter of incompatible time allocations that arise from the demands of family and work but a fundamental contradiction in the values that underlie the allocation of time: Women are expected to be committed to their work just like men at the same time as they maintain a priority to family. By today's standards, fathers face a similar contradiction: Men live in a culture in which there are new expectations that they be committed to family just like women (see, e.g., Daly, 1993; LaRossa,

1988) while at the same time maintaining their role as the primary provider (Cohen, 1993). Furthermore, the perception of the ever-deepening scarcity of time highlights the underlying contradictions in time commitments for men and women and makes the actual conflicts over time allocations that much more overt and challenging.

## His and Her Time

In the same way that Jessie Bernard made reference to "his and her marriages," it appears that men and women have a phenomenologically different experience of time. Numerous theories have been proposed to explain these differences between women and men.

### BIOLOGICAL DIFFERENCES

Kellerman (1989), for example, has pointed to biological differences as the basis for women and men's different experience of time. Although both men and women have biological rhythms, women's temporal rhythms tend to be more cyclical in nature. Women experience the cycles of menstruation, pregnancy, birth, and menopause. These cycles are not simply biological; they are experienced as psychological cycles and, as a result, influence the daily rhythms of thinking, feeling, and acting. Kellerman argues that women's experience of time as natural and cyclical is in contrast with societal linear time that is shaped by culture, technology, and industrial production. Linear time is the essence of masculine experience. Work and career continue to be the most salient aspects of identity for men, which is expressed in time as progression and achievement. As the pace of production in industrialized capitalist society has intensified, there has been a widening gap between intensified linear time (under capitalism) and women's cyclical time, which is relatively fixed in pace and duration. This is a gap between masculine linear temporality and feminine cyclical temporality.

Giving birth accentuates and dramatizes the difference between male and female conceptualizations of time. The biological clock, as experienced by women, refers not simply to "a determinacy of nature or a coercion of linear time, but to a reminder of the opportunity to locate oneself differently in time through relationship, continuity and connectedness that the possibility of giving birth symbolically offers" (McMahon, 1995, pp. 85-86). As a result, the "biological clock" metaphor has a decidedly linear ring to it, with its emphasis on endless ticking and time left, yet the decisions that women make about becoming mothers tend to be focused on the implications for connectedness and relationship (McMahon, 1995).

## SOCIAL-PSYCHOLOGICAL DIFFERENCES

Taking a social-psychological approach, Cottle and Klineberg (1974) offered some speculations about how men and women are socialized to have different orientations to time. Gendered time perceptions change according to the different demands that are associated with social roles for men and women. For example, under an ideology that stresses the importance of success (once for men only, now for both men and women) the future takes on greater importance. "Achievement" is a future-oriented goal that requires a focus on a recurring cycle of planning and accomplishment. This is part of our Western culture, which teaches women and men that all activity is directed toward the future. However, for men especially, there is an alienation from the past and the present that comes with learned definitions of achievement and future preparation. When the focus is on accomplishing goals, the day-to-day becomes unsatisfying because of "the devotion to preparing for the future" (Cottle & Klineberg, 1974, p. 122). Metaphorically, men's orientation toward time is like that of a stock market investor who monitors current investments with an eye to a payment of some kind in the future (Cottle, 1976). Because men are more likely to be preoccupied with achievement, they are more likely to see the present as a preparation for the future and to accept the uncertainties and ambiguities associated with a future orientation.

By contrast, Cottle and Klineberg (1974) argued that women are socialized to believe that nurturing people and sustaining interpersonal relationships is more important than achievement. Cottle (1976) referred to this as "expressive interaction." Women are socialized in expressive interaction, and as a result, they visualize their expectations as occurring in a series of uninterrupted presents and as ends in themselves (p. 79). This focus is strikingly similar to Gilligan's (1982) later influential work that argues that women are socialized under an ethic of care. For Cottle and Klineberg (1974), this orientation means that women are more engaged in the day-to-day experience of the present. Whereas for men, the present is a time of preparation, for women, the present is a time for having (Cottle, 1976, p. 79). Although these ideas reflect traditional, and perhaps stereotypical, categorizations of men and women's behavior, they continue to have saliency for understanding the gender divisions that mark family experience. Cottle and Klineberg (1974) offered some empirical support for these ideas, but their conclusions certainly need to be revisited in light of changes in gender practice since that time. Specifically, feminist writers have begun to question whether women's caregiving is a natural part of being female or a consequence of subordination (Baber & Allen, 1992). Although more psychologically oriented theories (such as Gilligan's) tend to support the ethic of care argument in which women are better suited to a lifelong involvement of child rearing and caregiving, sociological theories tend to emphasize the notion that women provide care because men with more power do not want to do it.

More recent research by Maines and Hardesty (1987) on the career and family plans of young adults, supported the idea that temporality is gendered. For the young men in the study, the future was cast as a linear life plan with education, work, and family organized in a sequential fashion with an accompanying set of strategies for how to realize these goals. There was a sense that the future was mapped and they felt a sense of control in getting to their destination. By contrast, the futures anticipated by the young women tended to be marked by less control and an awareness of impending disruptions or discontinuities. Parenthood and family responsibilities were seen as potentially problematic choices for women because they posed challenges for the way that they organized or synchronized their time. Therefore, although young men planned uncomplicated and progressive futures, young women anticipated work and family as competing commitments.

Other sociological theories claim that men and women have a distinctive experience of time because of differences in the nature of the demands that are placed on them and the degree of control that they are able to bring to their allocation of time. Hall (1983) has distinguished between monochronic and polychronic experiences of time. Monochronic time is a pattern of sequential behavior that is shaped by schedules, is task oriented, and is open to evaluations of success or failure. Polychronic time is patterned by a set of simultaneous interactions, focused on the present, and shaped by the involvement of people in transactions. Whereas monochronic time requires the sequential processing of one experience at a time, polychronic time usually involves the simultaneous processing of several things at once. It has been argued that men are more likely to have a monochronic time perspective and women a polychronic one (Hall, 1983). Monochronic time dominates the traditional masculine domains of business, government, the professions, entertainment, and sports. However, in the domestic domain, especially in traditional homes where the woman's role is pivotal, polychronic time takes over. Otherwise, "How else can one raise several children at once, run a household, hold a job, be a wife, mother, nurse, tutor, chauffeur and general fixer-upper?" (Hall, 1983). Women in these positions are more likely to be engaged in multiple tasks and responsibilities.

Although there is limited empirical support for this gendered experience of time, a number of researchers have come to similar conclusions about women's experience of time as polychronic. Hochschild (1989), for example, in her research on dual-earner families, reported that women more often do two or more things at once while in the home. This might include thinking out the shopping list while vacuuming and watching the 3-year-old child. Men, by contrast, are more likely to take on one task at a time, such as cooking dinner *or* taking a child to the park. In other research, women were said to average three tasks at one time (Berheide, cited in Thompson & Walker, 1989).

Davies (1994) argued that it is well recognized that women have a simultaneous capacity that allows them to carry out several activities at once. Not only is this seen as a positive quality, but it is presented in management courses as a useful organizational tool or skill. This ability is captured in the concept of "process time," which is based on the idea that any activity has fluid boundaries and is invisibly woven into other activities (Davies, 1994, p. 281). This is also captured in the expression "a woman's work is never done," which exemplifies the incompatibility between women's experience of time and com-modified work time that comes in finite, uniform, measured units that are exchanged for money (Adam, 1993). Specifically, "caring, loving and educating times, household management and maintenance times and their female times of menopause and pregnancy are not so much time that is spent, allocated and controlled as time lived, time made and time generated" (Adam, 1993, p. 172).

In a similar vein, women are more likely to report family time with children as an experience of mixed leisure and work (Shaw, 1992). The combination of planning, organization, responsibility, and enjoy-ment that women experience during "leisure" time may also reflect their polychronic disposition to family time experience. These dif-ferences in time use may go unrecognized by men and women in the home, but they are, nevertheless, a potential source of conflict. As these "time styles" are associated with different levels of commitment, responsibility, and distraction, there is potential for frustration and accusation in the ongoing negotiations for time use in the household.

Monochronic and polychronic conceptualizations of family time are useful starting points for understanding differences in time ex-perience for men and women, yet there is a need for more empirical research in these areas. These models of time may have been an apt description for the way that men and women experienced time in the early 1980s when they were first proposed. However, they must be reexamined in the context of how men and women live their lives now under a new set of temporal demands. Many questions arise. In light of the increases in the labor force participation of women, should women become more monochronic in their orientation in order to reduce stress in the way that they manage their work and family balance? Or should men become more polychronic as they move toward increased levels of commitment to family time? There are several possibilities for reconceptualizing this schema about gendered time. One is to think about a model of convergence in which men become more polychronic in light of their increased participation at home and women more monochronic as they spend more time in the paid labor force. Another possibility here is to think about both men and women becoming more polychronic—in light of the escalating demands that they both experience in their efforts to juggle the demands of work and home.

## MODELS FOR UNDERSTANDING
## GENDER AND TIME

There have been two traditional models that have been used to assess and explain the scarcity of time that men and women have in meeting their occupational and family demands. The first of these is the role overload model, which is based on the assumption that the temporal demands of paid and family work exceed the available time and energy available. As Burley (1991) pointed out, both members of dual-earner couples feel the effects of time-related conflicts, but women tend to mention time shortages more often and experience them to a greater extent than husbands. Overall, the literature indicates that women in dual-earner households generally make gains in economic well-being at the expense of increasing the number of demands on their time. However, there is a contradiction in the research literature insofar as some studies indicate higher life satisfaction among women with paid jobs, whereas other research shows that women in dual-earner families are particularly prone to time stress and role overload (Shaw, 1991). In her own research, Shaw (1991) found that this contradiction was experienced by women when they reported greater life satisfaction and greater time stress. The second model is an equity model that argues the greater the discrepancy in time spent in family work between spouses, the higher the probability of marital dissatisfaction and decreased psychological well-being (Burley, 1991). The vast majority of family time studies implicitly take this approach by using a ledger comparison of who does more to determine differential outcomes of satisfaction or equality.

## MEASURING THE GENDERED
## EXPERIENCE OF TIME

By far the most extensive literature pertaining to the gendered experience of time concerns the way that men and women allocate time. This is a large and complicated literature that compares the amount of time that women and men spend in paid work, unpaid work, and leisure time. On reviewing this literature, Godwin (1991) suggested that the contradictory conclusions that are reached in this research are a function of the many disciplines that have taken an interest in the division of domestic labor (e.g., economics, family economics, sociology). Furthermore, within any discipline many theoretical perspectives have been used (e.g., Godwin identifies no fewer than eight in sociology). The diverse values, assumptions, and motives associated with disciplines and theoretical perspectives results in different questions, methods, and results.

Part of the difficulty one encounters when trying to make sense of this literature concerns the methodological issues that arise in measuring time and time usage. General categories such as "unpaid work time" or "leisure time" are fraught with conceptual and methodological difficulties that make comparison of results difficult. Some studies fail to distinguish between the objectively observable behavior of each spouse or the couple and the subjective perceptions of the spouses (Godwin, 1991). Furthermore, diary events are often treated as separate entities or categories, when, in reality, they may be experienced in an overlapping or concurrent manner. Studies that have examined parental involvement with children have had to deal with a dizzying array of time categories. Pleck (in press), for example, in commenting on fathering time, outlines the complexity of measurement: There is the father's total time with the child, solo time, interaction time, physical and emotional caregiving time, time spent with the child with or without the mother present, and absolute versus proportional time (relative to the mother's). Time diaries catalog the amount of time that is spent in various activities, but little attention is directed toward temporal sequencing, planning activities associated with time, or general time stress (Shaw, 1991). There are also variations in the data in terms of family structures, the age and number of children, and the stage of the family life cycle.

The theoretical and methodological diversity that exists in the study of time allocations has resulted in few conclusive answers. In her comprehensive critique of time allocation studies, Godwin (1991) concluded that "despite the dozens of studies and the years of effort of researchers from the three disciplines, little cumulative knowledge about the causes of family time allocation exists and many questions remain without definitive answers" (p. 279). In light of these challenges, my purpose is to provide a brief overview of ongoing gender asymmetries in each of three domains: paid work, domestic labor, and leisure. Although time allocation studies play an important role in cataloging the way that time is distributed and used in families, it is beyond the scope of this book to try to present the details here. The discussion that follows focuses on the meanings and implications of time allocations for men and women's experiences of paid work, domestic labor, and leisure. In this regard, there is an effort to go beyond the "who does what how often" (Thompson & Walker, 1989, p. 861) approach to the distribution of family labor and instead to explore the meanings associated with their different experiences of time.

## The Politics of Time and Paid Work

An understanding of the gendered use of time begins with the idea that gender differences reside primarily in the way that the workload is divided between men and women. Despite the massive movement of women into the paid labor force, there is still a traditional division of labor. Women, despite high labor market participation, are still primarily responsible for domestic tasks and child care, whereas men are mainly responsible for paid work and the more durable maintenance work that is performed around the home (Elchardus & Glorieux, 1994). Although the traditional asymmetry in paid work is rapidly changing, men typically spend more time in paid work.

### GENDER DISPARITIES IN THE
### TIME GIVEN TO PAID WORK

The most recent figures for Canada, based on 1992 data, indicate that men with children (regardless of age) continue to do approximately 20% more paid work than women (Statistics Canada, 1994). Similar trends are reported in a U.S. study of time diary data showing that employed men spent significantly more time in paid labor than employed women (Firestone & Shelton, 1994). On average, women contribute less than one third of dual-earner family income in both Canada and the United States (Statistics Canada, 1994; Thompson & Walker, 1989). As a consequence, the responsibility for providing for the family still rests primarily on men's shoulders, and both women and men are ambivalent about women as providers (Thompson & Walker, 1989). Furthermore, women are more likely than men to have contradictory feelings about combining their paid work and family work and to feel guilty about their homes and children (Thompson & Walker, 1989). As this suggests, there is a continuing cultural mandate that women continue to give priority to their families and men continue to give precedence to their work. The result is that women's time is undervalued in relation to men: In continuing to make her primary allegiance to the family, her work, whether paid or unpaid, is typically poorly rewarded and of low status.

## CULTURAL VARIATIONS OF GENDERED TIME IN PAID WORK

Men continue to experience advantage in relation to the control of time as a result of their higher status (overall in the workforce) and the higher commodified value that is attached to their time. Studies of social stratification have shown that the higher one's rank within a hierarchy, the greater one's time advantages as manifested in less observability of their time and greater choice in the use of their time (Telles, 1980). In families where husbands have professional careers, there is a pattern of subordination of family life to professional life in which wives integrate their roles with the requirements of professional life in a way that advantages the husband's career (Fowlkes, 1987). As Shelton (1992) has pointed out, occupational status is negatively associated with women's and men's household labor time. In light of men's continued status advantages in the economic domain, there is a wider gap between their paid work and their household responsibilities. Although there has been slow progress in closing the wage gap between women and men, women who worked full-time, year-round earned just 72% the amount of their male counterparts (Statistics Canada, 1994). Inasmuch as women's work is consistently linked with lower power, prestige, and material rewards than men's work (Hunt & Hunt, 1987), men continue to enjoy advantages in the control of their time by virtue of their status advantages.

A gendered analysis of time also cannot overlook the fact that women's paid labor is ghettoized insofar as their jobs tend to be underpaid, of low status, precarious, and often with little opportunity of advancement (Thompson & Walker, 1989). This is largely attributable to the growth of the service sector with its disproportionately high percentage of female occupations (Presser, 1989). According to U.S. census data, between 1970 and 1986, employment in service industries grew at approximately twice the rate of total employment (Hendricks & Cutler, 1990). The overall result is that the value assigned to women's work time in service occupations is still considered secondary to men's (Pronovost, 1989). The implication is that it is "less costly" for women to sacrifice paid work time for the demands of the household. Indeed, when there are increases in the amount of family work to be done, it is wives, not husbands who typically respond by cutting back on time spent in paid work (Berk, 1985). An overview of the research that examines the effect of employed parents coping with a sick child revealed that women missed twice as many days as men to care for a sick child (Neal et al., 1993). This greater tendency of women to take time off for sick children, to take maternity leave, or to work part-time are some of the manifestations of the ongoing discrepancies in how time is experienced by men and women in their paid work.

## BLURRED BOUNDARIES
## BETWEEN WORK AND FAMILY

An examination of the gendered nature of social time must also be attentive to the relationship between the temporal norms and pressures of the domestic sphere on the one hand and the economic sphere on the other. Popular belief suggests that women have the choice between a commitment to work outside of the home or a commitment to the work of family in the domestic sphere. Yet as Le Feuvre (1994) pointed out, women's experience of time in the early stages of the family life cycle is tightly bound to the concomitant nature of two contradictory temporal forces: the temporal constraints of the domestic sphere that are associated with the presence of small children and the constraints of the economic sphere that are associated with laying the foundations of a future career. There is little option to switch between the two; rather, work is continuous in both and as a result there is an experience of conflicting temporalities.

The hours that men spend in their paid work can be seen as relatively homogeneous and discrete, but for women, nonwork concerns frequently impinge on and intermingle with their working time

(Hantrais, 1993). This points to the persistence of "asymmetrical permeable boundaries" in which work continues to intrude into family time for men, whereas family continues to intrude into work time for women (Pleck, 1977, p. 423). Research that examines family-work spillover (aspects of the family domain negatively affect aspects of the work domain) shows that dual-career women spend significantly more time in family-work than their husbands and this is associated with higher family-work spillover for women (Burley, 1991).

SCHEDULING PATTERNS IN PAID WORK

One of the ways that women's responsibility for time is manifested is in the way that men and women schedule their work lives. According to the 1985 Current Population Survey, mothers were 5 times more likely than fathers (42% compared to 8%) to indicate that child care was their primary reason for working evenings or nights (Presser, 1989). These differences support the notion that women generally are the "adapters" who arrange their work hours around the needs of their children for care, whereas husbands are the "accepters" who are willing to care for their children when mothers are employed (Presser, 1989, p. 531).

There is also considerable variation in the experience of work time for men and women. Whereas work involvement for both men and women has often been considered a static background characteristic, there is evidence to suggest that it varies on a weekly basis, seasonally and across the life course (Crouter et al., 1992; Moen, 1985; Stipp, 1988). When across-the-week time allocations were examined for employed and nonemployed mothers, employed mothers work more, sleep less, and have less leisure time than nonemployed women for all days of the week (Zuzanek & Smale, 1992). However, when employed mothers are compared to employed fathers, there tends to be a symmetrical pattern of time distribution for work, family, and leisure during the weekdays and an asymmetrical pattern during the week-ends. On weekdays, the overall workloads of employed mothers are lower than those reported by employed fathers on Mondays and Tuesdays, slightly higher on Wednesdays and approximately the same on Fridays, with the only difference being that employed fathers have slightly more leisure during the week. On weekends, however, the

asymmetry between employed men and women is evident with
employed fathers reporting workloads that are 1.0 to 1.5 hours lower
than those reported by employed mothers and with an additional 2.0
to 2.5 hours of free time per day (Zuzanek & Smale, 1992). For
employed mothers, weekends appear to be the time when they "catch
up" with domestic duties that go unattended during the week.
Weekends appear to be the primary frontier for balancing the asymmetry between employed fathers and mothers (Zuzanek & Smale,
1992).

Some research has argued that there is considerably more variation
throughout the year in time spent at work for women than men. For
example, women are more likely than men to be employed part time,
to work less than 12 months of the year and to have a discontinuous
pattern of employment marked by entering and leaving the labor force
more often (Hoffman, 1987). Men are associated with linear career
paths, whereas women are viewed as having a more cyclical path as
they adapt their work lives to match changes in their family situation
(Hantrais, 1993). The effects on family of these patterns of work time
seem to vary widely. In general, the data indicate that the employed
mother spends less time with each child, but this differed by social
class and the definition of child contact (Hoffman, 1987). In keeping
with this, Le Feuvre (1994) has reported that there are dramatic
differences in subjective meanings of time allocations for working-
class mothers and university graduate mothers in France. Working-
class mothers tend to work part-time and perceive their paid work as
a barrier to "the expression of their dominant core identity as wives
and mothers" (Le Feuvre, 1994, p. 172). By contrast, university
graduate mothers were more likely to see their time in paid work as
their main source of personal identity and satisfaction and their time
in domestic tasks as something they wished to distance themselves
from.

Fathers, by contrast, are more likely to be employed full-time and
in a continuous manner. The available research suggests that men in
higher occupational groups, especially executives and independent
professionals, work longer hours on the job (Hoffman, 1987). When
fathers spend more time at work, they and their wives are more likely

to report work-family conflict, whereas when wives work long hours, only they, and not their husbands, are likely to report increased role strain (Hoffman, 1987; Keith & Schafer, 1980).

## CHANGES IN FAMILY STATUS AND THE
## GENDERED EXPERIENCE OF PAID WORK TIME

A gender politics of time also gets played out with respect to the transitions from married to divorced and from divorced to remarried statuses. For men there is very little change in the annual number of hours that are worked in the years either leading into or following a divorce or remarriage (Gerner, Montalto, & Bryant, 1990). For women, by contrast, there are differences. Women who become divorced tend to increase the number of hours that they work in the year or two prior to the occurrence of the divorce and in the year or two following the divorce (Gerner et al., 1990). For women who remarry, the opposite effect was observed, with women who become remarried decreasing the hours of their paid work in the year of the remarriage and thereafter (Gerner et al., 1990). This decrease was attributed to women dropping out of the labor force at the time of remarriage rather than reductions in the hours of work. As these results suggest, marriage represents an economic relationship that provides a level of economic security for women that, in turn, affects their time allocations to paid work. When there is an impending disruption to this economic relationship, women invest more time in paid labor. When the economic stability of a marriage is reestablished, the investment in paid work diminishes.

## The Politics of Time in the Domestic Sphere

In the same way that there is a wage gap in the paid labor force, there is a gap in the work that men and women do at home (Hochschild, 1989; Le Feuvre, 1994). Although men have steadily increased their commitment to housework and child care, women continue to do the majority of these tasks.

GENDER DISPARITIES IN THE
TIME GIVEN TO DOMESTIC WORK

In an analysis of the 1987-1988 National Survey of Families and Households, Demo and Acock (1993) reported that mothers, across all family types, contribute approximately 70% to 90% of the total domestic labor that is done in the family. Put in another way, when the contribution of mothers is compared to all other family members combined, they do 70% of the domestic labor when they are in a first marriage or a stepfamily and roughly 87% when they are divorced or never-married mothers. When the total domestic labor of husbands and male cohabitating partners is compared to the contribution of mothers in all family types, men contribute one third of the work that mothers do (Demo & Acock, 1993) (when this is coupled with the earlier finding that women contribute approximately one third of family income, there is a remarkable symmetry amidst the imbalance!). The consistency of this finding across family types led the researchers to conclude that gender, not family type or statutory relationship, is the critical variable for explaining domestic labor. These results are consistent with a long line of research that has demonstrated women's ongoing responsibility for the majority of household labor (Berardo, Shehan, & Leslie, 1987; Berk, 1985; Pleck, 1985). Although the differences appear to be less pronounced in Canada, the disparities are similar with national data indicating that women spent approximately twice the time their husbands do in both domestic work and child care (Statistics Canada, 1994).

The only variables that are consistently related to a more equitable division of labor between spouses is level of education and employment status of the wife (Godwin, 1991). The results are not consistent across all samples, but there is less asymmetry in families where both spouses work and are more highly educated (Godwin, 1991).

The employment status of the mother is consistently reported as playing an important role in determining the distribution of time in the family (Godwin, 1991; Hilton, 1990). Employed mothers devote significantly less time to household chores than do nonemployed mothers (Sanik, 1990), and this pattern holds regardless of family type (Demo & Acock, 1993). Time devoted to employment seems to reduce the amount of time that is available for household work, with nonemployed mothers spending between 45 and 52 hours per week compared to 32 to 37 hours per week for employed mothers (Demo & Acock, 1993). This supports the "substitution effect" from economics, which posits that when one's own wages increase, his or her time in household production will decline (Godwin, 1991). This can be attributed to the fact that employed women tend to place a higher marginal value on their time available for household work than their nonemployed counterparts (Becker, 1965). Overall, it appears that employed women spend more time in activities that are considered "obligatory" (i.e., paid work, housework, child care, and personal care) than nonemployed women (Shaw, 1991; Zuzanek & Smale, 1992).

## WOMEN AND THE "SECOND SHIFT"

For the majority of women who are working full time in the labor force, this results in working "the second shift" at home (Hochschild, 1989) and ultimately being caught in "the double ghetto" (Armstrong & Armstrong, 1984) whereby they work in the home and for pay in jobs that are typically segregated, undervalued, and underpaid. According to traditional Marxist analysis, capitalism had the effect of separating men and women's work into public and private spheres where men produced exchange values and women produced use values in the home (Zaretsky, 1976). Because his work contributed directly to the production of commodities that could be sold for profit, his work was more highly valued in a capitalist economy, whereas her work was undervalued. There is a fundamental difference in the fungibility of the resources produced by each that allows for the emergence of an unequal exchange relation between men and women (Brines, 1994). As a consequence, women's time is undervalued and dehumanized (Forman, 1989). The net result of this undervaluing of women's time is that their entitlement to use time for their own purposes is greatly diminished. Because women's time is devalued in both the public and private spheres, women have carried greater responsibility for the second shift:

> Since [her] work comes second, she carries more of the second shift, thus providing support for her husband's work. Because she supports her

husband's efforts at work more than he supports hers, her personal ambitions contract and her earnings, already lower, rise more slowly. The extra month a year that she works contributes not only to her husband's success, but to the expanding wage gap between them and keeps the cycle spinning. (Hochschild, 1989, p. 254)

This explanation is consistent with the "economic dependency model," in which the rules governing the division of housework are tied to relations of economic support and dependency (Brines, 1994). According to this view, wives continue to perform most of the domestic tasks because they earn less than their husbands.

Although the second shift has become prominent in feminist and family science discourse, care must be used in interpreting this to mean that women typically work a double workload. Time studies indicate that although women may carry double responsibility, they do not work twice the hours of their employed husbands (Elchardus & Glorieux, 1994). In fact, there seems to be an established norm that limits the total workload to about 55 to 60 hours a week, which, when reached, seems to activate other mechanisms (such as paid or household help) to reduce the workload (Elchardus & Glorieux, 1994). It is as if there is a tolerance threshold or "ceiling" on household labor activity that, when reached, results in either ignoring or off-loading the remaining work. This is consistent with research that shows that in dual-career families, the amount of housework that is done is far less than in families where there are full-time housewives (Berardo et al., 1987). Women in dual-career families are still doing the majority of the household work, but there is a lower ceiling on the overall amount of work that is carried out.

## GENDER AND TEMPORAL
## COORDINATION IN FAMILIES

Women continue to carry the primary responsibility for the temporal coordination of family activities. Because time management constitutes one of the major elements of the socialization process, it is usually women as mothers who carry the primary responsibility for the temporal organization of their children (e.g., getting them up, fed, dressed, and off to school) (Le Feuvre, 1994). As part of this, mothers play a major role in the development of "time awareness," which

prepares their children to meet the socially imposed temporal impera-
tives and constraints (Le Feuvre, 1994). As this suggests, mothers play
the key role in helping the child to develop an attentiveness to the
temporal dimensions of all tasks and activity. Although the emphasis
in the literature tends to be on women's role in the development of
temporal awareness for children, it is imperative to look in future
research at the role that fathers play in this socialization process. How
does the father's conduct, as shaped primarily by the economic domain, convey temporal standards to children? One could hypothesize
that fathers, inasmuch as their time is more highly valued, are more
likely to convey a greater sense of urgency, rigidity, and precision with
respect to their time.

    In light of the perceived acceleration of time, women have become
"the time and motion experts" insofar as they carry the brunt of the
speedup in work and family life (Hochschild, 1989, p. 9). Their own
time may be undervalued in the family, but women generally carry the
responsibility for controlling the temporal organization of family life.
This can range from making decisions about the timing of childbirth
to juggling the timetables of all family members (Hantrais, 1993).
Specifically, women typically take responsibility for assigning other
household members with both routine and emergency scheduling
requirements (Hessing, 1993). This is particularly acute for the majority of mothers who are now in the paid labor force. For them, the day
involves getting children up early, making sure they are clean, dressed,
and fed, taking them to a caretaker or day care center, and arranging
for pick-ups and drop-offs throughout the day.

## GENDER AND THE CONTROL OVER
## TIME IN DOMESTIC ACTIVITIES

    There is evidence that men and women carry out different kinds of
household responsibilities that result in different levels of control that
they have over their time. Not only do men spend less time overall in
household activities, but the nature of the activities is qualitatively
different (Hochschild, 1989; Shelton, 1992). Whereas women's
household tasks tend to be focused on the daily reproduction of family
life (meals, laundry, cleaning), more of men's housework time is spent
on the long-term maintenance of the home. The major consequence

is that men have more discretion in the allocation and distribution of their household time: "They have more control over *when* they make their contribution than women do" (Hochschild, 1989, p. 8). The difference is that "the lawn can go unmowed for an extra day or week . . . but if work runs long [for the woman], a meal cannot be put off until tomorrow" (Shelton, 1992, p. 147). In this regard, Berk (1985) argued that it is the nature of the household "pie" of work that places demands on household members, which, in turn, determines gendered household labor time allocations. Furthermore, an analysis of investments of time by men and women supports the finding that men have more control over their time (Juster, 1985). The researchers were able to successfully predict only male investments in time on the basis of demographic and situational variables, and they concluded that male roles are more "purposive" and female roles are more "residually determined" (Juster, 1985, p. 202).

Although there are differences between men and women in the nature of the tasks they do in the household, there are also differences in the timing of household tasks. In families with young children, parents usually work together in the morning but have different experiences in the evenings (Berk & Berk, 1979). When wives are doing after-dinner chores, husbands are taking care of children. However, when mothers are again available for child care, husbands are often ready to quit for the evening. Furthermore, whereas men tend to do most of their family work on the weekends, women do family work on weekdays and weekends (Thompson & Walker, 1989).

Another manifestation of this gender disparity in the responsibility for domestic time arises in the literature on punctuality. Here the research suggests that although both men and women believe equally in the importance of punctuality, it is much more difficult for women to actually achieve it (Shaw, 1994). Men tend to complain about the time women take to get ready to go out, and women tend to blame themselves in terms of personality or organizational skills, but the underlying difficulty is that women quite often have to fit into the same time period more household and child care tasks (Shaw, 1994). Because women tend to have more work in the home, they are more pressed for time and therefore, have greater difficulty meeting punctuality standards within the home.

RESPONDING TO DOMESTIC
TIME DEMANDS: WOMEN'S STRATEGIES

In response to the greater load that women carry in managing paid and unpaid work, several strategies have been adopted as a way of coping with these demands (Hessing, 1993). At the most basic level, women have extended the hours of their workday to include the additional time in the morning, afternoon, and evening that is dedicated to domestic needs. A second strategy is to "borrow time," which involves anticipating future household needs and then performing them prior to their actual occurrence. An example of this is preparing for the next day the night before by making lunches and having children lay out their clothes for school. Another method of manipulating time in domestic work is "double time," which combines chores so that two or more are completed at the same time. Similar to polychronic patterns, a mother of young children might keep an eye on her toddler while making dinner and making a mental grocery list. Another tactic in household time management is "time cutting," which means eliminating certain chores or condensing the amount of effort necessary to fulfill certain chores. Finally, the "routinization of time" helps to create an efficiency of effort and a stability that brings order and predictable sequence to an otherwise stressful situation.

MEN AND DOMESTIC RESPONSIBILITY:
RESISTANCE, CHANGE, OR CONSTRAINT?

One of the core questions in the gendered politics of domestic time is, Why have men been so slow to increase their commitment for household and child care tasks? Asking the question in this way reflects a set of values and assumptions that is perhaps best captured by a model referred to as the "demand/response capability" (Coverman, 1985). Understanding men's participation in domestic work is a function of the *demands* placed on husbands to fulfill their domestic responsibilities along with their capacity to *respond* to those demands. Much of the literature that looks at husbands' contributions to domestic labor assumes this reactive stance: Husbands either respond to the forces of feminism and the increases in women's paid labor or they do not. Others have taken a more pessimistic view, suggesting that women do not place demands on husbands because they have accepted household inequalities as normative and their efforts must therefore continue as "labours of love" (Berk, cited in Hiatt & Godwin, 1990).

Most research has concluded that when women increase their labor force participation, there is only a minimal increase in their husband's participation in household work (Berardo, et al., 1987; Coverman & Sheley, 1986). However, it appears that men have changed at a slow but minimal rate in the past three decades. The reports vary in terms of magnitude, but two trends are evident: (a) Women's domestic work has remained at a constant and substantial level, and (b) despite changing gender roles, increasing family diversity and steady increases in female labor force involvement, women continue to do a much higher proportion of the household work than their male partners (Demo & Acock, 1993). For example, a major U.S. survey reports that whereas in 1975 men did 46% as much housework as women, this had risen to 57% in 1987 (Shelton, 1992). Comparisons of data from the 1960s and the 1980s suggests that although men did approximately one quarter of the household labor in the 1960s, they now do approximately one third to one half (Demo & Acock, 1993).

When husbands do respond to their wives' employment, it is usually in terms of time spent interacting with the children (Baruch & Barnett, 1986). For example, in a comparison of data collected in 1967 and 1986, Sanik (1990) found that fathers had tripled the amount of time that they spent in child care during that time but had not significantly increased the time they spent on household work. Nevertheless, most recent data indicate that fathers' engagement time (direct interaction) with children was about one third of mothers', and fathers' accessibility time (when the father is available to the child) was about half of mothers' (Pleck, in press). These findings are consistent with the conclusion reached by Voydanoff (1988) in her study of family-work conflict among employed men and women. Men felt more obligated to participate in child care activities than in household chores, whereas women took responsibility for both child care and household work. Although there is a discourse that celebrates the emergence of the "new, nurturing father" (Giveans & Robinson, 1985), the traditional demands of the breadwinner role (Hughes, 1958) continue to dominate the actions of working fathers (LaRossa, 1988; Shelton, 1992).

Some evidence suggests that the presence of husbands simply increases the amount of household work for wives insofar as married women spend more time in household work than single heads of households (Hartmann, 1981). In reviewing the literature on time commitments of one- and two-parent mothers, Maudlin and Meeks (1990) pointed out a number of inconsistencies in the research literature with some studies indicating that single-parent mothers spend more time in the care of the family and other studies pointing out that they spend less time than married counterparts. In their own research, they reported that family structure does not appear to affect time allocation decisions in market work or leisure activities, but it does affect household work (including child care). In their comparison of 74 single mothers with 200 married mothers, they reported that single mothers spend almost 2 hours less per day on household work than married employed mothers. Although the authors hypothesized that husbands create more housework than they perform, other research results contradict this finding. Demo and Acock (1993), for example, concluded that husbands produce about the same amount of additional work for their wives as they provide in return.

Understanding men's commitment to family time means analyzing the changing meanings of time for women and men in terms of the values that are associated with various temporal commitments and the incentives or barriers that enter into decisions to reallocate time. There are indications in the research literature that men are concerned about the amount of time that they spend with their families but that they feel somewhat powerless to change it. For example, a recent study of dual-career husbands' responses to work and family roles indicated that there is a significant relationship between husbands' temporal involvement in work and their concern with family time such that the more they worked, the more concern they expressed (Crouter et al., 1992). Consistent with this, an analysis of the meanings of family time for fathers suggests that men believe in the priority of "spending time with their children" but at the same time lament that "making" time for family is "costly," fixed in amount, and largely beyond their control to change due to the demands of their paid work (Daly, 1996). In keeping with this, LaRossa and LaRossa (1981) argued that men commit themselves to raising children and derive status from being fathers but they "do time" with their children rather than enjoy them.

These specific tensions are consistent with a literature that indicates that despite women's having to carry the overload of the second shift, men in general are less happy with the dual-earner arrangement than women and show more evidence of psychological distress (Hunt & Hunt, 1987). In keeping with this, fathers who are highly involved with children tend to feel less benefited by marriage and are more critical of the time that their wives spend with the children and their work schedule (Baruch & Barnett, 1986). At the same time, however, other research suggests that wives in dual-earner families report significantly higher degrees of role overload than do husbands (Rachlin, 1987) but that this does not appear to have any effect on satisfaction with progress toward improving life as a whole (McCullough & Zick, 1992). One explanation for this is that the satisfactions that come from paid work compensates for the increased strain caused by the multiple role demands these women face (McCullough & Zick, 1992).

As Berk (1985) has pointed out, the normative background that influences the mechanisms by which work is apportioned to men and women in the household is a vast and largely uncharted territory. Although the economic dependency model serves as an adequate explanation in the usual situation where wives earn less than their husbands and do the majority of the housework as a result, it is not a good explanation for situations where wives earn more than their husbands (Brines, 1994). In these situations, dependent husbands do less housework the more they depend on their wives for income (Brines, 1994). It seems that the more a man's financial identity as a provider is threatened, the less he can afford to further threaten it by doing a greater share of women's work at home (Brines, 1994). Displays of appropriate gender behavior continue to have a constraining effect on the way that domestic roles are enacted. Beliefs about mothering, competence in the household, and the separation of public and private domains continue to have a hold on the gendered division of labor in the household, such that women's time, in all its manifestations, is seen to be at the disposal of family members (Hantrais, 1993). The result is that women continue to feel "more responsible" for home and children (Hochschild, 1989), and as a result, are more likely to feel the constraints on time that they experience in attempting to manage paid work and household labor. One indication of this is that employed women appear to experience more anxiety than full-time homemakers over whether they are providing adequate mothering for their children (Guidubaldi et al., 1986, cited in Leslie & Anderson, 1988). Although the amount of time that men commit to household tasks is increasing, the ongoing disparity in the feelings of responsibility for these tasks has important implications for the sense of entitlement that women have to the use of their time.

Entitlements, which refer to the culturally recognized rights of persons to resource shares (Papanek, 1990; Restrepo, 1995), are differentially distributed within families on the basis of gender. As an important commodified resource (Robinson, 1977), time is unequally allocated within households. This unequal allocation is enshrined in a set of norms and customs that have traditionally placed responsibility for domestic work with women and "breadwinning" with men. The different entitlements of time for men and women in both the family and work domains has given rise to "time collisions" in gender relations (Pasero, 1994, p. 186). Whereas men's time spent at work is continuous and more highly valued, women's paid work continues to be seen as the "second income" and their paid work is undervalued. The net result is a continued unequal division of time allocation, utility, and value that sets a course of gendered "collision." Furthermore, insofar as both men and women are increasing the amount of time that they are spending in productive work, their overall leisure time is shrinking (Zick & McCullough, 1991). For dual-earner couples, there are losses in togetherness in almost all aspects of domestic life, including eating meals together, watching TV, and enjoying active recreation (Kingston & Nock, 1987). This lack of time together is related to marital quality such that the lower the shared time, the lower the marital quality (Kingston & Nock, 1987; Tuttle, 1994). Although both men and women feel the effects of less shared time together, there continues to be an unequal distribution of leisure time for men and women.

## Gender and the Distribution of Leisure Time

The research literature indicates that there are differences in the amount of time that men and women spend in leisure activities, the nature of those activities, and the meanings that those leisure activities have for them. Similar to the time discrepancies in paid work and domestic activity, there is a gendered "leisure gap" both in terms of the availability of leisure and the conflict between leisure and other demands (Henderson, 1991, p. 363).

### GENDER DISPARITIES IN LEISURE TIME

In an analysis of 620 cases of 1981 time diary data originally collected by Juster and his associates, gender was found to be significantly associated with total leisure time (Firestone & Shelton, 1994). Women spent significantly less time on leisure than men. This difference was particularly pronounced for domestic leisure activities within the home, where women spent 12 fewer hours on domestic leisure activities than men. These results are consistent with other research that has shown that men have more leisure time than women (Coverman & Sheley, 1986; Shaw, 1992). Overall, the results of the research indicate that women's involvement in paid work, housework, and child care has compressed their leisure time (Hochschild, 1989).

Although the general trends indicate that men experience advantages in relation to the amount of leisure time, the wife's employment status plays a key role. Employed women have less free or discretionary time than nonemployed women (Firestone & Shelton, 1994; Schor, 1991; Shaw, 1988, 1991; Shelton, 1992). For women, the amount of time that is spent in paid labor has a direct effect on the amount of "free" time that is available. Although *employed* women have the least amount of free time, nonemployed women have the most, and employed men seem to fall between these two groups in terms of the mean amount of free time per day (Cyba, 1992; Shaw, 1991). However, this seems to vary with the time of the week. For example, nonemployed women have the most free time during the week, yet they have less leisure time on the weekends than the other groups (Cyba, 1992). There are also fundamental differences between employed women and housewives with respect to their attitudes toward the family and leisure. Although housewives express a high regard for family and a low appreciation of leisure time, employed women show a strong preference for leisure time as an independent sphere of life and a lower preference for family (Cyba, 1992).

Most of the literature emphasizes leisure deficits for women, but there is some research that indicates that men whose wives are full-time homemakers may also experience a shortage in leisure. In a study that compared the amount of leisure time for men and women when the wife is a homemaker or is working part-time or full-time, the two groups that appear to spend the least amount of time in leisure activities are women who are employed full-time and men whose wives are full-time homemakers (Leslie & Anderson, 1988). Although the double day for employed wives has been emphasized in the research literature, it may be that some husbands of homemaker wives experience a work overload that has been overlooked. The double day for these husbands arises as a result of working longer hours than husbands of employed women combined with the expectation that they take over the care of the children when they come home to offer some relief to the wife who has been with them all day. This interpretation must be treated with some caution, for it may well be that these hard-working career men are able to afford, and have insisted on, their wives staying home.

## WHEN FREE TIME IS NOT
## LEISURE TIME: WOMEN AT HOME

There are indications that the free time that is available to non-employed women does not translate easily into a greater quantity of leisure activities (Le Feuvre, 1994; Shaw, 1991). According to time budget studies, women who work as full-time housewives have traditionally had the largest amount of free time, yet due to the monotonous and repetitive nature of housework, they perceive themselves to have little freedom because of being constantly "on call" for the husbands and children (Shaw, 1988). Full-time housewives tend to have more difficulty in separating or compartmentalizing their work and leisure experience. Household labor intrudes on leisure time (Firestone & Shelton, 1994). As such, the time experience of full-time housewives tends to be fluid, seamless, and difficult to demarcate. In contrast with employed men and women, it is more difficult for housewives to compartmentalize their time experiences in a way that facilitates the transformation of free time into leisure time. The result is that full-time housewives are less likely to experience autonomous leisure than women in paid employment, and this is due in part to the absence of the legitimacy that paid work seems to confer on autonomous leisure activities. More important, however, full-time housewives usually have only short sequences of time (i.e., "for a breather") interspersed with time that is largely constrained by the requirements of other household members (Le Feuvre, 1994).

Although employed women have less free time, they tend to get more satisfaction from it. For example, in a comparison of employed and nonemployed women, Shaw (1988) found that employed women have less free time than nonemployed women but have an increased quality of experience of leisure. There appears to be a trade-off between the amount of free time that is available and the quality of experience in different types of daily activities for women when they are employed. Hence, caution must be used when interpreting quantitative measures that are not accompanied by qualitative meanings that, in this case, result in very different meanings for free time and leisure time.

Other research has examined wives' attitudes toward their time use (Hiatt & Godwin, 1990). In a sample of 235 married, employed women, they found that an overwhelming majority wanted more time for leisure and recreation activities. This was especially true for wives who spend more time in employment. They wished to spend less time at that employment and more time in leisure activities. Over 80% of the sample wished to have more leisure time but were getting little: Women in the sample averaged less than 53 minutes per weekday (Hiatt & Godwin, 1990).

The relationship between leisure and women's employment seems to be a double-edged kitchen knife. From one perspective, the time that employed women spend on household labor comes at the expense of their leisure time (Shelton, 1992; Zick & McCullough, 1991). In this regard, free time for women has been called "residual" insofar as it is unlikely that women find the time for leisure in their daily lives (Langevin, 1984, cited in Le Feuvre, 1994). Other feminist writers reject the notion of "residual" time on the grounds that it is an androcentric idea (Harrington, 1991). Although men may have residual time for leisure after work, women are less likely to have residual time for leisure because of housework and child care, and if they did, their leisure time is most likely to be centered in the home and therefore confounded with other domestic activities. From another perspective, work outside of the home may be providing more impetus for women to develop a sense of entitlement to leisure. According to Henderson and Dialeschki (1991), employment seems to legitimize the right to leisure because it gives women money, household help, and a way to compartmentalize their day to plan better for leisure. However, even in light of the greater sense of entitlement that may accompany increased participation in the labor market, women are unlikely to experience dramatic increases in leisure because of reduced free time and increased time stress (Shaw, 1991).

Men and women tend to share views about the value and importance of spending leisure time together as a family, but women are more likely to define a part of that time as involving work (Shaw, 1992). Fathers, by contrast, are more likely to *perceive* caring for, or time alone with, children as leisure and a source of satisfaction (Freysinger, 1994). This may be attributable to the fact that men are more likely to see participation in family activities as a matter of personal choice and as an experience that is relaxing and enjoyable (Shaw, 1992). Women are more likely to speak about the planning and organizing involved in leisure activities and the psychological effort of making sure that everyone is happy (Shaw, 1992). Overall, however, women tend to find family leisure activities more satisfying, because they invest more work and effort in producing a positive outcome (Shaw, 1992). Although not addressed in the research, one might also expect that women would be more likely to carry the burden of blame when family leisure activities do not turn out as positively as planned.

## GENDER AND DIFFERENTIAL
## ENTITLEMENTS TO LEISURE TIME

There is mounting evidence to indicate that women believe they have no right to leisure, and in accordance with this, this belief places a limitation on their construction of time for leisure (Henderson & Dialeschki, 1991). This is in contrast with a literature that suggests that men see leisure as a right and are more likely to feel entitled to take time away from their spouses (Henderson & Dialeschki, 1991). Responsibility to their paid and unpaid work results in a diminished sense of entitlement to "free time" for women. On the basis of the notion that leisure time must be earned (i.e., work before play), some women may feel that they never "earn" leisure because the duties of domestic work are never done (Henderson & Dialeschki, 1991). Furthermore, women frequently lack the economic resources or opportunity to pursue leisure activities and, as a result, may feel that free time is controlled by their husbands (Green, Hebron, & Woodward, 1989). As Shelton (1992) concluded in her study of the ongoing disparities between women's and men's use of time, either the full-time demands of paid and household labor go unmet, or time comes at the expense of leisure.

Women may also have a reduced sense of entitlement to their own leisure as a result of their commitment to creating successful leisure experiences for their families (Shaw, 1992). There is a contradiction between the pleasure and satisfaction that women accrue in helping to create positive family leisure experiences and the organizational and emotional work that is committed to making these experiences successful. The "ethic of care" associated with this commitment may mean that the leisure needs of the family override, or at least are confounded with, their own rights and needs for leisure. As Henderson and Allen (1991) have pointed out, taking time for self is not likely for women if they do not value themselves as someone with a right to exist apart from their role as caretakers of the family. Research studies report that women feel guilty about spending time on leisure when the domestic responsibilities associated with, and reinforced by, the ideology of motherhood are continuously present (Allison & Duncan, 1987; Henderson & Dialeschki, 1991; Shank, 1986). The traditional ethic of care for women tends to be associated with a reduced entitlement to personal leisure and be experienced as a "leisure liability" (Henderson & Allen, 1991, p. 101). Put simply, the ethic of care has meant that women have tended to put the family first and the self last (Henderson & Allen, 1991).

Although the general trend in leisure studies indicates that women experience little sense of entitlement to leisure, there are signs that this may be changing. As women's contributions to all aspects of life are more valued and accepted in society, the acceptance of leisure as a right and a priority will also become more evident (Henderson & Dialeschki, 1991). Future research needs to monitor the nature of these changes and explore the implications for how women experience their lives. For example, there needs to be a close analysis of the correspondence between attitudes about leisure and manifested behavior (Henderson & Dialeschki, 1991). Furthermore, there needs to be more exploration of male-female, adult-child differences in the way that leisure is perceived, experienced and defined.

## CONSTRAINTS ON LEISURE TIME FOR MEN AND WOMEN

Marriage, household size, and family income have been identified in the literature as important family variables that are associated with the constraint to leisure. A recent study of men's and women's leisure found that marital status was significantly associated with total leisure time such that for both men and women, those who were married spent approximately 8 fewer hours per week on leisure than those who were not married (Firestone & Shelton, 1994). The responsibilities associated with marriage may operate in a bidirectional fashion between men and women in a way that reduces leisure for both. Henderson and Dialeschki (1991) found that, among married and single respondents, married women were perceived to have less leisure regardless of whether children were present or not. This may be attributed to the reduced choices for leisure that women are perceived to have when they are in a married relationship. It may also be a function of the fact that as part of our patriarchal heritage, men have used various strategies to control and regulate the kind and amount of leisure that their wives have (Green et al., 1989). These strategies range from the creation and reinforcement of guilty feelings associated with being a good wife and mother, to sulking, right through to the use of threats and violence (Green et al., 1989).

Household size also plays an important role in the amount of leisure that women have. In a study of 548 women in a university community, Harrington (1991) found that the greater the size of her household, the less likely it is that a woman finds time for herself, for her interests, or for enjoying her family life in leisure pursuits. Similarly, in a smaller time diary study of 60 couples, Shaw (1991) found that high family workload (which took into account the number and ages of the children) resulted in the least amount of leisure time for women. The relationship between family income and leisure has not received a lot of attention in the literature. There are indications, however, that with a higher family income it is possible to purchase household labor in the form of convenience products that will increase the amount of leisure time that is available (Firestone & Shelton, 1994). This hypothesis, however, needs to be examined in future research. Firestone and Shelton (1994) did find, however, that the higher the family income, the more time individuals spend on non-domestic leisure and the less the they spend on domestic leisure. Although these appear to be important variables in the way that we understand the patterns of family leisure, more research is necessary to examine these linkages.

Much of the current literature that discusses the unequal distribution of leisure between men and women is written from a feminist perspective. Although this research provides important insight into the discrepancies between men's and women's leisure experience, there is a very strong orientation toward understanding women's experience of leisure. The current research on leisure in families has not adequately examined the meanings of free time, family time, or leisure for men.

## The Gender Politics of Time Over the Life Span

It appears from the available evidence that there are marked differences between males and females in the way that they use their time throughout the entire life span. Studies that have examined how children use time indicate that there are dramatic gender differences in time allocations to household chores and leisure activities. For example, adolescent girls spend a significantly larger portion of their time in household chores than adolescent boys do (Cogle & Tasker,

1982; Maudlin & Meeks, 1990; Sanik & Stafford, 1985, 1986). Furthermore, the nature of these tasks tend to follow traditional gender prescriptions: Girls are more involved in food preparation and house cleaning, whereas boys are more involved in home maintenance, pets, and yard care (Cogle & Tasker, 1982; Maudlin & Meeks, 1990). There is also evidence that boys spend more time in leisure activities than girls (Meeks & Maudlin, 1990). Adult gender disparities in the patterns of time allocation appear to be established early on in the way that children use their time.

During young adulthood, the demands of work and family predominate the time use of both men and women (Bernard, 1984). Both men and women spend progressively less time doing domestic work and spend more time in discretionary activity over the course of the family life cycle (Freysinger & Ray, 1994). Furthermore, there is a tendency for women and men to spend an increasing proportion of time in individual activities, and this tends to be negatively related to marital satisfaction (Orthner, 1976). At the same time, however, when women and men do have high levels of communication and interaction in their leisure time, they report high levels of marital satisfaction (Holman & Jacquart, 1988).

Overall, women do more domestic work than men and have less time for leisure in both early and later family stages (Witt & Goodale, 1981). One explanation for these adult disparities is that these differences are established early on in life. Bryant (1990), for example, argues that parental expectations about the future adult roles their children will play lead parents to assign more housework to girls than to boys. The result of this early differential experience is that girls are predisposed to marriage and the responsibility of shouldering the bulk of housework within marriage (Bryant, 1992).

Moreover, there is evidence that gender disparities in the use of time continue into old age. An analysis of time use among 535 elderly people living at home found that women spent significantly more time in housework and cooking activities, whereas men spent more time reading, listening to the radio, engaging in recreation, traveling, and spending time away from the residence (Lawton et al., 1987). In a similar vein, wives tend to experience more stress when they are caregivers to their husbands than the inverse. Husbands caring for their impaired wives were more likely to find personal time and space away from their spouse, including leaving her alone, whereas women, when caring for impaired husbands, were much less likely to preserve their personal time (Miller, 1987, cited in Neal et al., 1993, p. 116).

Family structure and the course of family development also play an important role in shaping the constraints and opportunities for leisure time. Specifically, as family roles change across the life course, different amounts of time are available for leisure participation and different motivations to participate in leisure (Altergott & McCreedy, 1993). Furthermore, the changing number and presence of family members means that leisure is contingent on the coordination of family timetables (Altergott & McCreedy, 1993). Although women have been presented as universally "disadvantaged" in terms of time, the analysis of leisure time over the life course indicates that they are not disadvantaged at all points in time (Altergott & McCreedy, 1993). For example, in an analysis of the time use data of 782 adults (data collected by Juster and colleagues), it was found that the time demands and the contextual conditions for parenting families are great enough to lead both mothers and fathers to reduce their leisure time (Altergott & McCreedy, 1993). When examining total amounts of leisure, both men and women have lower amounts of leisure during the parenting years, leading the researchers to conclude that, in general, "mothers are not temporally disadvantaged when compared to fathers" (Altergott & McCreedy, 1993, p. 168). This low ebb in the amount of leisure time during the parenting years is in contrast to the higher amounts of leisure for those early and late in the family life cycle. Specifically, there are higher amounts of leisure before children arrive and higher amounts after retirement, which produces a family life course pattern of leisure that is curvilinear in nature. This curvilinear pattern is generally the same for single female parents, married men, and married women (Altergott & McCreedy, 1993). Although the pattern is the same, single mothers of preschoolers have the least access to leisure time. Gender disparities do emerge after the constraints of parenting are lifted, however. In the postparental period, men are more likely to convert their freed-up time into leisure, whereas women remain actively engaged in service to the household and the family (Altergott & McCreedy, 1993).

## Summary

The politics of time is central to our understanding of current gender politics. Although the history of gender politics has focused in the past on the control of the body or the importance of language, it appears that time has taken its position as a highly salient concern. With the rapid emergence of the dual-earner family and the corresponding inflation in the value of time, the analysis of time differences for women and men is central to the analysis of gender relations.

To fully comprehend the different experience of time for men and women means going beyond the "accounting" approach that is typical of time diary studies. Although these studies are essential for understanding disparities in time use between men and women, many questions remain concerning the values, meanings, and commitments of time as they are experienced on a daily basis. To fully understand the gender politics of time, it is necessary to be attentive to phenomenological differences, disparities in entitlements, and the structural constraints of home and the workplace that continue to shape the experience of time for men and women.

Although there are preliminary indications that women and men have a phenomenologically different experience of time, we have only begun to scratch the surface of this important issue. The experience of time for women and men has been discussed in the literature in terms of polychronic and monochronic characteristics, process versus clock time, or cyclical versus linear forms. The differences have been attributed to various forces in men and women's lives, including biology, the different social roles that they occupy, or the external demands that are placed on their time. There are, of course dangers in rigidly dichotomizing male and female behavior in this way. By emphasizing difference, interchangeability and shared characteristics of temporal experience may go unnoticed. Nevertheless, the current indications of gender difference point to the need to explore in greater detail the similarities and unique characteristics of temporal experience for women and men.

In contrast with the scant literature pertaining to phenomenological differences, the literature concerning time allocations for women and men is well advanced. Although this literature is theoretically and methodologically diverse with many contradictions, there are, never-

theless, a number of key trends. Overall, and despite dramatic changes
in the number of women in the paid labor force, it appears that there
are still strong residues of the traditional division of labor. There is
less asymmetry in the world of paid work than there once was, yet
men typically still spend more time on the job. Furthermore, and
perhaps more significant, women contribute, on average, less than one
third of the family income. The implication is that women continue
to give priority to their families and men continue to give precedence
to their work. Continuing gender discrepancies in pay and job status
indicate that women's time is still devalued and men enjoy greater
advantages in the control of their time. One implication of this is that
family responsibilities for women are more likely to "spillover" into
their work time, resulting in more day-to-day tensions in the management of the work-family balance. This has resulted in women having
to be more adaptable than men in meeting the care needs of their
children. Women are more likely than men to arrange their work
schedules in a way that will accommodate the demands of family
caregiving.

Within the domestic sphere, men are increasing their commitment
to the tasks of housework and child care, but women continue to do
the majority of these tasks. On average, men do approximately one
third the amount of domestic work that women do. This has been
popularly conceptualized as meaning that women work the second
shift when they arrive home. Employment status is an important
variable for understanding the distribution of household chores:
Employed mothers devote significantly less time to household work
than do nonemployed mothers. Time devoted to employment seems
to reduce the amount of time that is available for household work. In
light of the acceleration of time that accompanies the increased
workload in families, women have become the "time and motion"
experts in families. Women are more likely than men to carry responsibility for both routine and emergency scheduling in the family. This
is consistent with the traditional division of household tasks in which
women take responsibility for the daily reproduction of family life,
whereas more of men's housework time is spent on the long-term
maintenance of the home or the car. The major consequence of this
difference is that men have more discretion in the allocation and

distribution of their household time. Women have responded to the demands of the double day with a variety of strategies, including extending the hours of the day, doubling activity in the same period of time, or eliminating chores altogether.

When men do increase their contributions to work in the domestic sphere, it is usually in terms of time spent interacting with the children. Men have increased their responsibility to participate in child care activities, and women have held a steady course in their responsibility for both child care and household work. Although the research indicates that men are committed to increasing their share of domestic work, it appears that they feel constrained in their efforts to do so. Many forces come into play in perpetuating the discrepancies between the domestic work of men and women: real-time constraints imposed by the demands of work, beliefs about mothering and competence in the household, and the constraining effects of what constitutes a display of appropriate gender behavior.

Trends with respect to leisure time indicate that *employed* women have the least amount of free time, nonemployed women have the most, and employed men seem to fall somewhere between. Despite these differences in the amount of time, there appear to be dramatic differences for men and women in their respective entitlements to use free time as they wish to use it. In light of the fact that domestic labor is most likely to be seen as women's work, the demands of household responsibilities are more likely to intrude on women's free time. This is especially the case for women who are full-time housewives. Although they typically have the greatest amount of free time, they have the greatest difficulty separating that free time from their domestic work. By contrast, employment seems to legitimize the right to leisure for women because in addition to having control over money, they are better able to compartmentalize their day to include leisure. Nevertheless, men continue to see leisure as a right, whereas women, regardless of employment status, experience considerably more ambivalence about their entitlement to leisure.

Studies of gender distributions in time use over the life span suggest the disparities in the use of time begin early on in the life cycle and continue into old age. Although the research points to a nearly universal leisure disadvantage for women throughout the life cycle, there are some indications that both women and men experience very limited amounts of leisure during the early stages of parenting.

Persistent gender disparities in the responsibilities and entitlements associated with time draw our attention to the political essence of time use. Inequality, conflict, and differential entitlements continue to lie at the root the experience of time for women and men. In the next chapter, the focus shifts to the intergenerational politics of time. Although the emphasis is on differences in temporal control among the generations, the politics of gender are clearly evident.

# 8

# Intergenerational Politics
of Family Time

## Generations and Family Time

*Generation* is a term with a temporal essence that lies at the root
of an intergenerational politics of time. More specifically, the parent-
child relationship is the axis along which temporal norms are transmitted, stories of generations are passed on, and the meanings of the
culture are both preserved and modified. To be born is to have parents,
and to have parents is to be linked to the previous generation (Carr,
1986). Traditions, styles, ideals, and values are handed down through
parents. Through generations, "families persist through time" in a way
that is "different from the persistence of a thing but also from the
temporal integrity of an individual" (Carr, 1986, p. 109). Generations
play an important role in the relationship between the individual and
history. They bring collective representations that link a generation
with a certain part of history and act as reference points for experience, memory, and structured time (Pronovost, 1989).

In keeping with the importance of generations for giving families this sense of persistence is the idea that our social world consists of a set of "staggered and overlapping narratives" (Carr, 1986, p. 113). These overlapping narratives come from people in our social worlds who are at different generational stages. The intergenerational linkages give rise to a temporal continuity that comes in a "handed-down form" and that runs from predecessors to successors (Carr, 1986). Furthermore, these temporal sequences supersede the temporal boundaries of our lives by reaching back into the past before birth and stretching into the future after death. The individual is temporally embedded in a complex of relationships within the family that can be seen as "constituting a long-term co-biographical context" (Knipscheer, 1988, p. 427).

*Generations* has both objective and subjective dimensions. Objectively, a generation is a tool of classification that serves to categorize and locate individuals within a generational grouping or in a set of intergenerational relationships. It can, for example, refer to a particular cohort (such as the Beatle's generation) (Schuller, 1993). For Mannheim (1952), the concept of generations is the key for locating individuals in the historical and social process. Subjectively, being a part of a generation involves an awareness of collective membership in a group that shares experiences of history and age. By virtue of this shared membership, people of a generation are in a position to experience the same events and data that impinge on a "similarly stratified consciousness" (Mannheim, 1952, p. 297). This is the changing "Zeitgeist" that is part of being in a generation that is greater than the mere passing of years (Hendricks, 1982). Furthermore, it involves an awareness of how one's own generation is different from others, which in turn highlights the continuous passage of time (Schuller, 1993). The subjective experience of generation involves an ongoing project of "identification of" (Stone, 1981) the defining characteristics of one's generation and the "identification with" that group as a member who shares in the meanings and characteristics that are distinctive to that group. To be of a generation, according to Mannheim (1952), there must be contemporaneity, cognizance of historical consciousness, and a sense of group identity forged by the reinterpretation of existing phenomena.

The analysis of generations, for Mannheim (1952), plays a critical role for understanding the "accelerated pace of social change that is characteristic of our time" (p. 287). Although this work was published posthumously in 1952, Mannheim wrote about the problem of generations in the 1920s. The perception of the "accelerated pace of social change" is not a new one but, rather, one that was well under way with the proliferation of machines and industry. Mannheim (1952) hypothesized that the quicker the social and cultural change, the greater the chances that generation groups would react by producing their own "entelechy" or their own inner aim or way of experiencing the world (p. 310). On these grounds, Mannheim argued that the phenomenon of generations is much more than an age or biologically determined phenomenon but, rather, one that emerges and is constructed in response to the prevailing tempo and nature of social change. Accordingly, the rapid rate of social change in the 1990s that has been brought on by technology and the changing distribution of men and women's labor has resulted in the emergence of generations that must contend with newly arising temporal problems and challenges.

As Schuller (1993) has pointed out, the experience of being in a generation is at once becoming more predictable and uncertain. Drawing on the demographic analyses of Hagestad (1986), Schuller argues that because of the greater predictability and institutionalization of life cycle events and death itself, family time and the patterns of generational succession are becoming more uniform. At the same time, many of these generational experiences and sequences are historically unprecedented. The result is that the public and private understanding of the roles associated with many generational experiences are fraught with uncertainty, either due to the absence of role models or to the rapidly changing nature of models with the intervening changes in social mores (Schuller, 1993). For example, men who now become grandfathers in later life may have little to model their behavior on, for the great majority of older men in previous generations died either before retiring or very soon after (Schuller, 1993).

In keeping with this, the increasing family diversity of the post-modern era has implications for our understanding of the temporal continuity that is central to intergenerational relationships. Several trends suggest that it is more difficult to maintain the handed-down form (Carr, 1986) of one generation to the next. High geographic mobility for families as a result of globalization, free trade, and corporate downsizing has resulted in a spatial dislocation that has made the temporal linkages of generations more difficult to maintain. Reproductive technologies have created distinctions between social parenthood and biological parenthood that have resulted in a "genealogical bewilderment" and an uncertainty in the generational linkage (Daly, 1995; Edwards, 1991; Lifton, 1988). The increasing diversity of family forms through divorce, single parenthood, remarriage, or same-sex relationships has cast intergenerational ties into an unprecedented web of complexity. Ganong, Coleman, and Fine (1995) highlight the differences between nuclear families and stepfamilies in the way that family narratives are created and managed through the generations:

> Adults in nuclear families enter marriage with individual family-of-origin histories, but they go on to develop a mutual family culture with its own rituals and history. Children raised in nuclear families share that history as part of a common family culture. In stepfamilies, a parent and child(ren) have mutual experiences and shared recollections of of family life that does not include the stepparent (and any children he or she may have). This is important not only because some stepfamily members are excluded from "remember when . . ." stories but also because different histories can result in patterns of living or lifestyles that seem odd to those who were not involved in developing those patterns. (p. 289)

For those in stepfamilies or families who are formed through other paths, there is a greater probability that they will find themselves in "culturally ambiguous life phases interacting in ambiguous family relationships" (Hagestad, 1986, p. 689).

Although the claim can be made that family diversity has disrupted the degree of overlap in generational narratives, it can also be argued that increases in longevity may actually heighten the temporal linkages of generations. When the norm is for four or five generations to live concurrently rather than previous norm of two or three at the turn of the century (Bengston & Allen, 1993; Uhlenberg, 1980), then there is the potential for the rich overlapping of many historical narratives at any point in time. This has been referred to as the increased "verticalization" of the multigenerational family and it is characterized by frequent and highly valued interaction among generations (Knipscheer, 1988). Grandparents are typically thought of as being the keepers of the family stories. Due to increases in longevity, grandparents are in the role longer now than at the turn of the century, with most being in the role for an average of three or four decades (Norris & Tindale, 1994).

## Intergenerational Dynamics of Time Within Families

An intergenerational politics of time is concerned with the differences in power and dependencies between parents and children of various generations and their accompanying ability to control time. Within families at any given time, various temporalities intersect to create the potential for a variety of conflicts. For example, children, parents, and grandparents each have their own unique experience of time depending on their age, involvements, and attitudes. Depending on their stage in the life cycle, individuals interpret the sequence and grouping of events quite differently, perceive them negatively or positively, and are more likely to focus on the past, present, or the future (Pronovost, 1989). These are reflective of the different "developmental stakes" that they each have in the maintenance of existing structures and patterns because of their differences in generational position (Bengston, 1989). As an illustration, the desire of parents to launch their children "on time" may come into conflict with their children's ability to find work and establish supportive relationships for themselves. Similarly, middle-aged children may lament the further squeeze placed on their time as result of the increased demands from their aging parents.

Each generation has a different relationship to family time that is based on "historical collective memory" as well as the social horizon that is constituent of that generation (Pronovost, 1989, p. 39). Generations are socially constructed age groups with a "historical consciousness" that represent a dynamic interplay between the demographic reality of being born into an age cohort and the social meaning that is assigned to that reality through the emergence of political and social events (Bengston, Furlong, & Laufer, 1983). Individuals of different generations will interpret and evaluate events according to their own experiential reference points, which, in turn, lays the ground for competing views about, and claims for, family time among generations. On a clinical level, "time lines" have gained more attention as a tool for elucidating the proximity of life cycle events to the onset of family problems (Stanton, 1992). Specifically, the time line can serve as a useful tool for answering the "Why now?" question by linking family life cycle events and generational issues with the onset of family problems.

*Caring* lies at the root of most intergenerational family relationships: parents caring for their children as they grow and age and adult children caring for their parents as they become more needy as they grow old. Grandparents, too, count on a system of caring exchange in which they invest in the care of the younger generations whenever necessary, thereby "banking" this help for their own future needs (Norris & Tindale, 1994). Relationships that involve caring bring into play a set of competing dynamics between "process time" and "linear or clock time" (Davies, 1994). Most institutionalized forms of care work are shaped by the same dominant norms of clock time that govern all productive activity: rationalization, efficiency, and accountability. An orientation to caregiving that puts the receiver's interests first requires a fundamentally different conceptualization of time. Caregiving, by its nature, requires process time, which acknowledges that needs are not always predictable, that there are a plurality of caring activities occurring within any situation (e.g., physical, emotional, cognitive), and that care requires continuity in a way that is not primarily determined by abstract conceptual measures (Davies, 1994, p. 279). Hence, the needs and activities associated with caregiving requires process time that is enmeshed in the many unexpected exigencies of the caring relationship. This is in contrast to the quantitative calculations of "how much" time is required to carry out certain caregiving functions.

## Parents Controlling Children's Time

One of the most pronounced manifestations of the intergenerational dynamics of time occurs with respect to the efforts of parents to
control the time of their young children. Parents invest "prodigious
amounts" of time and energy in the hope of achieving continuity
between what was best in their own lives and what they transmit to
their children (Bengston, 1989). Indeed, Erikson's (1963) concept of
"generativity" is prescriptive in its tone: Parents have a responsibility
to provide guidance to the next generation. To this end, children's
time is actually highly structured, monitored, and controlled by the
timetables set up by adults. This is in contrast to romanticized notions
that childhood is a period of unencumbered free time. For the
developing child, the temporal limits of activities are gradually
modified from physiological needs to conventional patterns (Moore,
1963). From early on, children are taught to be punctual and to
exercise self-constraint in relation to time (Elias, 1992). In the process,
children learn the fundamental time values of the Western world: "Be
on time" and "Use your time wisely." As children grow older, there
are more intergenerational conflicts around timetables: Children increasingly want privileges, whereas parents wish to maintain control
(Roth, 1963).

One of the manifestations of the control that parents exercise over
their children is found in the "hurried child syndrome" (Elkind, 1981).
At a time when single-parent and dual-earner families are the norm,
there is an inevitable conflict between the pace of a child's life and the
imposed pace of a parent's schedule. In this regard, time awareness in
the family can be like a collective bargaining agreement in which
"children gradually learn to ignore their own natural rhythms . . . and
absorb the messages and attitudes about time sent by their busy
parents" (Erkel, 1995, p. 36). Behind the tendency for parents to hurry
their children is the rapid rate of social change where nothing is
permanent. For parents, coping with the stress that is associated with
this growing impermanence and pace of life means that they hurry
children. When stress induces parents to put their own needs ahead
of their children's, then children are expected to adapt to adult

schedules and timetables rather than adults adapting themselves to the pace of childhood (Elkind, 1981).

In addition to their early temporal socialization within the family, most children spend much of their time being directed in formal organizational settings. School is the most obvious, with bells and buzzers marking the beginning and end of the day and the transition from one activity to the next. The school day is organized into precise segments of time despite the circumstance that the learning speeds of children are different (Moore, 1963). The consequence of this temporal segmentation is that time is objectified: Class periods become standardized units that are stripped of contingencies brought to the experience by participants. The standardized school system has been likened to "assembly line learning" (Elkind, 1981, p. 49) that hurries children and ignores individual differences in mental abilities and learning rates. The net effect is that students are socialized early on to relinquish some control over how their time is spent. In some ways the reification of their time in school lays the groundwork for their experience in the paid labor force. The school tends to have "a peremptory claim on blocks of time and often about as disciplined an allocation of time as the job has to the adult wage earner" (Moore, 1963, p. 24). Students are socialized in school to meet deadlines, prepare for exams, and take responsibility for homework. On this basis, they learn to structure their out-of-school time, which in turn affects parents who must plan their activities, outings, and even work schedules to comply with those of the school (Pronovost, 1989, p. 48).

As more women have entered into the paid labor force in recent years, there has also been a tendency for the institutional control of children's time to shift downward. Although it is taken for granted that children's time is highly scheduled and controlled at the elementary school level, it is a more recent phenomenon that the preschool child is exposed to a more regimented day. As a result, there is a tendency to hurry very young children in the same way that older children have been hurried. What we are seeing is that the "heavily scheduled preschool child of today is a downward extension of the heavily programmed elementary schoolchild" (Elkind, 1981, p. 39).

The bureaucratic control of children's time is "stretching its arms beyond the public arena of schooling" into children's leisure time (Qvortrup, 1991, p. 29). The activities of children after school have become more structured due to the work commitments of both parents. The formal organization of children's leisure time into after-school programs, sports, and lessons of all sorts results in the further regulation of their time. Even summer camps have shifted to more specialized forms of training for children, including training programs in languages, computers, or tennis (Elkind, 1981). The significance of this greater specialization is that it reflects an attitude that suggests "the years of childhood are not to be frittered away by engaging in activities merely for fun. Rather, the years are to be used to perfect skills and abilities that are the same as those of adults" (Elkind, 1981, p. 9). This control over their time amounts to a "planned spontaneity" that excludes children from experiencing through their own explorations in favor of an organized experience of time that is "motivational, structured and role-oriented" (Qvortrop, 1991, p. 29). The problem, according to Elkind (1981), is that children need the opportunity to play their own games, make up their own rules, and abide by their own timetable, and adult intervention interferes with the crucial learning that goes on when children express this autonomy.

Competitiveness is also an important component of the structured nature of time for children. In a hurried culture, efficiency and organization are marks of success, and as a result, there is a natural tendency for children to become the "carriers of their parents' frustrated competitiveness in the work place" (Elkind, 1981, p. 30). Children's participation in organizational activity teaches them the rules of time use while at the same time diminishing their control over time. The organization of children's time has a similar effect on both the child and parents: Although it is intended to give working parents the reassurance that their children are safe and developing their skills, it results in a quickening of the pace of daily life and presents new challenges for the synchronization of family schedules. Inadvertently, children are socialized to juggle complex schedules. As an article in *Newsweek* suggested several years ago, children are "pencilling in playtime" (Kantrowitz & Witherspoon, 1986). More recently, a major corporation has observed and capitalized on this trend: CASIO introduced an electronic timetabling device called "My Magic Diary" for children that allows them to keep track of their daily appointments, assignments, and 50 names and numbers. This mirrors the proliferation of electronic notebooks among adults and portrays the escalating temporal regimentation of the child's day.

The dominance of such temporal routines in children's lives reflects the priority of clock time over process time. Play requires a process-time relationship, yet clock time almost always wins (Davies, 1994). Whether at home or in other forms of institutional care, children's activities are organized in relation to mealtimes, cleanup times, or a schedule of 1-hour blocks that are all based on clock-time assumptions. However, what children need, in the important activity of their play, is to be able to engross themselves for a long stretch of uninterrupted time so that they can develop their creativity, imagination, and concentration (Davies, 1994). Although research is limited, there are some preliminary indications that too much structure in children's activities may reduce the range of creative activities, limit the development of intrinsic motivation, and ultimately slow the child's social emotional and cognitive development (Barnett & Kane, 1985).

The research that examines the extent to which the child's day is regimented is very limited. An examination of the 1981 Time Use Longitudinal Panel Study data concluded that children spend more time in unstructured activities than in structured (Meeks & Maudlin, 1990). Age was a significant variable for explaining the amount of structured leisure, with preschool children spending the least amount of time in structured activities and 13- to 15-year-olds spending the most. However, this research did not support the hypothesis that children are overprogrammed when their parents are busy and preoccupied in their paid work. Specifically, mother's employment status or family income did not appear to affect the amount of time in structured leisure activities. Although this research does not appear to support the idea that children's lives are overly regimented, there are several shortcomings in the research that warrant further research in this area. First, the data were collected in 1981. In the intervening 15 years, not only are more women in the paid labor force, but there are now more structured opportunities for children that have developed in response to this trend. Second, in this study, it was not known how much time the child spends in unsupervised or structured leisure after school. This is one of the times when structured activities for children are organized. Finally, *structured* and *unstructured* are socially constructed classifications that are open to challenge. For example,

"games" "hobbies," "attendance at events" are classified as unstructured events when arguments could be made to categorize them as
structured. Other research that attends to some of these difficulties is
needed.

When children are not involved in externally controlled activities,
they are controlled by their parents (or at least we expect them to be)
through bedtimes, curfews, homework times, or mealtimes. In this
regard, home serves as a mechanism for the construction and reification of the conventional daily schedule. The daily conflicts that
parents and children experience over mealtimes and bedtimes are
indicative of the coercive nature of these scheduling efforts (Zerubavel,
1982). As children grow older, they are gradually promoted to a later
bedtime and are allowed greater control and discretion over when they
go to bed. The gradual transference of control over time is a function
of the child's growing maturity and privilege (Zerubavel, 1982).

Turn taking is another means by which parents socialize children
to operate within the sociotemporal order of the larger culture.
Research that has examined the ways that parents seek to foster a sense
of fairness and justice in the way that they play with siblings or friends
is also a function of learning to control time. These efforts to establish
fairness in turn taking within the home is an important prerequisite
to orderly regulation of access to social goods outside the home
(Zerubavel, 1982).

## Children Controlling Parents' Time

The effort on the part of parents to control their children's time
ironically results in a control of their own time (Qvortrup, 1991). The
work of child care has been objectified insofar as it is one item among
many in time budget studies (albeit a big one) that is seen to consume
parents' time. Elkind (1981) goes further when he claims that busy
parents treat children as objects, not as full subjects, when the goal is
to hurry them along. As the temporal demands on parents intensify,
children are more likely to be seen as time-consuming objects. This is
particularly acute in light of the fact that parenting standards have
risen at the same time. In the days when families were large and
parenting psychology was not part of the mass media, children helped

to parent each other while parents got on with the job of getting the housework done and the money brought home. For today's families, there is a new kind of diligence required in parenting. Children must be monitored for their safety from the perceived dangers of abduction or crime. Parents now are expected to play with their children, invest quality time in their development, be involved in their schooling, and overall, ensure that they are spending sufficient time with their children. Even when parents send their children to day care, the expectation is that the "responsible" parent will invest a good deal of time exploring options and monitoring quality. The effect, however, of these rising standards of parent care is that parents' time is increasingly controlled by the demands of their children.

Getting children to do housework provides a good example of children controlling parents' time. The time that parents commit to ensuring that their children complete household chores is often perceived to exceed the amount of time that it would take to complete the chore themselves (Zelizer, 1985). The message here is that the time spent socializing children to do housework involves a time commitment of the parenthood role that is greater than the time that might be freed up by virtue of the child completing the task. Nevertheless, controlling children's time in this way is perceived by parents to be part of their moral responsibility to their children. In a study that examined why parents ask their children to do housework, White and Brinkerhoff (1987) found that the actual work accomplished was a secondary consideration and that it was for the children's benefit that they assigned them chores. For approximately three quarters of the sample of parents, doing chores "builds character, develops responsibility and helps children learn" (White & Brinkerhoff, 1987, p. 210). The actual amount of household work that children do has been referred to as "negligible," with children under the age of 19 averaging 3 to 6 hours per week (Demo & Acock, 1993).

When mothers go into the paid labor force, there are indications that children, rather than husbands, increase their involvement in housework to make up for mothers' decreased availability (White & Brinkerhoff, 1987). In contrast, other research (Key & Sanik, 1990; Peters & Haldeman, 1987) indicates that women's employment status does not lead to a major reallocation of responsibilities to children. Mothers' paid work does not appear to adversely affect the amount of time that adolescents commit to their own capital development by way of school work and recreation (Key & Sanik, 1990). In comparisons of children's household work in one-parent and two-parent families, the results are more equivocal. In one study, children in both kinds of families did not contribute significantly more time to household work when their mothers entered the paid labor force (Key & Sanik, 1990). In a similar vein, Zick and Allen (1996) reported no statistically significant effect of mother's marital status on either adolescent boys' or adolescent girls' housework time. By contrast, other research has reported that children in single-parent families spent more actual time in household tasks than children in two-parent families, suggesting that in single-parent families there is more sharing of household responsibilities (Peters & Haldeman, 1987). One of the conclusions of this research is that employed mothers continue to shoulder the major part of domestic work, for it appears that the task of eliciting help from other family members is more burdensome and time-consuming than doing the work themselves (Key & Sanik, 1990).

In a review of the literature on maternal employment, Scarr, Phillips, and McCartney (1989) argued that the key issue in marital relationships is not maternal employment, but rather the attitudes, expectations, and ways that time is distributed in the family as a consequence. In a recent review of the literature pertaining to gender differences in work-family conflict (Neal et al., 1993), employed mothers had higher rates of absenteeism, were more likely than fathers to report child care as a source of worry or stress and were more likely to report high levels of work-family conflict. In fact, personal and family responsibilities was the major reason given for hours lost from work in a Canadian national study of child care needs (Lero et al., 1992). The stresses appear to be particularly acute for parents of infants and toddlers and those who had their children in some type of care outside of their homes (Neal et al., 1993). Children's control over parents' time may, in some cases, be more accurately be referred to as children's control over mother's time.

One of the stereotypes in the gerontology literature is of older parents who are frail and in need of care by their adult children (Norris & Tindale, 1994). "Caregiving" is a central focus in this literature, and it emphasizes the "burden" or the demands of time that aging parents place on their children. What is overlooked, or at least receives much less attention, are the demands that adult children continue to place on their aging parents. In an economic climate where unemployment and the cost of housing are both high, there is an increasing tendency for the empty nest to be refilled by the "return of the fledgling adult" (Clemens & Axelson, 1985). After launching their children, parents are at a time in their lives when they expect to have more discretion over the use of their time. When parents have to reassume responsibility for their children's welfare at a time when they wish to fulfill their own ambitions, the family relationships can become strained and conflictual. Although the first impression of the empty nest is that aging parents will have more time and money to spend with one another, the second and more enduring impression is that they are not free of the demands of children (Norris & Tindale, 1994). This unexpected control that children place over their parents' time can cause distress for all concerned.

The demands that grown children make of parents has a tendency to increase the frequency of the contact between them (Aldous & Klein, 1991). Specifically, when parents experience a high number of competing demands coming from their adult children, there tends to be more, rather than fewer contacts between them. For parents, and fathers especially, the needs expressed by adult children are more likely to be responded to with a sense of obligation rather than choice. This is especially the case when children are defined as "more needy," which calls out for obligatory concern on the part of the parent (Aldous & Klein, 1991, p. 606). Although this creates some dissatisfaction with "how adult children have turned out," it maintains parent-child contact and, in so doing, represents another means by which adult children exert some control over the parental use of time.

Adult children also place temporal demands on their aging parents through expectations about grandparenting. Although the dominant cultural image of the grandparent suggests that they have copious amounts of time at their disposal and constant availability to provide care, most grandparents also have busy lives and are constrained in the amount of time that they can give to the grandparenting role. Most people become grandparents in their late 40s and early 50s (Gee, 1991). Grandparenthood comes at a time when jobs and community responsibilities may be at their peak. It may also come at a time when dependent children are still living in the parental home or have returned to the parental home after leaving. Even parents in their 60s are typically very active and may find it difficult to fit grandparenting into a busy lifestyle. A 65-year-old grandmother makes this comment about her lifestyle:

> My life is extraordinarily busy; my hobbies, well I guess in my old age that is the thing that I am good at is in games. In my case, golf and bridge. My lifestyle is busy; it's unreal. (Norris & Tindale, 1994, p. 76)

When adult children place pressures on their aging parents to give time to their young children, they exert a subtle form of control over their parents' time. When grandparents are unable to meet these expectations because of their own fast-paced schedules, there is potential for resentment and conflict. A politics of time is concerned with these subtle expectations and constraints.

## Aging and the Intergenerational Politics of Time

An intergenerational politics of time also includes the claim on time made by aging parents on their adult children. As parents become more physically dependent, they too become objectified as a claim on their adult children's time. Although research indicates little intergenerational conflict when adult children and their healthy elderly parents live together (Fiske & Chiriboga, 1990; Suitor & Pillemer, 1988), there is a greater likelihood of intergenerational tension when adult children are faced with the additional time demands associated with caregiving responsibilities. In the 1970s and 1980s, considerable attention was focused on the financial "life cycle squeezes" arising from the interaction of men's occupational patterns and family life cycles (Oppenheimer, 1974). Since then, the focus appears to have shifted from an examination of men's financial squeezes to middle-aged women's time squeezes. Several demographic trends have had a profound impact on intergenerational patterns within families: increased life expectancy, decreases in fertility rates, higher ages at first marriage, rising divorce rates, and changes in the economic roles of women (Pett, Caserta, Hutton, & Lund, 1988). The net result for caregiving daughters is a rise in the competing time demands of their immediate family, aging parents, their own aging, and job responsibilities.

An analysis of the current research indicates that approximately one quarter to one third of employees provide care to an elderly person, that most (72%) adult children caring for parents are women, and that almost half of these caregivers were parents to children under the age of 18 living in their household (Neal et al., 1993). These middle-aged women are caught in a generational squeeze between the temporal demands of their own growing children and their parents. These caregivers have been referred to as the "sandwich generation" (Miller, 1981). The greatest impact of trying to manage caregiving responsibilities, paid work, family, and personal roles is with respect to time: Caregivers report that they have less time and energy available for meeting the demands of any of their roles—for work, caregiving, or themselves (Scharlach, 1994). Many of the challenges associated with providing family support to parents or relatives are rooted in concerns about time. Time—and more specifically, the planning of future time—is a significant dimension of the stress or pressure that is commonly reported by middle-aged caregivers: anticipating needs for giving assistance in the future and mobilizing family members to plan future assistance, minimizing the disruption of one's own future plans and allotting sufficient time to fulfil the growth needs of one's own children and spouse, and adjusting to uncertainties in the progression or timing of the health condition for the person being cared for (Rakowski, 1986).

Employed women who are caught in this generational squeeze are also likely to exhibit problems associated with the allocation of time in the workplace. Employers have referred to these as "productivity problems": unscheduled days off, lateness, absenteeism, leaving early, and emergency hours off (Neal et al., 1993). Indeed, in a study of the relationship between work and caregiving responsibilities, Scharlach (1994) reports that over 50% of caregivers report reduced productivity and time off from work in the previous month (an average of 8.8 hours) to respond to their caregiving responsibilities. However, over a third of the respondents reported working longer hours or working weekends to make up for the lost time (Scharlach, 1994). In light of this, it was not surprising that work was perceived by 48% as reducing their time and energy for caregiving, and that caregiving, in turn, resulted in a lack of personal free time for 21% of the sample (Scharlach, 1994). Furthermore, compared to caregiving sons, employed caregiving daughters were more likely to reduce the number of hours they worked, rearrange their schedules, and take time off without pay (Stoller, 1983, cited in Neal et al., 1993).

Caregiving pressures appear to be particularly high when a dependent relative coresides with the caregiver. In a study of 181 caregiving women, those who had a demented relative living with them spent the highest number of hours in a caregiving capacity regardless of their employment status (Pett et al., 1988). In keeping with this, studies of time allocation before and after the institutionalization of a relative indicate that caregivers gain, on average, almost 2 hours a day after institutionalization (Moss, Lawton, Kleban, & Duhamel, 1993). Although guilt and some dissatisfaction are common reactions to such a placement, the gain in caregiver time has an overall positive effect on the quality of the caregiver's life, with more time for other family members, leisure, and activities outside the home (Moss et al., 1993). The provision of "free time" for caregivers is one of the most important means by which the stress of heavy caregiving can be alleviated. Research with caregivers indicates that having predictable blocks of free time can provide a sense of relief because it provides a block of time that is preserved as their own (Rakowski & Clark, 1985).

Despite the potential benefits associated with blocks of free time, many women experience "role overload" within the family in relation to the "ethic of care" (Henderson & Allen, 1991). Although being a mother in a family is the primary manifestation of the care responsibilities that are carried by women, they are also typically responsible for the care of aging parents, the return of adult children to the home, the support of male partners during significant transitions in their lives, and even for the care of pets (Henderson & Allen, 1991). As this suggests, the intergenerational politics of time is a politics of generation *and* gender, for most caregiving responsibilities fall on women's shoulders. Furthermore, a conflict model of role interaction may be the most appropriate model for understanding the strained allocation of time associated with caregiving responsibilities. Excessive caregiving role demands inevitably produce feelings of stress and conflict (Scharlach, 1994). Although it is important to acknowledge that there are also many positive aspects of caregiving that arise in the course of carrying out these responsibilities, the strain on time accounts for the majority of negative implications.

The time demands on adult children imposed by caregiving responsibilities has been the focus in much of the research literature, but there is some evidence to suggest that aging results in the assignment of a qualitatively different meaning to time, which in turn can precipitate conflicts and misunderstandings between generations. Structural changes in demographics and the economy suggests that there will be a further expansion of time spent in retirement. Growth in the population of older persons, the extension of active, healthy life expectancy, and a lowering of the age of retirement are precipitating rather dramatic redistributions of time spent in work and retirement, with the result being that leisure has taken on added importance for the elderly (Hendricks & Cutler, 1990). The elderly can be considered to be "time rich" in that time is seen as an abundant resource over which they have a great deal of control (Shaw, 1994, p. 89). One implication of this is that punctuality is elevated as a supreme virtue. The practical consequence is that they can allow time for almost everything but then are more inclined to be impatient and disapproving of family and friends who are at different life stages and are unable to meet the same controlled time standards (Shaw, 1994).

## Summary

To be a part of a generation is to share in the collective consciousness of a group and to hold a stake in the interests, values, and activities that represent the historical and developmental character of that group. For each generation, time has different meanings, places different demands, and is susceptible to varying levels of control. The politics of time between generations is concerned with the responsibilities and commitments of family members to each other to allocate time in the name of care and socialization.

Generations also serve as an important venue for the development of our understanding of family time. As Mannheim (1952) pointed out in the early part of this century, generations play an important role for understanding the shared cultural meanings of a historically located group of people. By examining the way that traditions, styles, and values are handed down, generations can serve as reference points for understanding the way that families change over time. There have been a number of structural changes that need to be examined to understand the way that generations experience time. Due to changes in longevity, there is a greater chance of four or five generations living concurrently in comparison to two or three in the past. At the same time, there is more diversity in family structure due to divorce or reproductive technologies, which has meant that there is more uncertainty and a higher probability of breaks in the transmission of intergenerational narratives. The paradoxical nature of generations emerges at the center of these trends: Generational lines are longer, more complicated, and in some ways more cherished than ever before, yet on the other hand, our preoccupation with a fast-paced global world leaves little time or energy for nurturing the links with the past.

The provision of care is the medium through which the politics of intergenerational time is played out. On the surface, it appears that the control over time is unidirectional insofar as the care*giver* is seen as the one who makes decisions about the allocation of time. For example, parents of young children are seen as controlling the timetables of children or the adult children are seen as giving time to their aging parents at their discretion. Beneath this veneer, however, is a very different set of dynamics where the demands of the caring relationship requires a commitment of time from all parties. In this regard, the intergenerational politics of time must be seen as bidirectional; the dynamics of time control are conceptualized as involving a resonance between controlling the time of others and being controlled by the time demands imposed by others.

This bidirectional dynamic is routinely manifested in the care that parents show for their children by imposing control over children's time. One of the first tasks of parents with their newborn infants is to establish a routine of feeding and sleeping. This control over children's time becomes more sophisticated as children grow older. Parents impose expectations for chores, bedtimes, and curfews, and they are there to ensure compliance of the child with the temporal expectations of being on time for school, games, or appointments. As parents get busier in their own lives and feel the briskness of the pace, there is a tendency for the child's temporal world to become increasingly regimented and hurried.

However, in the process of controlling children's use of time, parents find that their own time is controlled by their children. Investing time in getting children to do housework is probably the best example of this. Although the work that children do has the potential to offset the amount of time that parents themselves put into household chores, quite often the time required to motivate, remind, or nag ends up being a net drain on parents' use of time. Children's needs for care as they are growing up are more likely to impose controls on mothers' use of time. As labor studies of absenteeism and work-family stress indicate, mothers are more likely to miss work and to experience stress when their children are sick or in need of care.

As the population ages, middle-aged children are increasingly called on to provide care for their aging parents. As parents become physically or mentally dependent, they can make a deepening claim on the time of their adult children. Sons are involved in the provision of care for their parents, but it is typically the daughters who are called on to give of their time. Employed women who are caught in a generational squeeze between the time demands of their own children and the caregiving demands of their parents are likely to experience stress and conflict, exhibit higher rates of absenteeism, and require emergency hours off from work. In this regard, an intergenerational politics of time is a politics of generation and gender.

# 9

# Toward an Integrated
# Theory of Family Time

Time permeates all values, decisions, and actions. When pace, schedules, and temporal conflicts are raised to the surface of consciousness, time shifts from being an embedded and hidden dimension of family experience to one that lies at the apex of all activity. In the family literature, much of the emphasis has been on the symptoms of underlying time problems: stress, work-family conflict, caregiving dilemmas involving both young children and aging parents, and strained marriages and parent-child relationships. To problematize time is to focus on time as the etiology of these family dilemmas. In keeping with this, it is necessary to look at both the patterns and the politics of family time. Time is inherently political when it is at the root of competing interests, inequalities, culturally sanctioned entitlements, and discrimination.

In this final chapter, there is an effort to present an integrated theory of family time that outlines and integrates the underlying premises of the theory, the primary implications for families, and an

agenda for future research. The intention underlying the construction
of this theory is to create a point of departure that will generate new
ideas and questions. To return to the metaphor outlined in the preface,
if theory making is like bread making, then the empirical research and
the conceptual ideas that have been expressed in the book are the
ingredients that come together to form the dough. They give the
theory an elastic and substantive base. Working together, these ideas
take on an energy that allow the dough to rise and to move toward its
final shape. The task in this last chapter is to knead and reshape that
theoretical dough in order to enhance the integration of the elements
and to infuse it with the energy of new questions.

## Locating Family Time in the Cultural Milieu: Diversity, Acceleration, and Control

Like the three hands on a clock, diversity, acceleration, and control
represent three dominant characteristics of time in a postmodern
world. Globalization, computer technology, and pluralization in
values and structures have shifted our attention away from the traditional modernist notion of progress, to a preoccupation with a
demanding and multifaceted present. Electronic webs and global
markets operate at a speed that requires a shift from a focus on a better,
more innovative future, to a present that seems barely comprehensible
in light of exploding information, communications, and demands on
our time and attention. Herein resides the new politics of time where
families are faced with the growing challenge of controlling time when
it is being expressed in an accelerated and more variant form.

A theory of time for families must be premised on the idea that time
is not monolithic but is expressed in many diverse forms. It is tempting
to think of minutes, hours, days, and weeks as standard units that
simply serve to ground us in day-to-day reality in the same way that
air and gravity do. However, when we awaken our senses to the
diversity of temporal experience, time emerges in a kaleidoscope of
meanings and forms. Time is diverse and it is pervasive: It is embedded
in individual activity, identity, history, institutional schedules, social
norms, and family relationships. At any reflexive moment in our lives,
we awaken to the realization that we are active participants in this

pluralization of time. For example, a family who comes together at the end of the day experiences (whether verbally or not), the different pace of the day's events as experienced by individual members (with all its accompanying stresses and strains); the compression of the world's tempo into a newscast lasting several minutes that plays in the background; the plans and expectations for the next day in terms of meeting schedules, timing meals, or covering child care; hopes and dreams for the future; the stream of interruptions emerging from the telephone or the fax machine; and perhaps the quiet realization that the fatigue one feels may actually be related to the process of one's own aging. Hence, temporal diversity, as one hand of the clock, passes over the daily construction of our lives and leaves us with a fragmented, variable, and often contradictory experience of time on many levels and in many domains.

Closely related to this diversity is the belief that the pace of our lives has escalated dramatically. Through information and telecommunications technology, we can participate in many temporal worlds—whether that be a simple phone call to a relative in a different time zone or being a member of a "virtual community" via the Internet. This diversity not only disembeds us from our spatial moorings as if we had lost anchor in a windstorm, but it quickens the temporal pace. The horizons of temporal demands have expanded beyond the immediate geographical context of our work and family lives. In the process of plugging into the global demands of world time, families have put on speed to keep up with the incessant flow of information. Call-waiting features on telephones or the use of cellular phones are premised on the idea of constant availability and an entitlement of interruption. Even within their immediate context, individual family members disperse on a daily basis into their own temporal worlds of work, school, or day care, resulting in an ever tightening funnel of commitments and obligations.

The accelerated pace that arises from the multiple demands of time means that families must be more attentive to developing strategies to control time. Time is political because it is susceptible to the forces of control. Survival in a face-paced technological world involves an awareness of the demands that are placed on the distribution of one's time, a vigilance to the value that is placed on those demands, and a deliberate effort to contain those demands into a manageable daily routine. As part of this, to control time is to preserve time for family experience. When the daily routine is one of dispersion into separate temporal worlds and home life is marked by accessibility and interruption, the time to care, listen, or be with one another is easily diminished. The preservation of family time becomes a more daunting challenge in the face of many competing demands, not the least of which is a heightened work ethic that seems to exact ever greater allegiance to the march of production. Although families must work for the preservation of their time together, individual family members must also seek control over their own balance of family, work, and leisure. Both women and men in dual-earner families are confronted with the challenge of a double day, yet employed women face the greatest difficulty in surmounting the demands of work on their time. Negotiations within families about control over time, efforts to create free time, compliance with the social rules, and norms about "appropriate" time use all lie at the heart of the politics of time in families.

## Family Time as an Unhappy Present

Against the backdrop of the postmodern forces of acceleration, diversity, and efforts at control, is the continued importance of family time. At the very concrete level of everyday experience, there is a taken-for-granted experience of family time: It is the private time that members can own and have discretion over, a time of retreat into an intimate world. It is a time to be with loved ones. In short, as part of everyday discourse, people talk about "spending time" with the family, and, indeed, typically wanting to spend more time with the family.

This construction of family time is based on the principles of togetherness, choice, and mutual engagement. Although these principles may be commonly understood, they may be more reflective of an ideal than a reality. We do retreat into our homes to be with our families, but the pace and demands of the competitive world of work are often brought home with us. Given the increases in the amount of time that we give to work and the escalation of the pace of work activities, the result is that the home becomes the site of a parallel set of tasks and responsibilities. Whether it be the duties of parenthood, the tasks of household cleanliness, or the incessant demands of a consumer-based culture, there is often little sense of engaged involvement with one another in the experience of family time. The ideal, however, persists: People want to spend more time with their families; people are willing to trade work time for family time; and people yearn for the sense of calm and togetherness that is deeply embedded in our beliefs about what family time is. Our ideology of what family time is leaves us in an unhappy present. We are caught between the nostalgic tugs of an uncomplicated past where families worked together on the farm with no need to "find" family time; and an uncertain future that pulls us along with the fantasy of a slowed-down intimacy. The past and the future maintain the dream of family time, but the present is the site of our disillusionment. Although we are sustained by a belief that it was or will be better, "real" good-old-fashioned family time is often viewed as being just beyond our grasp in our experience of the present. As an ideological construct, family time may be a proxy for all of our longings for a secure and loving environment—where simplicity, calm, quiet, and intimacy prevail. The reality, however, is that families too often are consumed by the outward forces of a fast-paced, work-oriented world. In this regard, time results in a phenomenon that I refer to as "centrifugal families."

## Centrifugal Families

As a child, I have memories of going to Waterloo Park for Sunday picnics. These memories reflect nostalgic moments of family time. Brothers and sisters, parents—sometimes cousins, aunts, and uncles—coming together under the canopies of large maples with blue sky beyond. Coolers, charcoal barbecues, chips, and pop added to the celebratory air. The playground was enormous, with a carnival atmosphere: swings squeaking, a giant metal horse carrying what seemed like dozens of children whooshing back and forth, and the sound of sand cascading down the shiny metal slide. At the center, however, was my favorite: the simple, push as you go, hop on, merry-go-round. I liked it because it was silent, fast, and dangerous. And in the limited experience of a small boy, the dizzying spin was intoxicating because I could delight in the disorientation and loss of control.

It was in the soft focus of this happy memory that I began to think of the simple merry-go-round as a metaphor for our contemporary experience of family time. The merry-go-round is the private world of the family. Picture, if you can, breathless parents running around the outside, pushing as they go, being joined periodically by their children in the effort to keep up speed. As they do in their work, they push all day long with the encouraging voices that keep saying "Faster! Faster!" It is as if the bars of the merry-go-round were the hands of the clock where they push ever harder to keep up with the accelerating tempo of our technological world.

Tired from pushing at the end of the day, they jump on to the merry-go-round, at once feeling the relief of no longer having to push, but at the same time feeling the outward centrifugal push and a heightened awareness of the world spinning around them. When their feet are pushing through the sand they are in pace with the busy world of work, but when they stop and land on the moving carousel, there is a more acute awareness of the blurring speed of the world around them. Once safely on the carousel, there is an effort to hold on and get steady in the face of the new forces coming from the center that propel them to the outside. When they can focus their gaze on the markings of the merry-go-round itself, they can feel more in control of their position. Overnight and on days off, the merry-go-round slows down, prompting the riders to jump to the outside and begin again their task of pushing the hands of time to keep pace. Families on the merry-go-round are centrifugal families: While pushing and working, they generate enough speed to keep pace with the demands of their environment; when they jump on, they must hold on tight to their family world while working against the dizzying effects of the fast world around that continues to draw them to it. As a result, it is hard to move toward the calm center of family time because they are expected to be ever diligent to keeping up speed. And to do that, they have to keep jumping off and *pushing*. Centrifugal families are caught in an endless cycle of generating speed, working to overcome the effects of that speed by pulling themselves toward the center, only to find themselves back on the outside creating the very centrifugal forces that they will seek to overcome.

Because of the speed, the dizzying effects, and the centrifugal forces, the merry-go-round can be a dangerous game. Like the child who loses his grip and flies off on a tangent that ends with a mouthful of sand, family members too, incur their casualties. Parents trip and fall when they push the wheel too hard. Through physical illness, addictions, stress, and depression, they become victims of their own centrifugal forces when they can no longer keep up with the wheel and it simply spits them into the sand. Jumping on and off the merry-go-round is the time when accidents are most likely to happen. When family members converge on the fast spinning wheel at the end of the day, the chance of mishap or conflict is high. The "supper hour" is an experience of family time when parents and children come together with the accumulated fatigue of the day and the spinning effects of their participation in the outside world. Energies are low and needs are high, making the times of reentry back onto the wheel particularly precarious. Children occasionally fly off the merry-go-round because it is going too fast. Without a secure mooring in the home, kids can fly out of reach from their parents. Adolescents who run away, use drugs, or commit suicide can no longer hold their grip on a wheel that is either spinning too fast or empty too often. Sometimes the kids land in the sand in the proximal zone and end up being gently trampled as parents keep pushing—either out of financial necessity or as a result of their own disorientation and uncertainty about how to live any differently. At other times, the kids are flung beyond reach with parents left wondering where they ever went wrong.

If families are to live differently, and if family time is something that is to be experienced as a reality rather than an ideal, then we face the inevitable question about our ability to do anything to change it. If the merry-go-round is going too fast, can we do anything to change it?

## The Fatalistic View

At one level, it seems that we have not progressed much beyond the dark days of the industrial revolution when people were slaves to the clocked rhythm of the machine. Although working conditions have become cleaner, brighter, and safer, the total number of hours of family labor continues to increase. Time pressures on families during the introduction of the factory system gave rise to a call for the family wage. In acknowledgment of the detrimental effects on families of long hours of labor for men, women and children, there was a formal movement to pay a man a sufficient wage to support his family. In some ways, it is an idea that might seem attractive again, especially if it was brought up to today's standards of providing a family wage to either the woman or man. It is, of course, unlikely that the idea of a family wage would carry any weight in today's economy. Nevertheless, it is ironic that we have returned to the conditions that gave rise to it in the first place.

The work clock continues to tyrannize in a way that leaves people feeling somewhat powerless to change. In a consumer culture where both the standard of living and the cost of living continue to rise, there is a perception and indeed a lived reality in many families that both men and women must work in the paid labor force out of economic necessity. It is as if the carousel has its own inertia, fueled by the fabricated needs of a culture that runs on advertising. The end result is that for many families, who are left breathless at the end of the day, time controls them. Time is externally based and unrelenting in its demands. Work permeates both public and private spheres: Not only is paid labor considered work, but now child care and domestic activity are classified as work. The result is that only small fragments of residual time are left to the discretion of the individual or the family to be enjoyed as rest or leisure. The fantasy of family time is left largely unfulfilled.

It is arguable that it is beyond the control of individuals to change the domineering effects of work time. For example, a Marxist view would suggest that the forces of capitalism continue to ride roughshod over individual and family interests. In times of economic prosperity, families exchange a high proportion of their time for income. In periods of recession or economic collapse with high levels of unemployment, families continue to feel a loss of control over their time because they have lost their place in the dominating structure of the workplace. This is the fatalistic view of time that keeps the hand of control centered in our political and economic structures.

## Families Taking Control

To control the pace of their lives, families have to first be aware that the wheel is spinning too fast. The fast spin is taken for granted, and unless there is something to disrupt that rhythm, it will continue unchecked. A child that is thrown from the merry-go-round or the parent who trips and falls occasionally serve as moments of epiphany that drive home the awareness that the cost of keeping the pace is too high. Structural changes in the economy—such as downsizing, unemployment, and the move toward a series of temporary jobs or contracts—can also have resoundingly clear effects on the awareness of pace. When jobs are lost, pace can take a dramatic turn. On a more positive note, some companies have moved to 4-day work weeks as part of downsizing and this has been embraced in a very positive way by most employees. For other families, there is a vague sense that lives are speeding along at precarious speeds, but unless someone gets hurt, or someone tells them to slow down, there is neither the incentive nor the wherewithal to change the pace. Hence, awareness of pace is a precondition for controlling pace.

In some families there is the question of whether they could even live without the dizzying effects of the merry-go-round. When a fast-paced life is the basis for taken-for-granted reality, there may be greater fear of what lies on the other side, even if we were able to slow down the wheel. Would we survive financially? Would we be bored with our lives? Would we know what to do with that time if we had it in abundance? In this regard, it appears that the tyrannizing effects of work can leave those unattended parts of our lives in a state of atrophy, with some question about whether they can be brought back to life at all. Specifically, have families lost the capacity in their busy lives to be spiritual, joyous, intimate, and loving? Are they still able to simply be together without feeling like they have to do something?

## Changing Paradigms

The more optimistic view suggests that we can take control over time and that it is worthwhile to do so. The traditional approach for taking control over time in our culture is the time management model.

Although originating in the world of business and originally designed to make men more efficient and productive in their work, time management strategies are now a necessary survival skill for all members of contemporary families. Time management is based on the assumption that the world is fast-paced and that it does place multiple and often competing demands on our time. The goal is to learn how to keep pace with these demands by being a better manager of time. Learning how to synchronize work schedules, squeezing grocery shopping into a lunch hour, or running errands during a child's soccer game make it possible to fit it all in. Although time management holds out the promise that we can control time in a better way, there is an underlying assumption that we continue at the same speed but simply do a better job of squeezing it all in. Time management, as a tool for personal or professional survival, is based on the same values as the world of work: enhancing productivity, increasing efficiency, and avoiding the greatest sin of all, wasting time. The question then arises as to whether this is really taking control over time, or whether it is simply an exercise of more fully complying with a temporal order that is externally based. When families try to "shoehorn" as much activity as possible into the day, they are only controlling time in a superficial way. Underlying their "expert" abilities at organizing their time is a merry-go-round that continues to spin with a momentum that is maintained by their busy lives.

In this regard, time management strategies do more to maintain the pace of the culture and do little to slow it down. In fact, one could easily argue that the discovery of greater efficiencies in time opens the possibility of fitting more in, with the end result that there is a further escalation of time. Like the dizziness that arises from pushing the merry-go-round, we are affected by the inebriating effects of pace that is experienced as both seductive and repulsive. Like other forms of addiction, we are beguiled by the tempo of our lives and express a devotion to pace. The dizzying speed of our lives keeps us in a trancelike state of preoccupation. At the same time, in moments of sobriety, we are repulsed by the realization of how constrained and hollow our lives have become. Time management does little to change the intoxicating effects of a fast-paced culture; it simply serves as a tool for living with the malaise.

If time management is part of the problem for families because it is based on the same values as a productive and efficient work culture, then we need to think about new paradigms that are designed with different values in mind. A new paradigm must be attentive to both the dynamics of control that exist between families and the society of which they are a part, and the dynamics of control that exist within families, where women and men, young and old vie for their entitlements to time.

A new paradigm of time must begin with the idea that decisions about time are decisions about values. When people experience time conflicts, not only are there competing demands placed on that time, but divergent underlying values shape how the time is spent. These values take many forms in families. At the most fundamental level, they concern the relative importance of work, individual interests, and shared activity in the family. Awareness of these values calls for a scrutiny of the trade-offs between money and time. For parents especially, the interplay between values and time is routinely played out in terms of decisions about spending enough time with children. Personal needs of family members also give rise to different priorities about time. In the same way that a distinction can be made between freedom *from* and freedom *to,* the values associated with time can be differentiated on the basis of time *for* various activities, and time *from* the constraints of various obligations and responsibilities.

Hence, if there is to be a redistribution of time in families, there has to be a reexamination of the underlying values that organize our decisions about how family time is allocated. A new paradigm of time is a political paradigm because it calls out for an interruption of the taken-for-granted flow of time. It calls out for an interruption of the typical powerlessness that is expressed about time. When families interrupt the experience of being controlled by time, they increase their consciousness of time. This is a necessary condition for examining the relationship between time and values. Only when families have had the opportunity to assess the values associated with time use can they make decisions about controlling time.

A paradigm that invokes the politics of time involves a fundamental shift from counting and cataloging time to questioning the meaning of time. It involves a shift from a time-management mentality based on ever greater efficiency, to a critical viewpoint toward time that actively seeks to interrupt the pace and questions and challenges the experience of being spun about by forces greater than ourselves. It is a paradigm in which families stop trying to keep pace and instead seek to create a pace—a pace that is attentive to individual and family well-being. To create a different kind of pace, there may need to be an acceptance that you can't "fit it all in." Rather, establishing priorities about time use may mean letting go of some activities. For families who are riding the carousel, it means moving closer to the center, where the outward force is not so intense. It means shifting the focus from the blurred images of the world around to the people moving with you on the wheel. As families move closer to the center of the wheel, they are still spinning but the outward forces diminish. They don't need to concentrate on holding on so tightly but, rather, can relax a little and enjoy the ride. Trends toward nesting, cocooning, or retreating are indicative of this desire to move toward a calmer center.

Families continue to live within a world that is fast-paced, and they will always be constrained by the tempo of that world. Hence, although they cannot outright reject the influences of a racing technological world, they can live in a world with a different consciousness of time and a more deliberate posture toward time. If the merry-go-round has inebriating effects, they can choose a different level of sobriety with time. This sobriety allows them some control in choosing slow over fast, being over doing, or recreation over production. Interrupting the pace of time in this way is a call for the private world of family experience to challenge the regime of the spinning commercial world. It is political in the same way as the radical who challenges the system. For, in this case, the system is fast and most of the cultural rewards are given to those who can do things faster and better. By contrast, the rewards associated with choosing to do it slow must be generated and supported from within the confines of family experience.

## The Micropolitics of Temporal Control Within Families

To think of families as a whole taking control over time is to focus on their mutual interests in time together. The politics of temporal control, however, must also be attentive to the diverse interests that exist within families. Although family members may have a shared interest in time together, the way that these interests are determined within families is also a matter of temporal politics. It is tempting to think of women and men sharing the task of pushing the merry-go-round, but when we look closely, we realize that they push with different intensity, jump on and off with different responsibilities, and have very different interpretations of their ride. A micropolitics of time within the home must be attentive to both gender and age differences.

The literature that examines the allocations of time for women and men in the workplace, the home, and the leisure domain all point to ongoing gender disparities in the value and control of time. As the research suggests, there are significant gaps in the paid value of the time of men and women, the disruptability of their time, and their entitlement to free time. In some ways, measures of time provide some of the most startling indicators of the inequalities that persist between women and men. A new paradigm for controlling time means interrupting the taken-for-granted inequities that exist for women and men in their use of time. It means arriving at a new consciousness in which one person's entitlement to free time is realized in an atmosphere of fairness and sensitivity (Restrepo, 1995).

These gender discrepancies in time are clearly evident in the caregiving literature. There has been a considerable amount of research that looks at the dynamics of providing care for both children and the aging population. Women are still more likely to be the primary caregivers and many of the strains associated with caregiving are rooted in concerns about time: worries about the future, concerns about leaving enough time for children and spouse, adjusting to the uncertainties associated with illness and independent living, and concerns about absenteeism or lateness because of caregiving responsibilities. In light of the projected inability of government services to meet the needs of an aging population, the temporal strains arising from caregiving will no doubt continue to rise. This will result in an intensification of the intergenerational politics of time, thereby requiring a heightened diligence to the way that decisions about time are made within families.

## Implications for Practice

Although some families may have it within their own power to take
control over time, others would benefit from the services of various
professionals. If time is one of the most demanding challenges of
family experience, then family life educators and therapists need to
take time seriously in their work. The temptation may be to offer tips
in time management, but this may do little to alleviate strain in the
long run. Although time management strategies call for an analysis of
priorities, more often than not it involves shuffling the same number
of activities into a different order. Rather, what may be more beneficial is a fundamental reevaluation of whether certain activities can be
managed at all. For example, reducing the number of hours worked,
changing the standards of cleanliness in the home, or choosing to
forego social obligations can create temporal "room" in day-to-day
living. Therapists and educators can also play a role in helping to
create a new consciousness of time. Working with clients to interrupt
the domineering flow of an externally controlled time structure can
help to shift the balance from a fatalistic experience of time in which
people are left with a feeling of having little control over time, to a
more humanistic position that allows them to be vigilant to their own
needs for a different kind of pace.

Family life educators and therapists can also play a role in helping
families to achieve a greater awareness of clocking and synchronization issues. The dramatic increases in the number of women in the
paid labor force has resulted in the daily emptying of the family home.
In contrast to the daily routines of families in agrarian societies or the
prototypical Parsonian families of the 1950s and 1960s, all family
members now typically dissipate into the external temporal order on
a daily basis. This daily ritual of dispersion represents a dramatic shift
from a temporal order that was once more predominantly localized
within the household to one that is more dominantly located in the
institutional organization of society. Even among families with preschool children, the majority are composed of dual-earner couples or
employed sole-support parents.

With the fragmentation of daily routines, there are many implications for therapeutic practice. Foremost among these is the experience
of autonomy and connectedness in families. From one perspective,

one could hypothesize that these rituals of dispersion result in greater levels of disconnectedness in families as each family member engages in separate activity. From another perspective, however, there may be less conflict and a greater appreciation of their time together when all family members spend a larger portion of their lives in separate activities. Therapy needs to be attentive to the implications of dispersion for the formation of family boundaries, levels of cohesion, or family enmeshment/disengagement.

The challenge of temporal synchronization is both a personal trouble and a public issue because it brings into play the efforts of family members to reconcile their internal routines with temporal structures such as day care hours, work schedules, or the accessibility of recreation and leisure facilities. Families can also be supported in their efforts to control time through changes at the policy level. Although a number of corporations created family-friendly work policies in the 1980s and 1990s, they were often policies that were superimposed on a traditional work ethic. For many employees, these policies were occasions for the experience of contradiction: On the one hand, the opportunity to be attentive to family needs was available, and on the other, there was an expectation for continued high performance through long hours and company commitment (especially for those with promotion aspirations). This contradiction may be particularly acute for men: Whereas women are more likely to take advantage of family-friendly policies for various forms of caregiving, men are more likely to be swayed by the demands of the job. Education and therapy need to work hand in hand to heighten awareness of these contradictions and to advocate for change.

Temporal orientation has become centrally important in some of the new family therapies that focus on narrative. These approaches, although relatively new, show promise for gaining insight into the way that people socially construct and reconstruct their life stories. This is in contrast to a more positivist tradition of life span and family development approaches that give precedence to the linear and unchangeable sequence of life events. The focus on the storying of people's lives through the use of narrative techniques places emphasis on the importance of present conditions for the interpretation of past events. In addition, it is an archaeological endeavor that allows for the discovery of events in the past that have been subjugated or lost from memory. Narrative techniques, although usually focusing on the reconstruction of the past, have the potential to examine the way that families restory their futures in the face of unexpected events. We often think about families as yearning for a nostalgic experience of families from the past, but they also live with the construction of their own ideals for what their family should be. Although they make efforts to gravitate toward this future horizon, they must contend with the daily frustrations and disappointments that divert them from this ideal. In addition, they must contend with unexpected death, pregnancy, infertility, divorce, or sickness, which can precipitate more dramatic reconstructions of their expected life plans. Narrative techniques, which focus on restorying the past and storying the future, are well suited to the task.

## An Agenda for Research on Family Time

Although there has been a call in the family literature to go beyond the dichotomization of family and work as private and public spheres (e.g., Feree, 1990), it appears that family time is a highly privatized segment of the family's reality that they seek to create and protect. The "protection" of family time or the desire for "time together" are celebrated parts of our family discourse that have strong connotations of time as a private and boundaried experience. Whether it is the nostalgic picture of the family Sunday drive or a more contemporary image of the family coming together to catch its breath around the microwave, "family time" is time that is set apart from the rest of the busy schedule. Inasmuch as "family time" is commonly understood as an important boundaried experience, the research is almost nonexistent. Consequently, there are many unanswered questions about the experience of family time.

### WHAT IS FAMILY TIME?

First, there is considerable work to be done in even sorting out what constitutes "family time." In keeping with the postmodern emphasis on diversity, one expects family time to be expressed in a variety of forms. The first task of research on family time is to examine the values that are associated with it. This involves questions that seek to determine where family time fits into the hierarchy of demands that are experienced by family members. Inevitably, there will be diversity within families regarding the importance of family time, resulting in questions that concern the balance between individual and shared constructions of family time. Research also needs to examine the extent to which there are specific barriers to spending time together as a family. Although there is literature that attributes family problems to time shortages, there is little information about the strategies that families employ to contend with these technological pressures.

The way that priority is assigned to family time is going to vary by the nature of family structure and also the inherited traditions that are passed on through the generations. Research needs to examine how different kinds of families assign priority to family time and to explore the transmission of these values and priorities from one generation to the next. This task is becoming considerably more complex, for generational lines are typically longer (4 or 5 generations living at one time) and more complex because of divorce, separation, and alternate family forms. Research needs to examine how families maintain continuity with the past when the links are staggered and diverse. Of particular importance here is to examine the presence and frequency of formal and informal rituals. In particular, questions arise with respect to who performs these rituals, who plays the role of keeper of tradition within families, and how these rituals are changing in the face of increasing family diversification. The way that family time is socially constructed within families and through the generations is a largely uncharted territory.

Of course, an analysis of family time in future research would be incomplete without giving attention to the diverse forms of family time that exist in different kinds of families. For example, there are different challenges associated with the construction of family time in stepfamilies. Specifically, different entitlements to family time are experienced by step and biological parents, such that biological group-ings may seek their own family time together apart from the time spent as a stepfamily. Presumably, numerous conflicts arise in the course of reconciling the temporal expectations and habits of what were once separate families. Here it would be interesting to examine how two different styles of clocking and sequencing are brought together to form new temporal structures within the blended family. Although there is considerable research that has examined the difference in time allocations for dual-earner and single-earner families, there has been little emphasis on meanings of family time for these kinds of families. Questions also arise with respect to how localized family time is within the nuclear family or to what extent it continues to be meaningful within the extended family.

## HOW IS FAMILY TIME
## CREATED AND CONTROLLED?

Research that examines the creation or control of family time must be attentive to how deliberate family time is. At one end of the continuum, family time can be conceived as a residual category or a spontaneous occurrence in family experience that simply represents what is left over after the commitments to work and the duties of the household are taken care of. At the other end of the continuum, family time can be conceptualized as a scheduled experience that is deliberately created for the purposes of bringing the family together.

If families are more deliberate about planning family time, then we need to know more about the strategies that are used to create and maintain this time. Is this a shared commitment within the family, or are certain interests being served in this process? More specifically, are one person's values about the importance of family time being imposed on the others? Many questions arise with respect to how roles are established and modified in the family in the process of making family time a valued experience. One expects mothers, fathers, and children to play different roles in creating opportunities for family time. As part of this, it would be interesting to examine whether one member takes primary responsibility for orchestrating family time. Similarly, attention needs to focus on how much control children have over the scheduling of family leisure. Little is known about the tactics that are used, the negotiations that are carried out, or the conflicts that arise in arriving at shared meanings of family time. Furthermore, there needs to be an analysis of both informal expectations and formal rules that exist within families to ensure a certain level of family time. Mealtimes, which have traditionally been one of the congregating moments for families, may also have changed. To what extent do families try to have "family time" during meals? It would be interesting to examine the family rules around mealtimes and to explore the meanings that are attached to these times. As these ideas suggest, there is a need to examine the micropolitics within families associated with the creation and control of family time.

At a broader level, little empirical research exists that explores the dynamics of control between families and the sociotemporal order. Do families see themselves losing ground in the battle with time? What are the impediments to the successful protection of family time from within the family and from outside the family? On a more practical level, if schedules are the tools of efficiency and control, then to what extent do family members perceive that they have the opportunity to modify schedules? Although the provision of flexible working hours is one part of the equation, the extent to which people feel entitled to take advantage of these opportunities is quite another. Research might also fruitfully examine the way that various family members fit on the "humanistic-fatalistic" (Lyman & Scott, 1970) balance of controlling time. Furthermore, questions arise regarding the degree to which families look to the marketplace to substitute purchased services for various aspects of household production as a way gaining control over their time. Although there is some market-based research that looks at the consumption patterns of fast food or house cleaning services, there is little research that examines the meanings of these trends for families.

## GENDER AND THE
## EXPERIENCE OF FAMILY TIME

In the same way that family members play different roles in creating family time, women and men have a different experience of family time. Individual meanings of family time can reflect a wide spectrum of possibilities, including definitions of family time as work, leisure, and mandatory commitment. Research is needed to extend Shaw's (1992) analysis about the experience of family time as "work" for both women and men. Here, questions arise with respect to the contradictions for men and women between the cultural constructions of family time as play with their personal experiences of family time as work.

There has been considerable attention given in the literature to measuring the amount of time that men and women commit to their paid work and the amount of time that they commit to household and child care tasks. In general terms, men work longer hours and are more highly rewarded in their paid work, whereas women continue to do the majority of household and child care work. More recent research has begun to examine some of the obstacles to bringing about changes in these allocations. For example, research has begun to look at the reasons why men rarely take family leaves even when they are available to them (Pleck, 1993; Haas & Hwang, 1995). Similarly, research has begun to look at the reasons why women feel disentitled to leisure, even when it is available to them (Henderson & Dialeschki, 1991). As these research trends suggest, underlying the more mechanical allocations of time, are a web of social-psychological processes that maintain these inequalities. Although there is still lots of work to do in sorting out the methodological issues associated with measuring allocations of time, there is even more work to be done in examining some of these underlying processes. Qualitative research that explores the way that these patterns of time are maintained in various spheres will play an important role in understanding the basis for these inequalities and may also provide clues for change. It is also apparent in the research that does exist, that gender inequality in the use of time persists throughout the life cycle. As this suggests, attention needs to be directed toward socialization practices whereby boys and girls learn different responsibilities and entitlements with respect to time use.

## LOCATING FAMILY TIME
## IN TIME AND SPACE

The relationship between time and space within the home also offers some possible avenues for exploration. The design of space in family homes has changed considerably over the years. Where once homes were more open with an emphasis on common space, they have become more divided to optimize individual privacy. The kind of space that families inhabit has an impact on their distribution of individual and shared time. Social class has a bearing not only on the amount of space that is available but presumably on the amount of time. Although one expects a positive association between social class and domestic space, one could hypothesize a negative association between social class and family time. Whereas middle- and upper-middle-class families who live in relatively spacious homes may have to create times where they come together in a common space, working-class families who live in cramped quarters may focus on finding time and space to be apart. In this regard, the physical structure of the home affects the experience of family time.

In this line of research, there is a challenge to map where and when families come together for their experience of family time. Traditional views of family time point to eating spaces or family rooms as the key sites of family time, but there are questions about the extent to which family time is tied to specific spaces. One plausible alternative when we think of centrifugal families is to think of families on the move where the links between space and time are tenuous. In this regard, family time might be better conceptualized as transsituational or spatially dislodged, where the car, the telephone, and perhaps even the computer become the mechanisms by which family time is mobilized. Future research needs to examine these time-space links.

Closely related to this are questions about when families have family time. With the "colonization of time" and the diminishing importance of Sundays as a "day of rest," there are few, if any, reserved or sacred times that are devoted specifically to family time. Research needs to examine the extent to which families have been successful in maintaining certain traditions or rituals that preserve family time. This line of analysis could examine the relationship between family time and their participation in cultural and religious institutions that have structures and ideologies that support the commitment to family time.

## TECHNOLOGY AND THE ACCELERATION OF TIME

The accelerated tempo of life for families gives rise to many questions in need of empirical attention. Although the evidence seems clear that spouses are spending less time with each other and parents are spending less time with their children, it is much less clear how families cope with technology and the accelerated pace of change. As Elkind (1981) and others have suggested, as parents get busier in their own lives, they are more likely to transfer this busyness to their own children. The result is that children are seen as living hurried and highly scheduled lives. The research that examines the extent to which children live fast-paced, highly structured lives is quite limited. There is a need to examine the pace of children's lives, the way that this pace has changed over time, and the implications that it has for their development. The literature tends to emphasize the negative aspects of this experience by focusing on children being "hurried" or not having enough time for spontaneous play, but it is quite reasonable to expect that there are positive and adaptive repercussions to these changes. These have not been well explored in the research.

Computer games, CD-ROM systems, televisions, VCRs, and cellular phones have taken their place in everyday family life. Perhaps more than any other force, technology has been tagged as being responsible for the general speedup of modern family life. As Rifkin (1987) has predicted, the nanosecond culture of the computer world is altering our state of consciousness in the same way that the automated clock did in the thirteenth century. Computers have hastened the speed of communications and have reduced the requirement for face-to-face contact. At the same time that computers seem to be increasing the tempo of everyday lives, there are also indications that family members are spending more time within the home due to technology. This can be attributed to the proliferation of technological gadgetry that is the focus of family entertainment whether it be computerized exercise equipment or hand-held computer games. It can also be a function of the incorporation of technological machines (computers, fax, e-mail) that make home-based work more feasible than ever before. As this suggests, the speedup of family life is not "out there" but is happening within the kitchens, family rooms, and home offices of the family home.

As technology precipitates a faster pace and perhaps a more isolated experience within families, many questions arise with respect to how families manage the tempo of their lives. If a "new kind of impatience" is one of the symptoms of our postmodern culture, how does it affect relationships within families? Have expectations for fast responses or immediate gratifications heightened in families? As the postmodern view suggests, the temporary needs of the present have come to dominate the willingness to wait for the gratifications of the future.

Has this heightened pace changed the long-term reciprocal exchanges that we have traditionally attributed to families?

If technology allows for a constant state of interruption in families, then we know little about the effects that this has on the organization of family lives. What kinds of boundaries do families have with respect to technological intrusions? Is there even a consciousness of "technological intrusion" or are families simply being carried along on the silicon wings of change?

Television continues to be one of the most important technological visitors in the family home. With the development of satellite technology and the popularity of home entertainment centers, families will continue to cocoon around the family television set. Although some of the research supports the stereotyped notions about families sitting passively together without interaction in front of the set, other research has shown that this is an important opportunity for family togetherness in a more active way. With the central importance of television in the lives of families, this is a line of research that needs to be developed further. What is the quality of the television-viewing experience in the home? Although the impact of television viewing on children is well advanced in the psychological literature, the escalating importance of television and the proliferation of viewing options will continue to influence the nature of family interaction in unforeseen ways.

## THE CHALLENGES OF
## TEMPORAL SYNCHRONIZATION

For families with dependents, whether children or an aging parent, one of the greatest challenges of synchronization is to provide the continuous coverage of care that is required. Research that examines the synchronization problems associated with day care and work schedules is well advanced. Nevertheless, as Presser (1989) has suggested, many questions still need to be answered. For example, when parents work nonstandard hours, there is a need to explore the consequences for children. As part of this, research needs to examine the implications of "sequential parenting," when mothers and fathers work different times. What are the alternative child care arrangements during nonstandard hours? For unmarried mothers who work longer hours and more nonstandard shifts, there are questions about the quality of their time with children when they return home tired and without another adult to turn to for help. Questions also arise about the consequences for children of having a stream of interchangeable caregivers over the course of their week.

Similar kinds of questions can also be asked regarding the care that is required for aging parents. How do adult children provide the "continuous coverage" that may be required by their aging parents? These questions reflect the personal troubles of synchronization, but there are also questions about the willingness of organizations to provide flexibility or to accommodate the scheduling needs of families. Although some research has begun to examine the implementation of various strategies, there is a need to look at the effectiveness of these strategies for meeting the care needs of various family members.

As Davies (1994) has pointed out, clock time, with its emphasis on productivity and efficiency, is not a good measure for understanding the various forms of care work that go on in families. Instead, she proposes that "process time," with its emphasis on the unpredictability of needs and the plurality of activities that occur within a caregiving situation, is a better way to conceptualize the experience of time in a caregiving situation. Although clock time has been used as the basis for understanding how much time is committed to caregiving relations in families, we know relatively little about the way that caregivers experience process time. To this end, research needs to explore the physical, psychological, social, and spiritual dimensions of time that is devoted to caregiving. It needs to examine the way that process time can undergird other activities when it is expressed in terms of private anxiety, worry, concern, or affection. This is time that is not easily compartmentalized into blocks of clock time but, rather, is like a ribbon that transcends specific situations. Process time is relationship time and there is a need to explore the ways that men and women experience care and relationship through time.

Many questions arise with respect to the responsibility for temporal synchronization within families. Hochschild (1989) has indicated that women appear to be carrying the brunt of the speedup work in families, yet there is a need to examine more closely the distribution of responsibility for coordinating schedules throughout the week. Research also needs to examine the process by which families talk about or coordinate their schedules. Does the "traffic control tower" model fit with the way that families synchronize their lives? Or is it more chaotic? What are the different patterns that families exhibit in organizing their schedules? Furthermore, there is some evidence to suggest that more families are beginning to "off-schedule" their work to minimize their reliance on outside caregivers. Research needs to examine the implications of this approach for marital satisfaction and family well-being.

New challenges of temporal synchronization also arise with the increasing diversity of family forms. For example, in families where there is joint custody of children, we know little about what it means for children to make the transition from one temporal world to another on a regular basis. Future research needs to examine the differences in the expectations for how time is spent with each of the parents, who takes responsibility for coordinating or controlling the transition from one temporal world to another, and what the conflicts are that arise in the process of trying to synchronize these separate temporal worlds.

The clocking of everyday lives is also shaped by the different rhythms that individual family members bring to the daily routine. Differences in morningness or nightness or differences based on age or physical health will have an impact on the way that family members participate in the pace and scheduling of their daily lives. When a family member unexpectedly takes ill, we typically gain a better understanding of the regimentation of the daily routine when we have to adjust the pace and sequence to accommodate the illness. Women have been identified in the literature as the family members that usually respond to these unexpected changes in the family's clocking behavior by missing work or rearranging their schedules. The empirical study of these time crises in the family could not only open an important window on how family members respond to the crises themselves, but also have the potential to bring into focus the habitual patterns of time sequencing and pace that serve as the taken-for-granted backdrop to these crises.

## Conclusion

Although we know a great deal about time in families, many unanswered questions command our attention in these times of rapid change. Through our questioning, however, we bring time ever closer to the surface of our consciousness and, in the process, are in a position to gain a better understanding of how time shapes and constrains our everyday lives. As we gain a better understanding of the patterns and politics of time in families, we gain a better understanding of the patterns and politics of families themselves.

# References

Adam, B. (1988). Social versus natural time. In M. Young & T. Schuller (Eds.), *The rhythms of society* (pp. 198-226). London: Routledge.

Adam, B. (1989). Feminist social theory needs time: Reflections on the relation between feminist thought, social theory and time as an important parameter in social analysis. *Sociological Review, 37,* 458-473.

Adam, B. (1990). *Time and social theory.* Cambridge, MA: Polity.

Adam, B. (1993). Within and beyond the time economy of employment relations: Conceptual issues pertinent to research on time and work. *Social Science Information, 32,* 163-184.

Adams, B. (1987). "Early birds" and "Night owls" among college students and married couples. *Sociology and Social Research, 71,* 245-249.

Adams, B. N., & Cromwell, R. E. (1978). Morning and night people in the family: A preliminary statement. *The Family Coordinator, 27,* 5-13.

Aldous, J., & Klein, D. (1991). Models of intergenerational relations in mid-life. *Journal of Marriage and the Family, 53,* 595-608.

Allison, M., & Duncan, M. (1987). Women, work and leisure: The days of our lives. *Leisure Studies, 9,* 143-162.

Altergott, K., & McCreedy, C. C. (1993). Gender and family status across the life course: Constraints on five types of leisure. *Society and Leisure, 16,* 151-180.

Arlow, J. (1989). Time as emotion. In J. T. Fraser (Ed.), *Time and mind: Interdisciplinary issues.* Madison, WI: International Universities Press.

Armstrong, P., & Armstrong, H. (1984). *The double ghetto: Canadian women and their segregated work.* Toronto: McClelland Stewart.

Ausloos, G. (1986). The march of time: Rigid or chaotic transactions, two different ways of living time. *Family Process, 25,* 549-557.

Avery, R. J., & Stafford, K. (1991). Toward a scheduling congruity theory of resource management. *Lifestyles: Family and Economic Issues, 12,* 325-344.

Baber, K. M., & Allen, K. R. (1992). *Women and families: Feminist reconstructions.* New York: Guilford.

227

Barnett, L., & Kane, M. (1985). Environmental constraints on the child's play. In M. G. Wade (Ed.), *Constraints on leisure* (pp. 189-225). Springfield, IL: Charles C Thomas.

Baruch, G. K., & Barnett, R. (1986). Consequences of father's participation in family work: Parents' role strain and well-being. *Journal of Personality and Social Psychology, 51,* 578-585.

Becker, G. S. (1965). A theory of the allocation of time. *Economic Journal, 75,* 493-517.

Bellah, R. N., Madsen, R., Sullivan, W. M., Swidler, A., & Tipton, S. M. (1985). *Habits of the heart: Individualism and commitment in American life.* New York: Harper & Row.

Bengston, V. (1989). The problem of generations: Age group contrasts, continuities and social change. In V. Bengston & K. W. Schaie (Eds.), *The course of later life: Research and reflections* (pp. 25-54). New York: Springer.

Bengston, V., & Allen, K. (1993). The life course perspective applied to families over time. In P. G. Boss, W. J. Doherty, R. LaRossa, W. R. Schumm, & S. K. Steinmetz (Eds.), *Sourcebook of family theories and methods: A contextual approach* (pp. 469-498). New York: Plenum.

Bengston, V., Furlong, M. J., & Laufer, R. S. (1983). Time, aging and the continuity of social structure: Themes and issues in generational analysis. *Journal of Social Issues, 39,* 45-71.

Berardo, D. H., Shehan, C. L., & Leslie, G. R. (1987). A residue of tradition: Jobs, careers, and spouses' time in housework. *Journal of Marriage and the Family, 49,* 381-390.

Berger, P. L. (1963). *Invitation to sociology: A humanistic perspective.* Garden City, NY: Doubleday.

Berger, P., Berger, B., & Kellner, H. (1973). *The homeless mind.* New York: Random House.

Berger, P., & Luckmann, T. (1966). *The social construction of reality.* Norwich, UK: Penguin.

Bergson, H. (1965). *Duration and simultaneity* (L. Jacobsen, Trans.). Indianapolis: Bobbs-Merrill.

Berk, R. A., & Berk, S. F. (1979). *Labor and leisure at home: Content and organization of the household day.* Beverly Hills, CA: Sage.

Berk, S. F. (1985). *The gender factory.* New York: Plenum.

Bernard, M. (1984). Leisure rich and leisure poor: The leisure patterns of young adults. *Leisure Studies, 3,* 343-361.

Berry, L. L. (1979). The time-buying consumer. *Journal of Retailing, 55,* 58-69.

Best, F. (1978). The time of our lives: The parameters of lifetime distribution of education, work and leisure. *Society and Leisure, 1,* 95-121.

Beutler, I., & Owen, A. (1980). A home production model. *Home Economics Research Journal, 9,* 16-26.

Boorstin, D. J. (1983). *The discoverers: A history of man's search to know his world and himself.* New York: Vintage.

Bose, C. E., Bereano, P. L., & Malloy, M. (1984). Household technology and the social construction of housework. *Technology and Culture, 25,* 53-82.

Brines, J. (1994). Economic dependency, gender and the division of labor at home. *American Journal of Sociology, 100,* 652-688.

Broderick, C. (1988). *Marriage and the family* (3rd ed.). Englewood Cliffs, NJ: Prentice Hall.

Brooks, P. (1984). *Reading for the plot: Design and intention in narrative.* New York: Random House.

Bryant, W. K. (1990). *The economic organization of the household.* New York: Cambridge University Press.

Bryant, W. K. (1992). Human capital, time use, and other family behavior. *Journal of Family and Economic Issues, 13,* 395-405.

Bryant, W. K., & Wang, Y. (1990). Time together, time apart: An analysis of wives' solitary time and shared time with spouses. *Lifestyles: Family and Economic Issues, 11,* 89-119.

Burley, K. A. (1991). Family-work spillover in dual-career couples: A comparison of two time perspectives. *Psychological Reports, 68,* 471-480.

Burton, J. R. (1992). Household technology: Implications for research and policy. *Journal of Family and Economic Issues, 13,* 383-394.

Butler, R. (1963). The life review: An interpretation of reminiscence in the aged. *Psychiatry, 26,* 65-76.

Carr, D. (1986). *Time, narrative and history.* Bloomington: Indiana University Press.

Charmez, K. (1980). *The social reality of death.* Reading, MA: Addison-Wesley.

Charmez, K. (1991, May). *Timemarkers and turning points.* Paper presented at the Interpretive Interactionist Conference, Carleton University, Ottawa.

Cheal, D. (1993). Unity and difference in postmodern families. *Journal of Family Issues, 14,* 5-19.

Christensen, K., & Staines, G. L. (1990). Flextime: A viable solution to the family/work conflict? *Journal of Family Issues, 11,* 455-476.

Clemens, A. W., & Axelson, L. J. (1985). The not-so-empty-nest: The return of the fledgling adult. *Family Relations, 34,* 259-264.

Cogle, F., & Tasker, G. (1982). Children and housework. *Family Relations, 35,* 395-399.

Cohen, T. (1993). What do fathers provide? Reconsidering the economic and nurturant dimensions of men as parents. In J. C. Hood (Ed.), *Men, work and family* (pp. 1-22). Newbury Park, CA: Sage.

Coontz, S. (1992). *The way we never were.* New York: Basic Books.

Coser, L. (1974). *Greedy institutions: Patterns of undivided commitment.* New York: Free Press.

Cottle, T. J. (1976). *Perceiving time: A psychological investigation with men and women.* New York: John Wiley.

Cottle, T. J., & Klineberg, S. L. (1974). *The present of things future: Explorations of time in human experience.* New York: Free Press.

Coverman, S. (1985). Explaining husbands' participation in domestic labour. *Sociological Quarterly, 26,* 81-97.

Coverman, S., & Sheley, J. F. (1986). Change in men's housework and childcare time, 1965-1975. *Journal of Marriage and the Family, 48,* 413-422.

Cowan, R. S. (1983). *More work for mother: The ironies of household technology from the open hearth to the microwave.* New York: Basic Books.

Cromwell, R. R., Keeney, B. P., & Adams, B. N. (1976). Temporal patterning in the family. *Family Process, 15,* 343-348.

Crouter, A. C., & Crowley, M. S. (1990). School-age children's time alone with fathers in single and dual earner families: Implications for the father-child relationship. *Journal of Early Adolescence, 10,* 296-312.

Crouter, A. C., Hawkins, A. J., & Hostetler, M. (1992). Seasonal stability and change in dual-earner husbands' psychological responses to work and family roles. *International Journal of Behavioral Development, 15,* 509-525.

Cunningham, J. B. (1989). A compressed shift schedule: Dealing with some of the problems of shift-work. *Journal of Organizational Behavior, 10,* 231-245.

Cyba, E. (1992). Women's attitudes towards leisure and the family. *Society and Leisure, 15,* 79-94.

Daly, K. J. (1988). Reshaped parenthood identity: The transition to adoptive parenthood. *Journal of Contemporary Ethnography, 17,* 40-66.

Daly, K. J. (1993). Reshaping fatherhood: Finding the models. *Journal of Family Issues, 14,* 510-530.

Daly, K. J. (1994). Uncertain terms: The social construction of fatherhood. In M. L. Dietz, R. Prus, & W. Shaffir (Eds.), *Doing everyday life: Ethnography as human lived experience* (pp. 170-185). Toronto: Copp Clark Pitman.

Daly, K. J. (1995). Reproduction in families. In R. Day, K. Gilbert, B. Settles, & W. Burr (Eds.), *Theory and research in family science* (pp. 229-242). New York: Brooks/Cole.

Daly, K. J. (1996). *Spending time with the kids: Meanings of family time for fathers.* Unpublished manuscript.

Darian, J. C., & Tucci, L. (1992). Convenience-oriented food expenditures of working-wife families: Implications for convenience food manufacturers. *Journal of Food Products Marketing, 1,* 25-36.

Davies, K. (1994). The tensions between process time and clock time in care-work: The example of day nurseries. *Time and Society, 3,* 276-303.

de Grazia, S. (1962). *Of work, time and leisure.* New York: Twentieth Century Fund.

Demo, D., & Acock, A. (1993). Family diversity and the division of domestic labor. *Family Relations, 42,* 323-331.

Desaulniers, S., & Theberge, N. (1992). Gender differences in the likelihood that work reduction will lead to an increase in leisure. *Society and Leisure, 15,* 135-155.

Dewey, J. (1957). *Human nature and conduct.* New York: Modern Library.

Dienhart, A. (1995). *Men and women co-constructing fatherhood through shared parenthood: Beyond the dominant discourse?* Unpublished doctoral dissertation, University of Guelph, Ontario.

Dollahite, D., & Rommel, J. I. (1993). Individual and relationship capital: Implications for theory and research on families. *Journal of Family and Economic Issues, 14,* 27-48.

Douthitt, R. A., Zick, C. D., & McCullough, J. (1990). The role of economic and demographic factors in explaining time-use of single and married mothers. *Lifestyles: Family and Economic Issues, 11,* 23-51.

Durkheim, E. (1915). *The elementary forms of religious life.* London: Allen and Unwin.

Edlund, M. (1987). *Psychological time and mental illness.* New York: Gardner.

Edwards, J. N. (1991). New conceptions: Biosocial innovations and the family. *Journal of Marriage and the Family, 53* 349-360.

Eichler, M. (1988). *Families in Canada today.* Toronto: Gage.

Elchardus, M., & Glorieux, I. (1994). The search for the invisible 8 hours: The gendered use of time in a society with a high labor force participation of women. *Time and Society, 3,* 5-27.

Elder, G. H. (1974). *Children of the Great Depression: Social change in life experience.* Chicago: University of Chicago Press.

Elias, N. (1992). *Time: An essay*. Oxford, UK: Blackwell.

Elkind, D. (1981). *The hurried child: Growing up too fast too soon*. Reading, MA: Addison-Wesley.

Elliot, B. (1994). Biography, family history and the analysis of social change. In M. Drake (Ed.), *Time, family and community* (pp. 44-63). Oxford, UK: Blackwell.

Elshtain, J. B. (1982). Feminism, family and community. *Dissent, 29*, 442-449.

Engels, F. (1967). *The origin of the family, private property and the state*. New York: International Publishers.

Erikson, E. (1963). *Childhood and society* (2nd ed.). New York: Norton.

Erkel, R. T. (1995). Time shifting. *Family Therapy Networker, 19*, 33-39.

Ferree, M. M. (1990). Beyond separate spheres: Feminism and family research. *Journal of Marriage and the Family, 52*, 866-884.

Firestone, J., & Shelton, B. A. (1994). A comparison of women's and men's leisure time: Subtle effects of the double day. *Leisure Sciences, 16*, 45-60.

Fiske, M., & Chiriboga, D. A. (1990). Change and continuity in adult life. San Francisco: Jossey-Bass.

Flaherty, M., & Meer, M. D. (1994). How time flies: Age, memory and temporal compression. *Sociological Quarterly, 35*, 705-721.

Flynn, C. P., & Rodman, H. (1989). Latchkey children and after-school care: A feminist dilemma? *Policy Studies Review, 8*, 663-673.

Foa, E., & Foa, U. (1980). Resources theory: Interpersonal behavior as exchange. In K. Gergen, M. Greenberg, & R. Willis (Eds.), *Social exchange: Advances in theory and research* (pp. 77-101). New York: Plenum.

Forman, F. J. (1989). *Taking our time: Feminist perspectives on temporality*. Toronto: Pergamon.

Fowlkes, M. R. (1987). The myth of merit and male professional careers: The role of wives. In N. Gerstel & H. E. Gross (Eds.), *Families and work* (pp. 347-361). Philadelphia: Temple University Press.

Fraser, J. T. (1978). *Time as conflict*. Basel, Switzerland: Birkhauser Verlag.

Freysinger, V. J. (1994). Leisure with children and parental satisfaction: Further evidence of a sex difference in the experience of adult roles and leisure. *Journal of Leisure Research, 26*, 212-226.

Freysinger, V. J., & Ray, R. O. (1994). The activity involvement of women and men in young and middle adulthood: A panel study. *Leisure Sciences, 16*, 193-217.

Friedman, W. (1990). *About time: Inventing the fourth dimension*. Cambridge, MA: MIT Press.

Galambos, N. L., & Garbarino, J. (1983). Identifying the missing links in the study of latchkey children. *Children Today, 2*, 40-41.

Ganong, L., Coleman, M., & Fine, M. (1995). Remarriage and step-families. In R. Day, K. Gilbert, B. Settles, & W. Burr (Eds.), *Theory and research in family science* (pp. 287-303). New York: Brooks/Cole.

Gee, E. M. (1991). The transition to grandmotherhood: A quantitative study. *Canadian Journal on Aging, 10*, 254-270.

Gergen, K. J. (1980). The emerging crisis in life-span developmental theory. *Life-span Developmental Behavior, 3*, 31-63.

Gergen, K. J., & Gergen, M. M. (1984). The social construction of narrative accounts. In K. J. Gergen & M. M. Gergen (Eds.), *Historical social psychology* (pp. 173-190). Hillsdale, NJ: Lawrence Erlbaum.

Gerner, J. L., Montalto, C. P., & Bryant, W. K. (1990). Work patterns and marital status change. *Lifestyles: Family and Economic Issues, 11,* 7-21.

Giddens, A. (1981). *A contemporary critique of historical materialism, power, property and the state.* London: Macmillan.

Giddens, A. (1984). *The constitution of society: Outline of the theory of structuration.* Berkeley: University of California Press.

Giddens, A. (1987). *Social theory and modern sociology.* Stanford, CA: Stanford University Press.

Giddens, A. (1990). *The consequences of modernity.* Stanford, CA: Stanford University Press.

Giddens, A. (1991). *Modernity and self-identity.* Cambridge, MA: Polity.

Gilligan, C. (1982). *In a different voice.* Cambridge, MA: Harvard University Press.

Giveans, D. L., & Robinson, M. K. (1985). Fathers and the preschool-age child. In S. Hanson & F. Bozett (Eds.), *Dimensions of fatherhood* (pp. 115-140). Beverly Hills, CA: Sage.

Gloor, D. (1992). Women versus men? The hidden differences in leisure activities. *Society and Leisure, 15,* 39-60.

Godwin, D. D. (1991). Spouse's time allocation to household work: A review and critique. *Lifestyles: Family and Economic Issues, 12,* 253-294.

Gonseth, F. (1972). *Time and method: An essay on the methodology of research.* Springfield, IL: Charles C Thomas.

Goode, W. J. (1960). A theory of role strain. *American Sociological Review, 25,* 483-496.

Green, E., Hebron, S., & Woodward, D. (1989). Women, leisure and social control. In I. Hamner & M. Maynard (Eds.), *Women, violence and social control* (pp. 75-92). Atlantic Highlands, NJ: Humanities Press International.

Greenberger, E. (1988). Working in teenage America. In J. T. Mortimer & K. M. Borman (Eds.), *Work experience and psychological development through the lifespan* (pp. 21-50). Boulder, CO: Westview.

Gurvitch, G. (1964). *The spectrum of social time.* Dordrecht, The Netherlands: D. Reidel.

Haas, L., & Hwang, P. (1995). Company culture and men's usage of family leave benefits in Sweden. *Family Relations, 44,* 28-36.

Hagestad, G. (1986). Time and the family. *American Behavioral Scientist, 29,* 679-694.

Halbwachs, M. (1992). *On collective memory.* Chicago: University of Chicago Press.

Hall, E. T. (1983). *The dance of life: The other dimension of time.* Garden City, NY: Anchor Press/Doubleday.

Hantrais, L. (1993). The gender of time in professional occupations. *Time and Society, 2,* 139-157.

Hareven, T. K. (1982). *Family time and industrial time: The relationship between the family and work in a New England industrial community.* Cambridge, UK: Cambridge University Press.

Hareven, T. K. (1994). The history of the family. In M. Drake (Ed.), *Time, family and community* (pp. 13-43). Oxford, UK: Blackwell.

Harrington, M. A. (1991). Time after work: Constraints on the leisure of working women. *Society and Leisure, 14,* 115-132.

Hartmann, H. (1981). The family as the locus of gender, class and political struggle: The example of housework. *Signs, 6,* 366-394.

Harvey, D. (1989). *The condition of postmodernity.* Oxford, UK: Blackwell.

Heidegger, M. (1962). *Being and time.* New York: Harper & Row.

Henderson, K. (1991). The contribution of feminism to an understanding of leisure constraints. *Journal of Leisure Research, 23*, 363-377.

Henderson, K. A., & Allen, K. R. (1991). The ethic of care: Leisure possibilities and constraints for women. *Society & Leisure, 14*, 97-113.

Henderson, K. A., & Dialeschki, M. D. (1991). A sense of entitlement to leisure as constraint and empowerment for women. *Leisure Sciences, 13*, 51-65.

Hendricks, C. D., & Hendricks, J. (1976). Concepts of time and temporal construction among the aged, with implications for research. In J. F. Gubrium (Ed.), *Time, roles and self in old age* (pp. 13-49). New York: Human Sciences Press.

Hendricks, J. (1982). Time and social science: History and potential. In E. H. Mizruchi, B. Glassner, & T. Pastorello (Eds.), *Time and aging: Conceptualization and application in sociological and gerontological research* (pp. 12-45). New York: General Hall.

Hendricks, J., & Cutler, S. J. (1990). Leisure and the structure of our lifeworlds. *Aging and Society, 10*, 85-94.

Hendricks, J., & Peters, C. B. (1986). The times of our lives. *American Behavioral Scientist, 29*, 662-678.

Hess, R. D., & Handel, G. (1959). *Family worlds: A psychosocial approach to family life.* Chicago: University of Chicago Press.

Hessing, M. (1993). Mothers' management of their combined workloads: Clerical and household needs. *Canadian Review of Sociology and Anthropology, 30*, 37-63.

Hiatt, A. R., & Godwin, D. D. (1990). Use of time and preferences for time allocation among urban, employed married women. *Lifestyles: Family and Economic Issues, 11*, 161-181.

Hill, R. (1986). Life cycle stages for types of single-parent families: Of family development theory. *Family Relations, 35*, 19-29.

Hilton, J. M. (1990). Differences in allocation of family time spent on household tasks among single-parent, one-earner and two-earner families. *Lifestyles: Family and Economic Issues, 11*, 283-298.

Hochschild, A. (1989). *The second shift.* New York: Avon Books.

Hoffman, C. (1987). The effects on children of maternal and paternal employment. In N. Gerstel & H. E. Gross (Eds.), *Families and work* (pp. 362-395). Philadelphia: Temple University Press.

Holman, T., & Jacquart, M. (1988). Leisure activity patterns and marital satisfaction: A further test. *Journal of Marriage and the Family, 50*, 69-77.

Horna, J. L. (1992). Family and leisure. In K. Ishwaran (Ed.), *Family and marriage: Cross cultural perspectives* (pp. 293-304). Toronto: Thompson Educational Publishing.

Horton, J. (1967). Time and cool people. *Trans-action, 4*, 5-12.

Hughes, E. C. (1958). *Men and their work.* Glencoe, IL: Free Press.

Hunt, J. G., & Hunt, L. L. (1987). Male resistance to role symmetry in dual-earner households: Three alternative explanations. In N. Gerstel & H. E. Gross (Eds.), *Families and work* (pp. 192-203). Philadelphia: Temple University Press.

Husserl, E. (1964). *The phenomenology of internal time consciousness.* Bloomington: Indiana University Press.

Jaques, E. (1982). *The form of time.* New York: Crane Russak.

James, W. (1952). *The principles of psychology.* Chicago: University of Chicago Press. (Original work published 1890)

Juster, F. T. (1985). Investments of time by men and women. In F. T. Juster & F. P. Stafford (Eds.), *Time, goods, and well-being* (pp. 177-204). Ann Arbor: University of Michigan, Institute for Social Research.

Kantor, D., & Lehr, W. (1976). *Inside the family: Toward a theory of family process.* San Francisco: Jossey-Bass.

Kantrowitz, B., & Witherspoon, D. (1986, March 3). Penciling in playtime. *Newsweek,* p. 57.

Keith, P. M., & Schafer, R. B. (1980). Role strain and depression in two job families. *Family Relations, 29,* 483-488.

Kellerman, A. (1989). *Time, space and society.* Dordrecht, The Netherlands: Kluwer.

Kelly, J. R. (1983). *Leisure identities and interactions.* London: Allen and Unwin.

Key, R. J., & Sanik, M. M. (1990). The effect of homemaker's employment status on children's time allocation in single- and two-parent families. *Lifestyles: Family and Economic Issues, 11,* 71-87.

Kingston, P. W. (1990). Illusions and ignorance about the family responsive workplace. *Journal of Family Issues, 11,* 438-454.

Kingston, P. W., & Nock, S. L. (1987). Time together among dual earner couples. *American Sociological Review, 52,* 391-400.

Knipscheer, C. P. M. (1988). Temporal embeddedness and aging within the multigenerational family: The case of grandparenting. In J. E. Birren & V. L. Bengtson (Eds.), *Emergent theories of aging* (pp. 426-446). New York: Springer.

Kubey, R. (1990). Television and the quality of family life. *Communication Quarterly, 38,* 312-324.

Kvale, S. (1977). Dialectics and research on remembering. In N. Datan & H. Reese (Eds.), *Life-span developmental psychology* (pp. 165-190). New York: Academic Press.

Lakoff, G., & Johnson, M. (1980). *Metaphors we live by.* Chicago: University of Chicago Press.

LaRossa, R. (1983). The transition to parenthood and the social reality of time. *Journal of Marriage and the Family, 45,* 579-589.

LaRossa, R. (1988). Fatherhood and social change. *Family Relations, 37,* 451-458.

LaRossa, R., & LaRossa, M. (1981). *Transition to parenthood: How infants change families.* Beverly Hills, CA: Sage.

Larson, R., Kubey, R., & Colletti, J. (1989). Changing channels: Early adolescent media choices and shifting investments in family and friends. *Journal of Youth and Adolescence, 18,* 583-599.

Lasch, C. (1979). *The culture of narcissism.* New York: Norton.

Laslett, P. (1972). *Household and family in past time.* Cambridge, UK: Cambridge University Press.

Lawton, M. P., Moss, M., & Fulcomer, M. (1987). Objective and subjective uses of time by older people. *International Journal of Aging and Human Development, 24,* 171-188.

Leete, L., & Schor, J. B. (1994). Assessing the time squeeze hypothesis: Hours worked in the United States, 1969-1989. *Industrial Relations, 33,* 25-41.

Le Feuvre, N. (1994). Leisure, work and gender: A sociological study of women's time in France. *Time and Society, 3,* 151-178.

Le Goff, J. (1980). *Time, work and culture in the Middle Ages.* Chicago: University of Chicago Press.

Lero, D., Goelman, H., Pence, A., Brockman, L., & Nutall, S. (1992). *Parental work patterns and child care needs.* Ottawa: Statistics Canada.

LeShan, L. L. (1957). Time orientation and social class. *Journal of Abnormal and Social Psychology, 47,* 589-592.

Leslie, L. A., & Anderson, E. A. (1988). Men's and women's participation in domestic roles: Impact on quality of life and marital adjustment. *Journal of Family Psychology, 2,* 212-226.

Levine, R. V. (1988). The pace of life across cultures. In J. E. McGrath (Ed.), *The social psychology of time: New perspectives* (pp. 39-60). Newbury Park, CA: Sage.

Levinger, G., & Huesmann, L. (1980). An "incremental exchange" perspective on the pair relationship: Interpersonal reward and level of involvement. In K. Gergen, M. Greenberg, & R. Willis (Eds.), *Social exchange: Advances in theory and research* (pp. 77-101). New York: Plenum.

Lewis, J. D., & Weigert, A. J. (1981). The structures and meanings of social time. *Social Forces, 60,* 432-462.

Lifton, B. J. (1988). Brave new baby in the brave new world. In E. H. Baruch, A. F. Adamo, Jr., & J. Seager (Eds.), *Embryos, ethics, and women's rights: Exploring the new reproductive technologies* (pp. 149-154). New York: Harrington Park.

Long, T. J., & Long, L. (1982). *Latchkey children: The child's view of self-care.* Washington, DC: Catholic University of America. (ERIC Document Reproduction Service No. ED 211 229)

Lopata, H. Z. (1986). Time in anticipated future and events in memory. *American Behavioral Scientist, 29,* 695-709.

Lukacs, G. (1971). *History and class consciousness: Studies in Marxist dialectics* (R. Livingston, Trans.). London: Merlin. (Original work published 1922)

Lyman, S. M., & Scott, M. B. (1970). *A sociology of the absurd.* New York: Appleton-Century-Crofts.

Lyotard, J. F. (1984). *The post-modern condition: A report on knowledge.* Minneapolis: University of Minnesota Press.

Maines, D. (1987). The significance of temporality for the development of sociological theory. *Sociological Quarterly, 28,* 303-311.

Maines, D., & Hardesty, M. (1987). Temporality and gender: Young adults' career and family plans. *Social Forces, 66,* 102-120.

Maines, D., Sugrue, N., & Katovich, M. (1983). The sociological import of G. H. Mead's theory of the past. *American Sociological Review, 48,* 161-173.

Mannheim, K. (1952). *Essays on the sociology of knowledge.* London: Routledge & Kegan Paul.

Marks, S. R. (1977). Multiple roles and role strain: Some notes on human energy, time and commitment. *American Sociological Review, 42* 921-936.

Matocha, L. (1992). Case study interviews: Caring for persons with AIDS. In J. Gigun, K. Daly, & G. Handel (Eds.), *Qualitative methods in family research* (pp. 66-84). Newbury Park, CA: Sage.

Maudlin, T., & Meeks, C. B. (1990). Time allocation one- and two-parent mothers. *Lifestyles: Family and Economic Issues, 11,* 53-69.

McCullough, J. & Zick, C. D. (1992). The roles of role strain, economic resources and time demands in explaining mothers' life satisfaction. *Journal of Family and Economic Issues, 13,* 23-44.

McGrath, J. E., & Kelley, J. R. (1986). *Time and human interaction: Toward a social psychology of time.* New York: Guilford.

McMahon, M. (1995). *Engendering motherhood: identity and self-transformation in women's lives.* New York: Guilford.

Mead, G. H. (1932). *The philosophy of the present.* La Salle, IL: Open Court.

Meeks, C. B., & Maudlin, T. (1990). Children's time in structured and unstructured leisure activities. *Lifestyles: Family and Economic Issues, 11,* 257-279.

Melbin, M. (1978). The colonization of time. In T. Carlstein, D. Parker, & N. Thrift (Eds.), *Human activity and time geography* (pp. 100-113). London: Edward Arnold.

Merleau-Ponty, M. (1962). *Phenomenology of perception* (C. Smith, Trans.). London: Routledge & Kegan Paul.

Miller, D. A. (1981). The "sandwich" generation: Adult children of the aging. *Social Work, 26,* 419-423.

Miller, D. F. (1993). Political time: The problem of timing and chance. *Time and Society, 2,* 179-197.

Miller, L. J. (1993). *Claims making from the underside: Marginalization and social problems analysis.* Paper presented at the conference "Studying Human Lived Experience: Symbolic Interaction and Ethnographic Research," Waterloo, Ontario.

Mills, C. W. (1959). *The sociological imagination.* London: Oxford University Press.

Modell, J., Furstenberg, F., & Hershberg, T. (1978). Social change and transitions to adulthood in historical perspective. In M. Gordon (Ed.), *The American family in social-historical perspective* (2nd ed., pp. 192-219). New York: St. Martin's.

Moen, P. (1985). Continuities and discontinuities in women's labor force activity. In G. H. Elder, Jr. (Ed.), *Life course dynamics* (pp. 113-155). Ithaca, NY: Cornell University Press.

Moen, P., & Moorehouse, M. (1983). Overtime over the life cycle: A test of the life cycle squeeze hypothesis. In H. Lopata & J. Pleck (Eds.), *Research in the interweave of social roles: Jobs and families* (Vol. 3, pp. 201-218). Greenwich, CT: JAI.

Moore, W. E. (1963). *Man, time and society.* New York: John Wiley.

Moss, M. S., Lawton, M. P., Kleban, M. H., & Duhamel, L. (1993). Time use of caregivers of impaired elders before and after institutionalization. *Journal of Gerontology: Social Sciences, 48,* S102-S111.

Neal, M. B., Chapman, N. J., Ingersoll-Dayton, B., & Emlen, A. C. (1993). *Balancing work and caregiving for children, adults, and elders.* Newbury Park, CA: Sage.

Needham, J. (1943). *Time: The refreshing river.* London: Allen and Unwin.

Neugarten, B. L. (Ed.). (1973a). *Middle age and aging.* Chicago: University of Chicago Press.

Neugarten, B. L. (1973b). Personality change in late life: A developmental perspective. In C. Eisdorfer & M. P. Lawton (Eds.), *The psychology of adult development and aging.* Washington, DC: American Psychological Association.

Neustadter, R. (1992). Beat the clock: The mid-20th century protest against the reification of time. *Time and Society, 1,* 379-398.

Nickols, S. Y., & Fox, K. D. (1983). Buying time and saving time: Strategies for managing household production. *Journal of Consumer Research, 10,* 197-208.

Nock, S. L., & Kingston, P. W. (1984). The family work day. *Journal of Marriage and the Family, 46,* 333-343.

Norris, J., & Tindale, J. (1994). *Among generations: The cycle of adult relationships.* New York: Freeman.

Nowotony, H. (1992). Time and social theory: Towards a theory of time. *Time and Society, 1,* 421-454.

Nowotony, H. (1994). *Time: The modern and postmodern experience.* London: Polity.

Nyedegger, C. (1986). Timetables and implicit theory. *American Behavioral Scientist, 29,* 710-729.

O'Malley, M. (1990). *Keeping watch: A history of American time.* New York: Viking.

Olson, D., Sprenkle, D., & Russell, C. (1979). Circumplex model of marital and family systems: Cohesion and adaptability dimensions, family types and clinical applications. *Family Process, 18,* 3-28.

Olson, P., Ponzetti, Jr., J. J., & Olson, G. I. (1989). Time demands on families: Is there a bottom line? *Lifestyles: Family and Economic Issues, 10,* 311-323.

Oppenheimer, V. (1974). The life cycle squeeze: the interacting of men's occupational and family life cycles. *Demography, 11,* 227-246.

Orthner, D. K. (1976). Patterns of leisure and married interactions. *Journal of Leisure Research, 8,* 98-111.

Orthner, D. K., & Mancini, J. A. (1990). Leisure impacts on family interaction and cohesion. *Journal of Leisure Research, 22,* 123-137.

Owen, A. J. (1991). Time and time again: Implications of time perception theory. *Lifestyles: Family and Economic Issues, 12,* 345-359.

Padilla, M. L., & Landreth, G. L. (1989). Latchkey children: A review of the literature. *Child Welfare, 68,* 445-454.

Papanek, H. (1990). To each less than she needs, from each more than she can do: Allocations, entitlements and value. In I. Tinker (Ed.), *Persistent inequalities.* New York: Oxford University Press.

Parsons, T., & Bales, R. (1955). *Family socialization and interaction process.* New York: Free Press.

Pasero, U. (1994). Social time patterns, contingency and gender relations. *Time and Society, 3,* 179-191.

Peters, J. M., & Haldeman, V. A. (1987). Time used for household work. *Journal of Family Issues, 8,* 212-225

Pett, M. A., Caserta, M. S., Hutton, A. P., & Lund, D. A. (1988). Intergenerational conflict: Middle-aged women caring for demented older relatives. *American Journal of Orthopsychiatry, 58,* 405-417.

Piaget, J. (1970). *The child's conception of time.* New York: Basic Books.

Pleck, J. H. (1977). The work-family role system. *Social Problems, 24,* 417-427.

Pleck, J. H. (1985). *Working wives/working husbands.* Beverly Hills, CA: Sage.

Pleck, J. H. (1993). Are "family supportive" employer policies relevant to men? In J. C. Hood (Ed.), *Men, work and family* (pp. 217-237). Newbury Park, CA: Sage.

Pleck, J. H. (in press). Paternal involvement: Levels, sources and consequences. In M. E. Lamb (Ed.), *The role of the father in child development.* New York: Wiley.

Pleck, J. H., & Staines, G. L. (1985). Work schedules and family life in two earner couples. *Journal of Family Issues, 6,* 61-82.

Popcorn, F. (1991). *The popcorn report: Faith Popcorn on the future of your company, your world, your life.* Garden City, NY: Doubleday, Currency.

Pouthas, V., Droit, S., & Jacquet, A.-Y. (1993). Temporal experiences and time knowledge in infancy and early childhood. *Time and Society, 2,* 199-218.

Presser, H. B. (1989). Can we make time for children? The economy, work schedules and child care. *Demography, 26,* 523-543.

Pronovost, G. (1989). The sociology of time. *Current Sociology, 37,* 1-124.

Quinn, P., & Allen, K. (1989). Facing challenges and making compromises: How single mothers endure. *Family Relations, 38,* 390-395.

Qvortrup, J. (1991). Childhood as a social phenomenon: An introduction to a series of national reports. In M. Bardy, J. Qvortrup, G. Sgritta, & H. Wintersberger (Eds.), *Childhood as a social phenomenon.* Vienna, Austria: European Centre for Social Welfare Policy and Research.

Rachlin, V. C. (1987). Fair vs. equal role relations in dual-career and dual-earner families: Implications for family interventions. *Family Relations, 36,* 187-192.

Rakowski, W. (1986). Future time perspective: Applications to the health context of later adulthood. *American Behavioral Scientist, 29,* 730-745.

Rakowski, W., & Clark, N. M. (1985). Future outlook, care-giving and care-receiving in the family context. *The Gerontologist, 25,* 618-623.

Reiss, D. (1981). *The family's construction of reality.* Cambridge, MA: Harvard University Press.

Restrepo, D. (1995). *Gender entitlements in Colombian families.* Unpublished doctoral dissertation, University of Guelph, Ontario.

Rettig, K. D. (1988, November). *A framework for integrating family relations and family resource management.* Paper presented at the Theory Construction and Research Methodology Workshop, National Council on Family Relations, Philadelphia.

Rheingold, H. (1993). *The virtual community.* Reading, MA: Addison-Wesley.

Rifkin, J. (1987). *Time wars: The primary conflict in human history.* New York: Henry Holt.

Ritterman, M. (1995). Stopping the clock. *The Family Therapy Networker, 19,* 44-51.

Robinson, J. P. (1977). *How Americans use their time: A social psychological analysis of everyday behavior.* New York: Praeger.

Robinson, J. P. (1990). The time squeeze. *American Demographics, 12,* 30-33.

Rodgers, R. H., & White, J. M. (1993). Family development theory. In P. G. Boss, W. J. Doherty, R. LaRossa, W. R. Schumm, & S. K. Steinmetz (Eds.), *Sourcebook of family theories and methods: A contextual approach* (pp. 469-499). New York: Plenum.

Rodman, H. (1990). The social construction of the latchkey children problem. In N. Mandell (Ed.), *Sociological studies of child development* (Vol. 3, pp. 163-174). Greenwich, CT: JAI.

Rodman, H., Pratto, D. J., & Nelson, R. S. (1985). Child care arrangements and children's functioning: A comparison of self-care and adult-care children. *Developmental Psychology, 21,* 413-418.

Rorty, R. (1990). *Contingency, irony and solidarity.* Cambridge, UK: Cambridge University Press.

Roth, J. A. (1963). *Timetables: Structuring the passage of time in hospital treatment and other careers.* Indianapolis, IN: Bobbs-Merrill.

Rothman, S. M., & Marks, E. M. (1987). Adjusting work and family life: Flexible work schedules and family policy. In N. Gerstel & H. E. Gross (Eds.), *Families and work* (pp. 192-203). Philadelphia: Temple University Press.

Rubin, L. (1976). *Worlds of pain: Life in the working-class family.* New York: Basic Books.

Rubin, L. (1994). *Families on the fault line: America's working class speaks about the family, the economy, race and ethnicity.* New York: HarperCollins.

Rubin, R. M., & Riney, B. J. (1994). *Working wives and dual-earner families.* Westport, CT: Praeger.

Russell, P. (1992). *The white hole in time: Our future evolution and the meaning of now.* San Francisco: HarperSanFrancisco.

Rutz, H. J. (1992). The idea of a politics of time. In H. J. Rutz (Ed.), *The politics of time* (American Ethnological Society Monograph Series, No. 4, pp. 1-17). Washington, DC: American Ethnological Society.

Sanik, M. M. (1990). Parents' time use: A 1967-1986 comparison. *Lifestyles: Family and Economic Issues, 11,* 299-316.

Sanik, M., & Stafford, K. (1985). Adolescents' contribution to household production: Male and female differences. *Adolescence, 20,* 207-215.

Sanik, M., & Stafford, K. (1986). Boy/girl differences in household work. *Journal of Consumer Studies and Home Economics, 10,* 209-219.

Scarr, S., Phillips, D., & McCartney, K. (1989). Working mothers and their families. *American Psychologist, 44,* 1402-1409.

Scharlach, A. E. (1994). Caregiving and employment: Competing or complementary roles? *The Gerontologist, 34,* 378-385.

Schor, J. B. (1991). *The overworked American.* New York: Basic Books.

Schuller, T. (1993). A temporal approach to the relationship between education and generation. *Time and Society, 2,* 335-351.

Schutz, A. (1962). *Collected papers I: The problem of social reality.* The Hague: Martinus Nijhoff.

Schutz, A. (1964). *Collected papers II: Studies in social theory.* The Hague: Martinus Nijhoff.

Schvaneveldt, J. D., Pickett, R. S., & Young, M. H. (1993). Historical methods in family research. In P. G. Boss, W. J. Doherty, R. LaRossa, W. R. Schumm, & S. K. Steinmetz (Eds.), *Sourcebook of family theories and methods: A contextual approach* (pp. 99-116). New York: Plenum.

Schwartz, B. (1975). *Queuing and waiting: Studies in the social organization of access and delay.* Chicago: University of Chicago Press.

Schwartz, B. (1982). The friction of time: Access and delay in the context of medical care. In E. H. Mizruchi, B. Glassner, & T. Pastorello (Eds.), *Time and aging: Conceptualization and application in sociological and gerontological research* (pp. 75-111). New York: General Hall.

Seltzer, M. M., & Hendricks, J. (1986). Explorations in time. *American Behavioral Scientist, 29,* 653-661.

Seltzer, M. M., & Troll, L. E. (1986). Expected life history: A model in non-linear time. *American Behavioral Scientist, 29,* 746-764.

Seymour, J. (1992). "No time to call my own": Women's time as a household resource. *Women's Studies International Forum, 15,* 187-192.

Shank, J. (1986). An exploration of leisure in the lives of dual career women. *Journal of Leisure Research, 18,* 300-319.

Shaw, J. (1994). Punctuality and the everyday ethics of time: Some evidence from the mass observation archive. *Time and Society, 3,* 79-97.

Shaw, S. (1985). The meaning of leisure in everyday life. *Leisure Sciences, 7,* 1-24.

Shaw, S. (1988). Leisure in the contemporary family: On the leisure of Canadian wives and husbands. *International Review of Modern Sociology, 18,* 1-16.

Shaw, S. (1991). Research note: Women's leisure time-using time budget data to examine current trends and future predictions. *Leisure Studies, 10,* 171-181.

Shaw, S. (1992). Dereifying family leisure: An examination of women's and men's everyday experiences and perceptions of family time. *Leisure Sciences, 14,* 271-286.

Shelton, A. (1992). *Women, men and time.* New York: Greenwood.

Shorter, E. (1977). *The making of the modern family.* New York: Basic Books.

Silverstone, R. (1993). Time, information and communication technologies and the household. *Time and Society, 2,* 283-311.

Simmel, G. (1950). *The sociology of Georg Simmel.* New York: Free Press.

Smith, G. T., Snyder, D. K., Trull, T. J., & Monsma, B. R. (1988). Predicting relationship satisfaction from couples' use of leisure time. *American Journal of Family Therapy, 16,* 3-13

Sorokin, P. A., & Merton, R. K. (1937). Social time: A methodological and functional analysis. *American Journal of Sociology, 46,* 615-629.

Staines, G. L., & Pleck, J. H. (1983). *The impact of work schedules on the family.* Ann Arbor: University of Michigan Press.

Stanton, M. D. (1992). The time line and the "Why now?" question: A technique and rationale for therapy, training, organizational consultation and research. *Journal of Marital and Family Therapy, 18,* 331-343.

Statistics Canada. (1994). *Women in the labour force: 1994 edition* (Catalogue number 75-507E). Ottawa: Supply and Services.

Stipp, H. H. (1988). What is a working woman? *American Demographics, 10,* 24-27.

Stone, G. (1981). Appearance and the self: A slightly revised version. In G. P. Stone & H. A. Farberman (Eds.), *Social psychology through symbolic interactionism* (pp. 187-202). New York: John Wiley.

Strauss, A. (1964). Introduction. In A. Strauss (Ed.), *George Herbert Mead on social psychology: Selected papers.* Chicago: University of Chicago Press.

Strauss, A. (1975). *Chronic illness and the quality of life.* St. Louis, MO: C. V. Mosby.

Strober, M. H., & Weinberg, C. B. (1980). Strategies used by working and non-working wives to reduce time pressures. *Journal of Consumer Research, 6,* 338-348.

Suitor, J. J., & Pillemer, K. (1988). Explaining intergenerational conflict when adult children and elderly parents live together. *Journal of Marriage and the Family, 50,* 1037-1047.

Telles, J. L. (1980). Time, rank and social control. *Sociological inquiry, 50,* 171-183.

Thompson, E. P. (1967). Time, work-discipline and industrial capitalism. *Past and Present, 36,* 57-97.

Thompson, L., & Walker, A. J. (1989). Gender in families: Women and men in marriage, work and parenthood. *Journal of Marriage and the Family, 51,* 845-871.

Tiryakian, E. A. (1978). The time perspectives of modernity. *Society and Leisure, 1,* 125-153.

Toffler, A. (1980). *The third wave.* New York: William Morrow.

Tuttle, R. C. (1994, November). *The effects of work schedule and child care options on marital happiness.* Poster presented at the National Council on Family Relations Conference, Minneapolis.

Uhlenberg, P. (1980). Death and the family. *Journal of Family History, 5,* 313-320.

Urry, J. (1994). Time, leisure and social identity. *Time and Society, 3,* 131-149.

Veblen, T. (1934). *The theory of the leisure class: An economic study of institutions.* New York: Modern Library. (Original work published 1899)

Ventura, M. (1995). The age of interruption. *Family Therapy Networker, 19,* 19-31.

Voydanoff, P. (1988). Work role characteristics, family structure demands, and work/family conflict. *Journal of Marriage and the Family, 50,* 749-761.

Voydanoff, P., & Kelly, R. F. (1984). Determinants of work related family problems among employed parents. *Journal of Marriage and the Family, 46,* 881-899.

Vuchinich, S. (1987). Starting and stopping spontaneous family conflicts. *Journal of Marriage and the Family, 49,* 591-601.

Weber, M. (1958). *The Protestant ethic and the spirit of capitalism* (T. Parsons, Trans.). New York: Scribners.

Weigert, A. (1981). Time in everyday life. In A. J. Weigert (Ed.), *Sociology of everyday life* (pp. 196-241). New York: Longman.

Wells, H. G. (1931). *The time machine.* New York: Random House.

White, L. K., & Brinkerhoff, D. B. (1987). Children's work in the family: Its significance and meaning. In N. Gerstel & H. E. Gross (Eds.), *Families and work* (pp. 204-218). Philadelphia: Temple University Press.

White, M. (1989). *Selected papers.* Adelaide, Australia: Dulwich Centre.

White, M. (1992). Deconstruction and therapy. In D. Epston & M. White (Eds.), *Experience, contradiction, narrative & imagination: Selected papers of David Epston & Michael White, 1989-1991* (pp. 109-151). Adelaide, Australia: Dulwich Centre.

White, M., & Epston, D. (1990). *Narrative means to therapeutic ends.* New York: Norton.

Whitrow, G. J. (1988). *Time in history.* Oxford, UK: Oxford University Press.

Winter, M., Puspitawati, H., Heck, R. H., & Stafford, K. (1993). Time-management strategies used by households with home-based work. *Journal of Family and Economic Issues, 14* 69-92.

Winton, C. A. (1995). *Frameworks for studying families.* Guilford, CT: Dushkin.

Witt, P. A., & Goodale, T. L. (1981). The relationship between barriers to leisure enjoyment and family stages. *Leisure Sciences, 4,* 29-49.

Wylie, M. S. (1995). Mobile therapy. *The Family Therapy Networker, 19,* 11-12.

Young, M. D., & Schuller, T. (1988). Introduction: Towards chronosociology. In M. Young & T. Schuller (Eds.), *The rhythms of society* (pp. 1-16). London: Routledge.

Zaretsky, E. (1976). *Capitalism, the family and personal life.* New York: Harper & Row.

Zelizer, V. A. (1985). *Pricing the priceless child: The changing social value of children.* New York: Basic Books.

Zerubavel, E. (1976). Timetables and scheduling: On the social organization of time. *Sociological Inquiry, 46,* 87-94.

Zerubavel, E. (1979). *Patterns of time in hospital life.* Chicago: University of Chicago Press.

Zerubavel, E. (1981). *Hidden rhythms: Schedules and calendars in social life.* Chicago: University of Chicago Press.

Zerubavel, E. (1982). Schedules and social control. In E. H. Mizruchi, B. Glassner, & T. Pastorello (Eds.), *Time and aging: Conceptualization and application in sociological and gerontological research* (pp. 129-152). New York: General Hall.

Zerubavel, E. (1985). *The seven day circle.* New York: Free Press.

Zerubavel, E. (1987). The language of time: Towards a semiotics of temporality. *Sociological Quarterly, 28,* 343-356.

Zick, C. D., & Allen, C. R. (1996). The impact of parents' marital status on the time adolescents spend in productive activities. *Family Relations, 45,* 65-71.

Zick, C. D., & McCullough, J. L. (1991). Trends in married couples' time use: Evidence from 1977-78 and 1987-88. *Sex Roles, 24,* 459-487.

Zuzanek, J., & Smale, B. J. A. (1992). Life-cycle variations in across-the-week allocation of time to selected daily activities. *Society and Leisure, 15,* 559-586.

# Author Index

# Subject Index

# About the Author

Kerry Daly is Associate Professor in the Department of Family Studies at the University of Guelph, Guelph, Ontario, Canada. He received his PhD in Sociology from McMaster University, Hamilton, Ontario. His research interests focus on the social meaning of time, the social construction of fatherhood, and the nature of adoptive relationships. He is coeditor of *Qualitative Methods in Family Research* (Sage, 1992), and coauthor of *Adoption in Canada* (Health and Welfare Canada, 1993). He has published articles in the *Journal of Marriage and the Family,* the *Journal of Family Issues, Qualitative Sociology,* and the *Journal of Social Issues.* He is married, has two children ages 10 and 12 and, in moments of quiet, wonders where the time has gone.